Chasing Evil

Chasing Evil

SHOCKING CRIMES, SUPERNATURAL FORCES AND AN FBI AGENT'S SEARCH FOR HOPE AND JUSTICE

John Edward
and
Robert Hilland
with Natasha Stoynoff

THORNDIKE PRESS
A part of Gale, a Cengage Company

Thorndike Press, a part of Gale, a Cengage Company.

Thorndike Press® Large Print Nonfiction.

The text of this Large Print edition is unabridged.

Other aspects of the book may vary from the original edition.

Set in 16 pt. Plantin.

LIBRARY OF CONGRESS CIP DATA ON FILE.
CATALOGUING IN PUBLICATION FOR THIS BOOK
IS AVAILABLE FROM THE LIBRARY OF CONGRESS.

ISBN-13: 978-1-4205-3224-1 (hardcover alk. paper)

Published in 2026 by arrangement with St. Martin's Essentials, an imprint of St. Martin's Publishing Group.

Printed in the United States of America
1 2 3 4 5 6 7 30 29 28 27 26

For my kids, Justin and Olivia . . .
I hope this makes you proud.
— JOHN EDWARD

To my children, Connor and Caitlyn. As you journey through life, do not be afraid. You are never alone. Have faith. Thank you for letting me be your dad. I love you both more than I can possibly express.

And to the 10 percent of FBI Agents who do 90 percent of the work.
— ROBERT HILLAND

CONTENTS

This book is based on real events. All details are true to the best of the authors' memories and contemporaneous notes. Some names and details have been changed to protect privacy.

In accordance with my obligations as a former FBI employee pursuant to my FBI employment agreement, this book has undergone a prepublication review for the purpose of identifying prohibited disclosures but has not been reviewed for editorial content or accuracy.

The FBI does not endorse or validate any information that I have described in this book. The opinions expressed in this book are mine and not those of the FBI or any other government agency.

— Robert Hilland

"Evil prospers when
good men do nothing."
— attributed to JOHN PHILPOT CURRAN

"The arc of the moral universe is long,
but it bends toward justice."
— DR. MARTIN LUTHER KING JR.

Prologue

LITTLE NOAH

DUBLIN, VIRGINIA
March 25th, 2015

The phone rang. *John.* Thank God.

As soon as I picked up, his words were spilling out. He was on fire.

"Bob, you walked right over him!" said John, his sense of immediacy palpable.

"What?"

"Bob. STOP WHERE YOU ARE RIGHT NOW. Turn around. Go back in the direction you came."

I turned around and started walking back to the tires.

Five-year-old Noah had been missing for three days, and I was stumbling around in the dark, at midnight, trying to find the little boy. I was searching the area between the junkyard and the steep hill behind his parents' trailer. Hundreds of volunteers had been searching tirelessly, day and night.

"STOP! He's right there. You just walked over him!"

I started to backtrack. I had the phone in one hand, the flashlight in the other.

"Stop! You're going the wrong way. You need to go back up the hill. They're telling me you need to go *back up.*"

John was talking a hundred miles a minute.

"Go back up the hill and look for that *Star Wars* toy — the X-wing fighter plane. Bob, the boy is there. *I'm telling you.*"

I could hear the emotion in John's voice, and that was unlike him. He was usually clinical and composed when we worked together.

Noah was different for him.

The pure, guileless spirit of that red-haired little boy made the worried, loving father in both of us take over. It was personal. We felt Noah's innocence and yearning.

He touched our hearts.

Whatever horror befell him, his own father couldn't protect him. It was now up to John and me . . .

1

Two Worlds

BOB HILLAND, *Police Officer, FBI Agent*

After seven years as an NJ police officer, I joined the FBI in 1997 as a special agent assigned to the New York office.

I remember the first time I looked into the eyes of evil: the day I first saw killer John Smith.

It was in the fall of 1991, and I was a 23-year-old patrolman in West Windsor Township, New Jersey.

New to the force, I would become painfully aware of the unsavory, dangerous characters that were part and parcel to the job.

I almost died once after a drugged-up jackass dragged me down the highway. I was on routine duty and spotted a stalled pickup in the middle lane of a three-lane roadway. I pulled over to investigate.

As I approached the truck on foot, I could see wild hair and a tattooed neck through the half-open window.

"Good afternoon, sir," I said. "What seems to be the . . ."

The driver slowly turned to look at me, pupils dilated and fixed. He took a drag from a joint (laced with PCP, I'd learn later). A crazy-eyed Jesus on acid.

"Out of the car!" I ordered, pulling the door handle. It was locked.

At 6'8" and 250 pounds, I was an intimidating figure. Coworkers at the department nicknamed me "Big Bird" for my size — and later, for the number of collars I brought in.

But Crazy Eyes didn't flinch. He took another drag and turned away.

I reached through the window for the lock — big mistake. He raised the window, trapped my arm, slipped the truck in gear, and sped off — yanking me with him.

My body slammed against the truck and

bounced off the road like a rag doll as I fought from getting sucked under the tires.

"Pull over!" I yelled. "You're going to kill me!"

Crazy Eyes swerved and slammed against a concrete barrier, releasing my arm and sending me flying. I landed in the middle of four lanes of speeding oncoming traffic.

I scrambled to safety and chased the guy in my car, finally pulling him over and dragging him out of the truck before wrestling him to the ground and cuffing him as backup arrived. At the hospital later, doctors were shocked I had no broken bones or ruptured organs.

After the incident, I realized that the driver was the same man I'd spoken to several days earlier about kicking his drug habit.

That guy was drugged up, but his crazy eyes were not the eyes of evil — that was reserved for murderer John Smith and his cold, soulless gaze.

At the end of my shift one day in the fall of 1991, I passed through the department's dispatch area on my way to meet colleagues for a drink.

Through the lobby's bulletproof glass, a figure caught my attention — a thin, pale man sitting with another officer. He was fortyish and had a meek disposition. He would

INCETON PAC

Serving the Princetons, West Windsor, Montgomery, Plainsboro, Rocky Hill and surrounding areas.

A close encounter

WW cop survives, spares his attacker

By John P. McAlpin
Staff Writer

See **ENCOUNTER**, Page 15A

Staff photo by Mark Czajkowski

Officer Robert Hilland describes his encounter this week with a motorist who dragged him 75 feet through Route 1's rush-hour traffic in a pickup truck.

As a patrolman, I was dragged down a highway by a criminal high on PCP.

April 1992 — police photo of John Smith seven months after he reported his second wife, Fran, missing (COURTESY OF THE FBI)

have disappeared into the colorless background except for his reddish hair and those eyes. Killer eyes. A devil with an innocuous name . . . John Smith.

He looked up and our eyes locked.

His were like a shark's the second before it rips you apart.

From that first moment, it was a battle of wills between Smith and me. We stared, each challenging the other to look away.

I couldn't. I was seeing something difficult to comprehend — an evil spirit hiding in a human body, daring me to expose it.

We remained locked in our staring contest until the officer asked Smith a question and he looked away.

The date was October 4, 1991, and Smith had come to the department to report his second wife, Fran, missing. I would later learn that Fran was not his only wife to have disappeared. Seventeen years earlier in Ohio, he'd reported his first wife, Janice, missing.

Little did I know at the time that this scrawny man with the eyes of a killer shark would change my life forever.

Little did I know that I'd spend much of the next three decades searching for his missing wives, trying to find justice for them. And

Fran was outgoing and enjoyed posing for photos. (COURTESY OF THE FBI)

Janice Hartman's high school yearbook photo. She went missing in 1974, a few days after her divorce from Smith was final. (COURTESY OF THE FBI)

that they would haunt the rest of my days and come to me at night in my dreams.

My role as defender and protector began in childhood, out of necessity.

The eldest of five children, I grew up in a dysfunctional family plagued by trauma, apathy, and alcoholism. As a boy growing up in Brooklyn and later in New Jersey, I took care of and protected my younger siblings. I was the family guardian.

My father, Bob Sr., was Archie Bunker with a drinking problem — the world was black and white to him. My mother, Virginia, grew up with an alcoholic and absent father after losing her mother at an early age. Her upbringing was so tough that the city of New York put her in a shelter to protect her from her own father. Both my parents had unresolved traumas that affected every aspect of our family dynamic. I tirelessly tried to keep the family together while striving to win my parents affirmation.

As a teen I pumped iron and excelled in sports and academics. And I grew, towering over my family, my classmates, my teachers.

I never considered myself a fighter and never looked for trouble. But if I saw a bully picking on a weaker kid, I jumped in with my body and fists. In high school, I was suspended a few times for brawling. It didn't bother me much. My instinct was to protect the innocent and vulnerable and take down the abusers. If that got me in trouble, so be it.

You'd think my instincts would've led me to the police academy, but being a cop never occurred to me. When I joined the police force at age 22, it was by accident. (Although, I've learned since that there are no "accidents" or "coincidences" in life.)

I was a junior at Rutgers University studying history when a buddy asked me to go with him to take an entrance exam at the local police department. I aced the test, and if it's true that biology is destiny, my physique sealed my fate. The department had a winning softball team with a couple of vacancies, and I knew how to swing a bat.

I'd only been on the force for a year, still a rookie, when that drugged-up maniac dragged me down the highway in '91. I could take the beating; I was used to it. I wanted the tough assignments others didn't. I wanted to go after the bad guys no one wanted to touch. I liked going into battle, fighting the good fight, then walking off the field when it was over — no accolades or awards required.

My work gave me the validation I needed, the approval I never got from my parents.

It gave me purpose.

Six years after I looked into John Smith's predatory eyes, I began a new job: FBI special agent working on New York City's Cold Case Squad. The squad reexamined unsolved homicide investigations that were stuck in limbo, some for decades.

Our downtown Manhattan office was blocks from the World Trade Center and across from the Supreme Court buildings where *Law & Order* actors ran amok playing cops and criminals. On coffee breaks, I'd sit on a bench behind 26 Federal Plaza and see them with their cameras and lights, their imaginary world next to our very real one.

It was 1997, the era of Walkmans, fax machines, and pagers. Slow-as-a-snail technology compared to today, but back then it was cutting edge. The streets of New York City bustled with an energy and pace I hadn't known in Jersey, and I thrived on it.

Inside my new office, the pace was different.

My first day on the job, I found my officemate, Richie DeStano, asleep at his desk with glasses resting on the end of his nose and hands folded on top of his belly. His desk was strewn with coffee-stained files, empty cartons of chow mein from nearby Chinatown, and crumpled coffee cups. He was short and balding, my physical opposite. Someone nudged him awake. With a yawn, he got up and gave me a tour.

"Homicides can be some of the easiest cases to work," he said. "Bad-Guy-One kills Bad-Guy-Two over money, drugs, power, or a woman. Change the names, dates, and locations, and it's the same case over and over."

He grabbed an armload of files from his desk and dumped them on mine.

"Your first cases. Some are old dogs that won't ever be solved. For others, your murderers are already in prison for something else, or maybe even dead. Don't kill yourself on them. We got hundreds more," he said.

Then he pointed at me with a warning.

"And remember," he added, "*big cases, big problems . . . little cases, little problems.* No cases . . . get the picture?"

I nodded, to be polite. But I was the kind of guy who went big and all the way; I didn't do anything on a "little" scale.

I made my way through the mountain of files he'd slapped on my desk — faded yellow reports with crime photos dating back years, and sometimes decades.

Does anyone care about these victims anymore?

Someone had to.

A year later, in the summer of 1998, I was called to testify in some old cases from my police officer days. When court was over, I stopped by my old department to catch up with the guys, walking past that thick, bulletproof glass where I'd seen Smith years earlier. Everybody yelled:

"Hey, Big Bird!"

"Birdman!"

"The Bird!"

Detective Matt Dansman pulled me into his cubicle.

"How's the FBI treating you, Bird? Are they making you run after Russian spies or something?"

Dansman's desk was piled high like DeStano's, with the addition of an unusual item — a cheesy fortune teller's crystal ball. Dansman sometimes consulted with psychics on cases, and the guys teased him about it, giving him the novelty gift as a joke.

It was a sunny day, and as we talked, a beam of light from a window hit the crystal like a laser. It threw a rainbow of colors onto a bookshelf next to us, illuminating a binder with words in black magic marker:

BETTY "FRAN" SMITH — MISSING PERSON. As we chatted, I got up and pulled it off the shelf, opening it.

The photo on the first page gave me a jolt.

There he was, that guy from six years earlier with the evil eyes.

Oh, no, not this monster. I turned the page to find photos of his missing wives — Janice Hartman and Fran Smith. Again, I felt a thunderbolt — but this one was different. These women in the photos were strangers to me, but I felt an immediate, emotional, all-encompassing need to help them. As if they were urging me to.

"What's the status on this, Matt?" I asked, trying to be nonchalant.

"Dead in the water," he said. "No bodies, no evidence, no crime we can prove. That guy got away with at least two murders that we know of."

I couldn't take my eyes off the women; Fran's smile was full of mischief, and Janice looked like someone's sweet kid sister.

"There must be a way to breathe new life into it. Shake the trees a little?"

"Nope. We did everything. Between here, Ohio, and Connecticut, there's nothing left."

I looked into Fran's lively eyes and remembered Smith in the police lobby, filling out the missing person report on her. Days before, she'd been alive and smiling, like in this photo. I remembered Smith's eyes challenging me, daring me to catch him.

"Do you mind if I look into it?" I asked.

"Are you kidding? Be my guest!"

It was a reckless move, taking on a hopeless case that was out of my jurisdiction when I had dozens waiting for me on my desk in New York. But as I said, I liked tough assignments. I liked figuring out the impossible. At home, I had a dozen Rubik's Cubes I twisted and turned until I solved their three-dimensional puzzles. I liked mysteries.

But this went deeper. I was a no-nonsense, follow-the-facts guy. I was brought up a churchgoer and did not subscribe to superstition, hocus-pocus, or the supernatural. Had I believed in such things, I might have said destiny or cosmic forces pulled me to this case. Whatever it was, I couldn't explain it.

I made a silent vow: no matter how long it took, I was going to find Janice and Fran and put this monster behind bars. Forever.

"The answer is no, absolutely not," my supervisor, Stan Nye, said the next day at the New York office. "You're juggling dozens of cases here already without taking on Jersey's work, too."

"Stan, this guy Smith is bad news. Let me do some preliminary work and see what develops?"

Nye shook his head.

I got quiet. My voice took on a tone of urgency.

"This case means a lot to me. Would it be alright if I ran it past Buckbee?"

Dennis Buckbee was Nye's boss, and no one wanted to deal with him — especially Nye. Buckbee had the temperament of a hurricane. He was born yelling at everyone.

"You've got some set of balls, Bob. Go ahead. If he's good with it, so am I."

An hour later I was in Buckbee's office lining up photos of Smith, Janice, and Fran on his desk.

"New Jersey made an official request for our help," I told him. It was almost the truth.

"So? Forward it to Newark. This doesn't involve New York. We don't even have venue."

FBI offices were territorial and sensitive about poaching cases from other divisions. It was the kind of bureaucracy I hated. I was ready with an answer after skimming the details in the binder.

"We could open the case in New York as a kidnapping," I suggested. "Smith had a girlfriend in Connecticut he drove to see the weekend Fran went missing. The timeline shows he traveled through New York at the time of her disappearance. He could have dumped her body in New York."

Buckbee looked at the photo of Smith and grimaced.

"You know, we had a case like this in Pennsylvania a few years back. Guy killed his wife, reported her missing, had a girlfriend in Ohio. As hard as we tried, we couldn't make the case against him stick. Your Smith reminds me of that arrogant cocksucker. But let's be honest, the connection here to New York is weak. Our only interest here is *your* interest, correct?"

Damn it.

"Correct," I said.

Buckbee gathered the photos and handed them back.

"Open the case, Bobby. Run down outstanding leads and report back to me. Get the state and local cops to contribute. I don't want this case to take up all of your time. If this thing becomes a problem, I will shut it down. Do you understand?"

Absolutely. You bet. No problem.

I worked late into the night, sifting through police reports, statements, evidence receipts, search photos, and documents spanning decades of investigative work. I was so immersed I almost didn't hear the phone.

"Bobby, it's me. I haven't heard from you, and I've been worried."

Damn it.

"Alex, I'm sorry. I meant to call . . ."

The life of a cop's wife is thankless, especially if the cop is an obsessive workaholic, like me. Alex and I'd known each other in high school but didn't start dating until years later, in the fall of '91, a few weeks before I locked eyes with Smith.

We married on Valentine's Day, 1992, five months after our first date. Before I joined the FBI we had our son, Connor, and daughter, Caitlyn — now aged three and one. In that time, I'd missed family dinners, first words, and first steps because of my intense dedication to work.

When I was home, I tried to be the father I never had. Every day, I hugged my children tight and told them I loved them.

"Are the kids okay?" I asked.

"Caitlyn's asleep but Connor's molars are coming. He's miserable."

"I'm sorry. I have a new case. I'll be home in an hour. Or two. Assuming traffic isn't bad . . ."

Silence.

"Another new case?" she asked, sadly. "I hope you don't get too wrapped up in this one. You're hardly home as it is."

I paused. I knew I was standing on the edge of a high-diving board, about to jump into the deep end of the Smith case. She sensed it, too.

"Will you still be up when I get home?" I asked.

"Probably not," she said. "I'll see you when I see you."

Click.

I got home well past midnight. The house was asleep. I tiptoed into Caitie's room and inhaled the sweet baby powder scent. At the crib, I touched her cheek.

"I love you, Caitie-bear," I whispered.

I went to Connor's room. He was curled up like a ball hugging a teddy bear. I sat on the edge of his bed and tucked the blanket around him.

"Goodnight, little buddy. I love you."

At age 30, my days and nights were filled with blood, violence, criminals, and murderers. When I finally made it home, my innocent children were points of light in a dark world.

* * *

JOHN EDWARD, *psychic medium*

John Edward was wary of cops.

His dad was a cop and like me; he was named after his father.

Born John Edward McGee, Jr., in Queens, New York, the psychic had deep respect for the badge and uniform, something his Irish American police officer father, John McGee, Sr., instilled in him at a young age.

But John Sr. was also a hard-drinking, distant alpha male who didn't understand his intuitive, sensitive son. As a kid, John saw colorful auras around people and could tell you who was calling on the phone before you answered it. He was into vibrations instead of sports.

John's father hated anything that smacked of supernatural "nonsense" and was vocal about it. But John's mother, Perinda, was a self-confessed psychic junkie. John was their only child, but her side of the family — she had ten siblings — was big, Italian, and boisterous, and they embraced the mystical.

Once a year, Perinda whipped up a cake, put on the coffee percolator, and invited two dozen friends and family over for a house party starring a special guest — a psychic, who'd set up shop in John's bedroom and, one by one, tell people their future.

"Make sure Johnny's not home," his father would say. "I don't want him around that crazy stuff."

Even though he exhibited psychic abilities, young John was a skeptic like his father — a "huge doubter," he recalls.

That changed when he was fifteen. At one of his mother's psychic parties, John agreed to get a "reading" with the guest psychic to prove his mother and the other devotees wrong. He was the one proven wrong. The psychic — Lydia Clar — told the teen-ager details about his past and present she couldn't have known.

And she made a pronouncement about his future: He had an exceptional ability to communicate with those who'd passed, to bridge the gap between the physical and nonphysical worlds. His destiny, she informed him, was to teach and help others. One day he would be known internationally for his work as a psychic medium.

"You're the reason I'm here today," she said. "I'm supposed to put you on this path."

John was stunned.

After that day, he studied books on psychic phenomena, spirit guides, metaphysics, and spiritualism. He honed his abilities, communicating with the Other Side using energy. He saw pictures, heard words, and felt sensations. Soon, he was doing readings for friends and at local psychic fairs.

By sixteen he was making a name for himself in the psychic community on Long Island, where he lived with his mother and grandmother after his parents eventually split.

His father was not happy about this new path.

"You're not allowed to use my last name," John Sr. demanded. "I won't have you besmirch the family name."

John Jr. obeyed and used his middle name instead, creating the name he'd become known as professionally: "John Edward."

His father had a second command for his son: he must never engage with law enforcement and risk embarrassing him.

"How come whenever a psychic works with the police, they always say, 'The body will be found near water'?" his father asked, with a smirk. "The planet's 90 percent water. That's stacking the deck in a psychic's favor. Psychics are not helpful on cases. Real cops don't use psychics."

But it was inevitable that clients would reach out to John hoping to find lost loved ones.

One woman who booked an appointment his first year wanted to locate her missing niece.

The niece and her live-in boyfriend both struggled with mental issues. One day, she vanished. Her purse, credit cards, wallet, and jacket were all home but she was gone, without a trace.

During the reading, John immediately got details. The young woman had been murdered, and he saw the scene like a movie clip in front of him.

"I described who I thought was the perpetrator," John remembers, "and the details fit the girl's boyfriend, down to his looks, the car he drove, and where he lived. And then I got a name — Timothy."

The client immediately latched onto the name.

"My son Timothy passed," she said, tearfully. "They must be together in the afterlife; he's bringing her through!"

John didn't feel that he was getting *that* Timothy, but the woman insisted. Her emotional outburst and need to connect with her deceased son soon derailed the reading, shutting down any new information.

Investigators later arrested the niece's next-door neighbor — named *Timothy.* His looks, car, and location were similar to the information John got in the reading about the boyfriend.

The experience shook John up. "I decided

I never wanted to point fingers at anyone ever again," he says. "What if the innocent boyfriend had been arrested? It shut me down for working on other missing person cases."

Against his father's wishes, John attempted to work with police twice.

In 1989, the year John's mother died, one of his aunts asked if he'd help out with a case she'd seen in the newspaper — the murder of undercover DEA agent Everett E. Hatcher on Staten Island. It was the first murder of a DEA agent in New York City since 1972.

The suspected killer was mobster Costabile Farace, an associate of the Bonanno crime family. The FBI issued a manhunt, putting Farace on the Ten Most Wanted list.

"Do your thing. Find him!" his aunt urged. She was proud of John's ability.

"It doesn't work that way," he told her, as he scanned the news article she'd left for him on his grandmother's staircase. "I can't just think of someone and . . ."

A minute later, the staircase turned black and fell away. He steadied himself against the railing as information about the murder came to him in a dizzying rush. A minute after that, he was on the phone with police.

"The photo of the suspect in the newspaper, he doesn't look like that anymore," John told the officer. John's own body began to move into a bodybuilder pose as he talked to the cop.

"This guy's been in prison. He's jacked. He's huge now, like a body builder. You need to use another picture."

The cop passed John to the FBI agent in charge of the case, and John repeated the information, frustrated.

"Listen, my dad's a New York City police officer. I have great respect for the uniform. I'm not a crackpot, this is not a prank."

The next day, the newspapers released a new photo of the suspect — this time with his pumped-up physique, in the bodybuilder pose John was making.

John was a wreck.

He kept waiting for his father to find out he'd called the cops and then confront him, outraged: "Are you fucking nuts calling the cops? Are you crazy? Keep that shit to yourself!"

His father never found out, but the fear was there for John.

Ten months after the Hatcher murder, mobster Farace was found shot to death. John never heard back from the police and never found out if his information had been helpful to them.

The second time John contacted the police

about a case was after seeing a news item on TV about a bank robbery in Denver, Colorado.

"You're not finding the robber because you're looking for a woman," John told the cop manning the tip hotline. "But they're showing me it's a man. You should be looking for a man, they tell me."

The cop on the other line paused, confused.

"Who's 'they'?"

John sighed.

"That's a whole other conversation."

* * *

In 1990, the blockbuster romantic-fantasy, *Ghost* — a film about a murdered banker (Patrick Swayze) who tries to help his girlfriend (Demi Moore) with the help of a psychic (Whoopi Goldberg) — hit movie screens, shining a spotlight on psychics solving crimes.

John received calls from law enforcement looking for help, but now he vowed to stay away from that kind of work. His other attempts frustrated him.

His mediumship was still a sideline, anyway. He was studying for his master's degree in healthcare and public administration and working as a phlebotomist at a hospital. He learned ballroom dancing (he met future wife, Sandra, on the dance floor and married in 1995) and eventually became an instructor.

"My male ego didn't see psychic work as a viable or acceptable path forward," he says. "I didn't think of it as a real option. The image of my father's disapproving face if I told him I was pursuing a career flipping tarot cards and talking to dead people was not something I wanted to see."

But as word spread about his abilities, the hospital switchboard where he worked lit up with people looking for him, wanting sessions. In 1995, he quit his jobs and began working as a full-time psychic medium.

By the summer of 1998, at the age of 28, John was conducting seminars and readings and working on his first book, *One Last Time.*

That June, he appeared as a guest on the highly rated late-night talk show *Larry King Live,* describing his work and giving on-air readings. The phone lines at CNN blew up. His appearance ignited a media frenzy.

John Edward became a staple on the morning radio shows in the tri-state area and across the country that summer. His celebrity grew. And yet, he continued to turn down requests to work with police.

"I didn't want to waste their time or appear to be disrespectful or get in their way," he says.

His father's disapproving voice, years later, still rang in his ears.

"Psychics are not helpful," said John Sr. *"Real cops don't use psychics."*

John didn't get involved. He was guarded. He refused to go there.

Until the day in the summer of 1998, after I reopened the Smith case and heard John on the radio.

That's when John Edward got a call from *me.*

2

The Psychic, the Background, the Game Plan

THE COPS

Detective Matt Dansman, *New Jersey Police*
Detective Dave Minor, *New Jersey Police*
Sergeant Brian Potts, *Wayne County Sheriff's Office, Ohio*
Detective Sergeant Frank Barre, *Milford, Connecticut, Police Department*

THE SMITH LIST

Unknown girl in Smith's wallet photo
Sheila Sautter, *girlfriend of Smith*
Sherrie, *Fran's sister*
Deanna, *Fran's daughter*
Janice Miller, *prostitute in Milford, Connecticut*
Michael Smith, *John Smith's brother*
Ethel, *John Smith's grandmother*

THE WILD CARD

John Edward, *psychic on radio*

The Psychic

I first heard of psychic medium John Edward in the summer of 1998, a few weeks after I started on the Smith case. During my morning commute to Manhattan, I'd flick on the radio as I drove along the New Jersey Turnpike or waited to get into the Holland Tunnel.

One particular day, I was driving from the FBI's downtown Manhattan office back to West Windsor, New Jersey, for a big meeting about the case. Stuck in traffic by the Holland Tunnel, I switched on the radio in search of some classic rock tunes.

Instead, I got *The Big Show* on 95.5 WPLJ. Scott Shannon was a radio legend and his co-host was DJ Todd Pettengill.

". . . And we're back with John Edward! Every time we have John on the show, the switchboard lights up like the Fourth of July! For those of you who aren't familiar with my good friend Mr. Edward, he is a famous psychic who has the unique ability to communicate with those who have crossed over. He sees, feels, and hears energy and states the information out loud for the subject to validate. John has noooo idea who we're putting on the phone for him to read.

"First up we have Karen from Corona, Queens. Karen, you're on with celebrity psychic medium John Edward."

"Hello, John."

"Hello Karen. Right away I can tell you that there's a female energy around you. This person is above you. I believe it's your mother. Who has the 'Cat'-sounding name like Cathy or Kathleen?"

"My mom. Her name was Katherine."

"Okay, and this person's passing was very sudden. I feel an impact. Was she in a car accident?"

"Yes, yes, she died in a car accident last year."

"She's telling me she had a sister cross over in the same accident."

"Yes, Aunt Flo, her sister, died in the same accident!"

"And where's the B sound like Betty, Bennie . . ."

I turned the radio off, fuming, and shook my head.

"How about B for bullshit," I said out loud. "Is that the B you're looking for?"

Why did people believe such crap?

The purpose of the West Windsor meeting was to gather investigators who'd been on the case since in 1974 when Smith's first wife, 23-year-old Janice Hartman, went missing in Wayne County, Ohio.

I was eager to review the past details of the case, get up to speed to current day, and brainstorm new leads. I'd already pored through piles of reports and filings on the case and had a notebook filled with details, questions, and timelines in front of me.

But I wanted to hear that information from human voices, from the officers and agents who'd been there, face-to-face with Smith and others involved. I needed to know what they felt in their guts — a nuance you won't find written in any police report. This would help me envision the puzzle, the Rubik's Cube of moving pieces, that made up the case. I'd get a sense of what was missing, which way to twist and turn it.

The Background

In the conference room, I sat around a table with Detectives Matt Dansman, Dave Minor, and other investigators from the New Jersey department. On speaker phone, several investigators from Ohio and Connecticut waited.

After everyone filled their coffee cups, I stood up and placed photos of Smith, Janice, and Fran on the table.

"Any time we revisit old homicide cases," I began, "the intent isn't to second-guess or criticize the initial investigation. In fact, I have been very impressed with what I've read in your reports."

Smith and 19-year-old Janice married in 1970.
(COURTESY OF THE FBI)

I tapped the tip of my pen under each photo.

"Cases like this don't go unsolved due to a lack of effort, they go unsolved due to a *lack of evidence.* And clearly that's what we have here."

Everyone nodded.

"But now, the passage of time could work in our favor. Witness relationships and loyalties change. People reluctant to cooperate then are willing to provide information now. And we have the luxury of 20/20 hindsight, the evolution of forensics, and the general wisdom we all accrued over time. There's no doubt in my mind that if we put our heads together, we'll shake out new leads and create an investigation strategy."

I rolled up my sleeves.

"Let's get started. First, does anyone know where Smith is now?"

They all shook their heads.

A voice piped up from the speakerphone.

"Nobody's seen or heard from him since we made that run at him in 1996 at Kent State," said Sergeant Brian Potts, from the Wayne County Sheriff's Office in Ohio. "He was working as a salesman at a used car lot. We found out he was driving around with a suspended license and had him pulled over and arrested. We interrogated him for hours. Dansman and Minor were there."

Dansman and Minor nodded.

They hoped Smith would slip up and say something incriminating about Janice or Fran, said Potts, "but we got nothing. He sat there for hours, taking it all in like a sponge. He never asked to leave or even go to the bathroom. He just kept making that stupid ass sound every time we caught him lying."

The officers groaned in unison.

"Sound?" I asked, looking around the table. "What sound?"

Potts cleared his throat.

"It was bizarre. A cross between a cat

being run over and a woman screeching in pain. Kinda like . . ."

Officer Minor leaned toward the phone and let out a high-pitched shriek: *"WRRREEEEEAAANNNNNN!!!!!"*

Everyone chuckled.

"You're kidding," I said.

"No joke," said Potts. "Whenever we had that guy cornered in a lie, he would make that stupid sound."

Minor sat back in his chair. "Never heard anyone make a noise remotely close to that, before or since. And Bob, there was one other thing. Dansman?"

Dansman reached for a file folder and pulled out a wallet-sized photograph sealed in a plastic bag, which he handed to me. It was a picture of a heavyset woman with brown eyes and long dark hair.

"When we searched Smith at Kent PD, he had this photo in his wallet," said Dansman.

"Who is she?"

"Smith wouldn't tell us, Bird. He'd only say she was his girlfriend from New Hampshire. We didn't know where to begin trying to ID her. We don't even know if she's alive."

I scribbled notes on a yellow legal pad.

"Okay, what about this girlfriend in Connecticut? Tell me about Sheila Sautter."

They told me Sheila had been Smith's

girlfriend for eight years, living as his common-law-wife in Milford, Connecticut, before he met, married, and got a condo with Fran in Jersey.

While married, Smith would visit Sheila on weekends, telling Fran he owned a house there with tenants and had to go to make weekly repairs.

"He was essentially living a double life for years," said Dansman.

"Did Fran suspect anything?" I asked.

"Seems so . . ."

In the weeks leading up to her disappearance, Dansman explained, Fran was recovering from a broken hip, her family told police. She suffered from osteoporosis and slipped on a wet floor while getting out of the bathtub. I'd seen the medical reports and photos. She was housebound, in pain, unable to sleep, and unable to get around without a walker.

". . . meanwhile, Smith was working long hours at his job," Dansman continued.

"And then he'd disappear on weekends," I said, "so, Fran would have been angry and frustrated, right?"

"Right," said Dansman. "She wasn't stupid, she suspected he had a girlfriend in Connecticut. She talked to her daughter, Deanna, and sister, Sherrie, about it. Deanna wanted her mother to walk away from the marriage and offered to drive up from Houston with a U-Haul to get her and her stuff."

"And Sherrie, the sister?"

"Sherrie told Fran she should confront Smith with a list of demands, things she needed to continue with the marriage. Like going to his workplace and meeting his colleagues, going to the storage unit where her new furniture and belongings were supposedly kept, putting her name on a joint bank account and credit cards . . ."

". . . and let me guess," I jumped in. "At the top of the list was to go to Connecticut with Smith and see this house and meet his tenants."

"Bingo," said Dansman.

"I'm guessing she didn't follow her daughter's advice, or she'd be alive in Houston right now."

"Exactly. Smith was Fran's fifth husband — she married one of them twice, so four husbands, five marriages — and she was too stubborn, maybe embarrassed, to walk away from another marriage."

"What happened next?"

Dansman gulped down some coffee.

"She confronted Smith with the list. And then evaporated off the face of the earth."

I checked the timeline in my notes.

"So, the last time Fran was seen was

Saturday, September 28, 1991 . . . six days before I saw Smith filing the missing person report."

They all nodded.

"She spoke to her daughter that morning, excited because it was her first time leaving the condo since the accident. She and Smith planned to go to Toys"R"Us to buy presents for her grandson. The last person to see her are two neighbors who lived in the same condo building?"

"Right," said Dansman. "The paramedic and his wife. Fran was walking with crutches toward the lobby exit door with Smith behind her, and the paramedic and his wife were walking in, so they held the door open for her. They later told us her face was red, blotchy, and swollen — as if someone had hit her. But because she was limping with crutches, they figured her injuries were the result of an accident."

"Any neighbors hear an argument or fight that day between Smith and Fran?"

"Nope. Nothing."

I leaned back in my chair and crossed my arms.

"So, after the phone call that morning with her daughter and the neighbor seeing her leaving the condo, she's never heard from or seen again."

"Right," said Dansman. "We went to their condo after he reported her missing and Fran's clothes, makeup, even her toothbrush were still there. She just vanished."

A silence fell over the room.

"And what was your take on the girlfriend, Sheila. Did she know about Fran?"

A deep voice with a Northeastern accent came through the speakerphone. It was Detective Sergeant Frank Barre, from the Milford, Connecticut, Police Department.

"Eventually," said Barre.

It was a relationship of convenience for her, said Barre. She suspected Smith might have a girlfriend in Jersey, but she didn't have money to live on her own and was glad to have her house and her dogs.

But one day Smith woke Sheila up "and told her, 'Just so you know, I'm married . . . and my wife is missing. Don't be concerned if the police come talk to you. She left me and went back to her family in Florida.' Sheila was shocked by that."

"When we began showing up at her door asking questions, she was horrified," said Barre. "This thing has been like a bad dream for her."

"The day we executed a search warrant at the house, Sheila did a consensual call with John."

"We thought we had him a couple of times," said Barre. "She got him to admit he'd failed a polygraph and was lying to police. He told her the police would never find any physical evidence to use against him. And here's the clincher," the detective continued. "At one-point, Sheila pleaded with Smith, saying she loved him and would stand by him no matter what, and, 'Let's do the right thing. Let's work together to help find Fran and Janice.' "

"What did he say to that?" I asked.

"He said, 'It's too late to help them.' "

Dansman slid a cassette tape of the phone call across the conference table to me.

I pulled out a black-and-white mugshot from my notebook and placed it on the table. The young woman in the picture looked sad and bruised. It was taken seven years earlier, in 1991.

"Okay, and you talked to this prostitute in Milford?"

"Sort of," said Barre.

In the summer of '92 the Milford police got an anonymous call from a man saying he dropped off a prostitute at Smith's house and recognized the house from a recent newspaper story about Fran's disappearance, with a headline like, SERIAL KILLER LIVES IN MILFORD!

“The guy freaked out and called us from a pay phone,” said Barre. “We sat on the house and identified the girl as Janice Miller.”

I added her name to my notes and underlined it.

“What’s her story?” I asked.

“Wish I could tell you. We tried to talk with her, but she was so strung out on drugs she couldn’t speak to us about anything, even if she wanted to.”

I scribbled more notes.

Last on my list was Smith’s younger brother, Michael, who lived in Ohio. Sergeant Potts and another detective interviewed him early in the case.

“We both got the impression he knew something but wouldn’t tell us,” Potts said, over the speakerphone.

“At one point he looked like he was about to talk. He looked stressed and you could see he was hanging on to something. We kept talking, trying to solicit his help. But then his grandmother, Ethel, barged into the room. She grabbed him by the hand like a little boy and told him not to say another word to us.”

“How did that end?”

“Ethel gave us a ‘go to hell’ look and escorted us out of the house. It was clear something was going on there.”

I made a few more notes.

"I'll send out leads to the Cleveland Division to gather as much information on Smith's family as possible."

I took one last look at the photos of Smith, Janice, and Fran in front of me, and ripped the top page off my notepad.

The Game Plan

"First, we need to find out where Smith is right now and do a workup on him. Where does he work? Is he married again? Let's hope not. Let's use any financial records, credit card statements, and telephone data we can find to put together a timeline of his activities in the last few years."

I held up the wallet photo in plastic.

"Next, let's try to identify this woman. And find the prostitute, Janice Miller, assuming she's alive."

Everyone scribbled down their tasks.

"And lastly, I need each of you to make a list of other people you think might be relevant to the case. Anyone who might hold a little piece of information, even the smallest bit. We need to leverage the information we already have to develop a spreadsheet of new leads and data points."

I stood up and scanned the room. Some of them seemed eager to revive the case and work together, others looked like they couldn't care less.

"Looks like we have a game plan," said Dansman, one of the eager ones.

"Right now, that's all we've got."

Dansman got up.

"Okay, Bird. You're driving this one."

I gathered the photos.

"Let's shake the trees and see what falls."

Back at the New York office, I was greeted by my doubtful office mate and thirty large boxes, just arrived from Butte, Montana, stacked on top of one another.

DeStano stood in the middle of the room, eyes bugging out over his reading glasses, shaking his head.

Weeks earlier I'd sent a records check request to the FBI's data center in Butte, Montana, for any activity linked to Smith's name, Social Security number, and date of birth.

We both stared at the fortress between our desks.

I checked the cover sheet on the nearest box: "JOHN SMITH, date of birth 04/02/1951."

"That's a hell of a lot of John Smiths," said DeStano, stabbing at a dumpling with a chopstick. "Looks like they sent you every

John D. Smith in the country. Must be thousands of hits in there."

My eyes glazed over.

"Please don't tell me I've got to sort through all these to find him."

"Why," asked DeStano, mouth full, "are you even bothering with this case?"

I still found it difficult to explain.

"I'm not sure," I said. "Maybe I want to solve the case from my old department that no one else could solve."

"You're setting yourself up for failure, Bobby. Some cases can't be solved, no matter how hard you try or how good you are."

DeStano circled the boxes and put an arm around me — as much as he could, seeing he was a foot shorter.

"Don't forget what I said from Day One. Little cases, little problems. Big cases . . ."

He pointed at the boxes with his chopstick and left the room.

I dropped into my chair by my desk. *What have I gotten myself into?*

It was going to be a long night.

Hours later, as I was sifting through a pile of papers from the first box, the phone rang.

I looked down, saw the home number on the caller ID, and picked up, filled with remorse.

"Alex, I'm sorry, I meant to call . . ."

"Bobby, I haven't heard from you and I've been worried."

Damn it.

3

Your Worst Nightmare

THE COPS

Detective Matt Dansman, *New Jersey*

THE SMITH LIST

Janice Miller, *prostitute in Milford, Connecticut*

THE WILD CARD

John Edward, *psychic on radio*

We began making progress fast.

I took the wallet picture of the unknown woman to the FBI photo lab and had it blown up. I could see tiny lettering in the lower right corner, too small to read. When the photo came back enlarged, I could make out a copyright and a company name: "Glamour Shots." I looked it up in the phonebook; it was one of those photo studio chains in shopping malls where women get dolled up and pose like Marilyn Monroe or something.

I checked the state of New Hampshire, where Smith said the girlfriend lived, and found three locations. I made copies of the photo and sent one to each studio, in hopes an employee might still be around who remembered the woman and have contact information in their files.

"You think someone's going to be able to ID this woman after all these years, just by seeing the picture?" Dansman asked.

"You got any better ideas?"

He didn't.

A few days after the big meeting, Dansman picked me up at home. We'd tracked down the prostitute, Janice Miller, through a simple records check. She was in a women's prison north of Milford for drug possession and prostitution. We arranged to talk to her that afternoon. Hopefully she'd be sober this time.

I was wrestling with Connor in the living room when Dansman pulled up in his unmarked cruiser and honked.

"Okay, little buddy, got to go to work now."

Connor pulled at my pant leg.

"No Daddy, I want you to play with me!"

"When I get home tonight, we'll play Rescue Heroes, okay?"

Alex walked in carrying Caitie and I gave them kisses.

"Will you be home for dinner?"

"I'm not sure. I'll call from the road when I have a better idea. We're driving up to Connecticut."

"What's in Connecticut?"

"A prostitute."

"What, there aren't enough prostitutes in New York?"

"Oh, you're funny. You should take that show on the road."

"You never know. One day I might."

"See you later. Love you."

The prison was surrounded by a twelve-foot-high barbed-wire fence.

A guard checked our ID at the first checkpoint and activated a series of large, motorized gates that slowly pulled open for our car to pass.

At the next checkpoint, we relinquished our holstered guns and pagers, but I kept an array of contraband essentials — two Snickers bars and a couple of packs of chewing gum.

We also carried the mug shot of Miller taken close to the time she knew Smith. She had long, blonde-ish hair and was sickly thin — her face gaunt and blue eyes sunken, typical of a street addict.

"Man, she looks like a hundred miles of bad road," said Dansman.

We went through another set of heavy steel doors that buzzed open remotely — very *Get Smart* — before reaching the visitor's room. The woman who appeared minutes later in a maroon jumpsuit was a shocking contrast to the photo we held — she was now plump, with short hair and a bright smile.

After introductions, we sat down and I slid a paper bag across the table.

"A token of our appreciation for your time," I told her.

She peeked in, smiled at the Snickers and gum, and slid the bag out of sight into her lap.

Her grin evaporated and her eyes went dark when I took out a photo of Smith and slid it across the table.

"Oh, him. Yeah, I remember John. I'm afraid to ask, but why is the FBI interested in him?"

"People close to Smith have a tendency to disappear," I said.

"People? Like, more than one?"

"Two wives, to be specific."

Janice looked like she was going to be sick.

"I thought I was done with him," she whispered, reaching for a bottle of water with trembling hands. "Does he know you're here talking to me?"

"No. No one knows we're here," I told her.

She breathed a sigh of relief.

"Man, do I need a cigarette."

She popped a piece of gum in her mouth and leaned forward.

"What do you want to know?"

Dansman and I took out notebooks and pens.

"For starters, how did you meet Smith?" I asked.

She told us they met in the summer of '92 in Bridgeport, Connecticut, when she was hooking to support a drug habit. He picked her up and took her back to his place in Milford for $40 of "straight sex" and then drove her back to Bridgeport.

"It was quick and it was over," she said.

"Then what?" I asked.

"After that . . . things got kind of strange."

"How so?"

"Each night after that he came back and picked me up. He never wanted sex though. We drove around endlessly. Sometimes he'd drive me to work, watch me go on dates, and take me home at the end of the night. He would follow me in his car and park down the street while I was turning tricks. It was bizarre. Most times when I was done and got back into his car, John acted like he had picked me up from a normal job."

"And the other times?"

"Other times he was pissed off at me and acted like he had just caught me cheating on him or something. One day he couldn't do enough for me and the next day he was so pissed it scared the hell out of me."

She paused.

"He was a real sugar daddy to me. He gave me money, bought me food, and even drugs. But mostly, he wanted to talk."

"What about?"

"A lot of things. About growing up in Ohio and his family out there. And about his ex-wives."

I made eye contact with Dansman.

"Was it *two* wives?" I asked.

"Yeah. I remember he said the last one . . . I think her name was Fran, divorced him and went back to Florida. When he told me about the other one, though, he really freaked me out."

"Why?"

"I remember him saying his first wife was dead, that someone killed her. Then he said, 'And guess what her name was?' He stared right into my eyes with a smile and said, 'Her name was the same as yours . . . *Janice.*' When he said that my blood ran cold and I wanted to get out of the car."

"What did you do?"

"Nothing. I giggled like it was no big deal.

Inside though, my heart was beating like a jackrabbit. Girls on the street, we develop a sixth sense about danger, it's what keeps us alive. With John, my sixth sense was always on. I never dropped my guard when I was around him. Something didn't feel right to me. Like there was another side to him."

After a few weeks, Smith asked her to move in.

"Now he's offering me food, clothing, *and* shelter. And the best part was, I don't even have to blow any strange guys, let alone him. So I said yes and moved in. It was a no-brainer."

"And how did that go?" I asked.

She took a deep breath.

"I'll tell you how it went. It was like living in an insane asylum."

She described months of lies, gaslighting, control, and terror. At one point, Smith stole her clothes and returned from the attic carrying big garbage bags.

"He looked me up and down, and said, 'I'm guessing you're a size four?' Then he starts pulling out women's clothes from the bags, coordinating colors and outfits for me like we're in a department store."

"Did John say where he got those clothes?"

"He said they had belonged to Fran, but that didn't make sense. They were all different sizes. And why didn't she take her clothes? Some had tags on them, like they'd never been worn. And some were torn like they'd been ripped off someone. I could smell a woman's perfume. It was strong."

Smith had two house rules, Janice said. She wasn't allowed to have friends over when he wasn't home, and she wasn't allowed to go into the attic. *Ever.*

"So," I smiled, "tell me about the time you went into the attic."

Janice smiled.

She looked while Smith was at work one day, she said. To get to the attic, you had to go through a square cut-out in the hallway ceiling outside of John's bedroom. She stood on a chair and pushed the square open. On her tiptoes, she was high enough to scan the attic.

"What did you see?

Boxes and garbage bags. "One had fallen over and I could see clothes inside," she said. "And that perfume. I could smell the same perfume that was on the clothes he brought down to me before."

Later that night, when Smith realized she'd been in the attic, he went crazy.

"Did he hit you?"

"No," she said, looking down. "It would have been better if he had."

"What does that mean?" I asked.

She looked up and into my eyes.

"He scared the hell out of me. When you work the streets, you get smacked around sometimes, it comes with the territory. But even though John never laid a hand on me, he terrified me."

"Why?"

"Because when he yelled, it came from deep inside his soul. Like he became possessed and transformed right in front of me. The night of the attic thing, he was inches from my face screaming. I could feel his breath and the froth from his mouth went everywhere. He was like a dog trying to attack but held back by a leash. It was a total freak-out."

She stopped and tried to calm herself, taking a sip of water.

"I froze. I though he was going to kill me. My heart was racing. After screaming at me for what seemed like forever, he pulled back, contained himself, and walked away. It was like the demon left him."

"And the next time you saw him?"

"He acted like it never happened. He was like Jekyll and Hyde. Living with John was like living with a hundred different personalities, and you never knew which one you were going to get."

They shared a bed, she said, and she'd wake up in the middle of the night sometimes to find him gone.

"I'd hear agonizing yells coming from another room. I was shit scared. The first time it happened, I went downstairs to figure out what was going on. John was sitting on the couch in the dark, his face buried in a pillow. He was screaming like he was being tortured.

I sat next to him and put my hand on his shoulder, you know, to try and comfort him. He jumped back and looked at me. He was disoriented, confused. He had been crying. I gave him a hug and tried to kiss him but he pulled back. I felt bad for him. I tried to give him a freebie . . . you know. But when I tried, he couldn't get it up. That sent him over the edge again. He called me a fucking whore and told me to get away from him. So, I did."

"Did you ever have sex with John other than the night he first picked you up?" I asked.

"No. Just that one time."

When Smith suggested a trip to Ohio to meet his family, Janice remembers being afraid.

"I had this feeling something bad was going to happen, so I pretended to call my mother and made sure John could hear me. I put the receiver to my ear and listened to a dial tone but 'told' my mother I was headed out of town with John and I asked him for the address of his family in Ohio."

"Why did you do that?"

"I wanted John to think I had people out there who'd be concerned about where I was, or if something happened to me, people who'd look for me."

"What made you feel that way?"

Janice reached for another piece of gum, her hands still shaking.

"I can't explain it. When you live and work on the street you get a sense for things, a feeling when something bad is going to happen. John always gave me that feeling. It was like at any moment my worst nightmare would come true."

An uncomfortable silence filled the room.

"What is your worst nightmare?"

Her eyes filled with terror.

"I never feared death when I was on the streets. Hell, sometimes I welcomed it. What I feared was dying at the hands of some cold-blooded stranger. It's what all the girls feared. Sometimes these guys got violent. And there I was living with this dude I had a terrible feeling about. I felt a quiet, unspoken, pure evil. Like a storm about to hit, but before it does there is this quiet, unspoken calm. Right before the storm hits, you can sense the instability in the air. That's what John was like. I was always waiting for the storm."

I felt my stomach tighten at her description. *Pure evil.* She saw it in him, too.

"Did you go to Ohio?"

"Yeah, we went," she said. "I met his whole family — his brother, Mike, his grandparents, and his mother, Grace."

"What did you think of them?"

"They were all very nice, especially Mike. Grace was indifferent to me, like she was bothered by my being there. John was very close with his grandmother, Ethel. He seemed closer to her than with his own mother."

"Why do you say that?"

"You could see it, even feel it. Ethel doted on him like he was this perfect little boy. It was a bit much, but John ate it up. With his mother, Grace, it was different. I felt like John and Grace held secrets about each other, it was very strange. They spoke in whispers, out of sight from everyone. One minute they were fine, and the next minute they were cold and distant to each other."

"You mentioned he lied a lot," I said.

"About everything."

"Did you ever catch him in a lie so big he couldn't explain it away?"

Janice nodded.

"He came home from work one night wearing a wedding band. I'd been with him for months and never saw him wear a ring. I asked him, 'John what's up with the wedding ring?' I could tell by the look on his face that he forgot he was wearing it. He looked down at his hand and his face turned bright red.

He stuttered and told me some bullshit story that his boss at work told him to wear the ring because it would show 'normalcy' in his life, whatever the hell that is. John used that word a lot, 'normalcy.' "

Anytime she tried to confront him about his lies, she added, "he became nervous and made this high-pitched squeal, like a scared little girl."

Dansman and I nodded. I still had the sound of Minor screeching like a tortured cat ringing in my ears.

"Was there anything special about that day?" I asked.

"Yes! It was my birthday! I specifically remember because he took me out to a nice restaurant for my birthday and I jokingly told him that people would think we were having an affair because he was wearing a wedding ring and I wasn't."

"When's your birthday?"

"September 28."

I recognized the date but couldn't place it. Why was it so familiar?

While Janice paused and took another sip of water, I flipped through my notebook, scanning notes and timelines. And then I saw it. The timeline of Fran's disappearance. *The last time anyone saw Fran alive was on September 28, 1991.* When Smith came home wearing the ring, it was the one-year anniversary of the day Fran disappeared. The day, I was sure, he murdered Fran.

I shuddered.

All of a sudden, Janice was in tears. Dansman and I looked at each other in confusion.

"What is it??" I asked.

"You guys need to go to Bridgeport," she said.

"Why? What's in Bridgeport?"

"When I was working the streets in the early nineties, a lot of my girlfriends were killed. Some nut was going around killing them. The Bridgeport cops set up a task force. Go there. Ask about Pam Safford, Lisa Distassio, and Karla Storer. They were my friends."

Her sobs grew louder.

"The cops were looking for a clean-shaven white guy with glasses. I can't tell you how many nights I sat in the Bridgeport Police Department looking at pictures of hundreds of men. The cops wanted to know if we recognized any of them or had any problems with them. I was so high that none of them looked familiar and all of them did. It wasn't like we were paid to look at their faces."

I realized the enormity of what she was saying.

"Janice. *Are you saying you think John killed your friends?*"

Tears streamed down her face. She grabbed my hands.

"Please go to Bridgeport, Agent Hilland," she pleaded. "They never caught the guy who killed them. I can't tell you John killed them . . . but I can't tell you he *didn't.*"

Dansman and I exchanged another glance. As in, *Holy shit, how many women did this guy murder?*

I squeezed her hands to reassure her.

"Don't worry, Janice. I promise we'll get to the bottom of this."

"I'm so sorry," she whispered.

She covered her face with her hands and wept more; my heart went out to her. She'd been through hell and back with Smith, and others.

"What are you sorry for?" I asked.

"I'm sorry for everything. I'm sorry if he hurt my friends or his wives. He won't stop until you've put him in jail, Agent Hilland. *You've got to stop him.*"

Back in the unmarked cruiser, there was no doubt in either of our minds where we were going next: Bridgeport, Connecticut.

As Dansman drove, I looked out the window and thought about everything Janice told us, overwhelmed by her revelations.

"We've got to get this guy, Matt," I said.

"Yeah, but how?" he asked, turning on the radio.

". . . and the next caller is Jeannie from Astoria. You're on with psychic John Edward . . ."

"Oh, man, I love this guy," said Dansman. "He's unbelievable."

Oh, no. I leaned my head back in disgust. Not this psychic guy again.

"My aching ass, Matt! You don't really believe this bullshit, do you? These callers are paid actors! This is an infomercial!"

"Shhhhhh. Listen, Bird, I'm telling you. This guy is legit."

"Jeannie, who's the female I see as next to you . . . a sister or a cousin? I see a darkness in her chest. This person had cancer, either in her lungs or breast. I'm getting an 'S' name like Susan, Samantha . . ."

"My sister, Suzanne! She died of breast cancer four years ago."

I reached over and turned the radio off.

"Hey, come on Bird! I was listening to that!"

"He's a wack job."

"Bird, you're a close-minded asshole, you know that?"

"Hell, Matt. Why don't we call him up and ask him how to catch Smith? I'll tell you why. Because we can't solve cases with crystal balls like the one on your desk."

We remained silent for the rest of the drive. How a cop could believe in psychics was beyond me. We were supposed to be like Sergeant Joe Friday on *Dragnet:* just the facts.

No hocus-pocus. No mumbo-jumbo. No damn way.

4

Wounded Women of the Night

THE COPS

Detective Matt Dansman, *New Jersey*

Bridgeport, Connecticut:

Detective Sergeant John Kennedy

Detective Linda Mastranardo

Detective Bill London

Detective Dan Sullivan

Detective Arthur Bradshaw

THE SMITH LIST

Unknown girl in Smith's wallet photo

Karla Storer, *drug addict and prostitute*

THE WILD CARD

John Edward, *psychic on radio*

We weren't prepared for what we saw as we arrived in Bridgeport.

The city looked like an abandoned, ravaged, desolate war zone. Broken bottles, rats, and trash littered the sidewalks in front of burned-out buildings with boarded-up windows. Drug dealers and hookers populated the streets, brazenly conducting business out in the open.

"This is Bridgeport?" Dansman asked, as they watched a large rat run from a pile of garbage with chicken bones in its mouth.

"I thought Bridgeport was supposed to be nice. What a shithole."

I strode into the lobby of the Bridgeport Police Department with Dansman trailing behind and pressed my credentials against the dispatcher's glass window.

"Bob Hilland with the FBI. Is there anyone in your Detective Bureau we can speak with?"

Minutes later, Detective Sergeant John Kennedy emerged through a heavy metal door and introduced himself.

"We got a tip you had some prostitute murders a few years back," I said.

Kennedy paused, then gestured for us to follow him down the hall to the Detective Bureau.

"Why is a New York FBI agent and a detective from Jersey interested in Bridgeport hooker cases?"

"We're working on an old missing person case out of Jersey," I said. "A lead sent us to the Woman's Correctional Facility in

Danbury to interview a woman who worked the streets back in the day."

We turned and went down another hall.

"So, what do you want . . . her arrest file?"

"Not exactly," I said. "We were told there was a task force looking at a string of related cases."

Kennedy stopped walking and turned toward me.

"Are you kidding?"

"No. Why?"

"Do you have a perp in mind?"

"Not sure. We've got a guy we think is good for two missing women and used to live in Milford. And he had a thing for a particular prostitute from Bridgeport."

Kennedy started walking again, "Follow me guys, back here."

The detective bureau at the very back of the station was in a seventies time warp: an open area of old metal desks, yellowing "WANTED" posters, and calendars of scantily clad women posing on hot rods. The bullpen smelled of cigarettes, old coffee, cheap aftershave, and stale pastrami.

Kennedy bellowed down the hall.

"Artie, Bill, Linda, Dan! I need you guys in the conference room!"

They were some of the detectives who'd been on the task force, Kennedy explained, but the force had also included detectives from five neighboring towns, the state attorney's office, and the state police.

After the group assembled in the conference room, Kennedy introduced us to Detectives Linda Mastranardo, Bill London, Dan Sullivan, and Arthur Bradshaw.

"They want to talk to us about our dead hooker cases."

The group looked surprised. Tired. Curious.

I briefed them on the Smith case, our meeting with Janice, and our suspicion that Smith could be the serial killer they were looking for.

"What's your guy's name?" Bradshaw asked.

"John Smith."

The detectives laughed.

"No, really. His name is John Smith."

I slid the mug shot of Janice Miller across the table.

"I remember her," Mastranardo said. "She took at least three collars here in the early nineties. A heroin junkie. Pretty bad, as I recall."

"Which one of them wasn't?" said London. "What's Smith's connection to our cases?"

"Not sure yet," I said. "Janice told us she feared for her life when she was living with

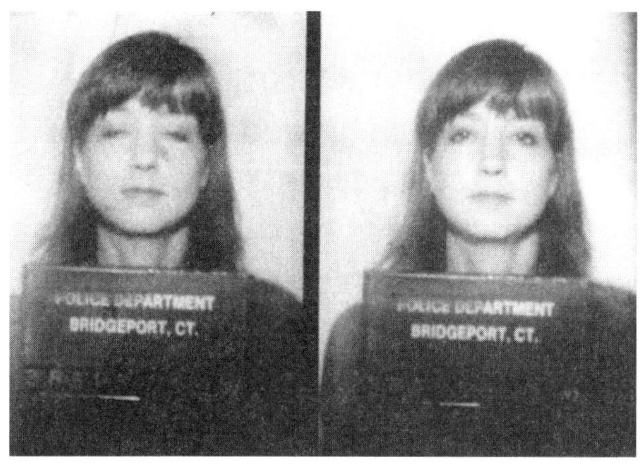

Janice Miller's mug shot after her arrest for prostitution: "I thought he was going to kill me." (COURTESY OF THE FBI)

him. And that Smith kept garbage bags filled with different women's clothing in his attic."

The energy in the room shifted. The detectives looked at one another, taken aback.

"Are those clothes still around?" asked Bradshaw.

"I doubt it. Smith sold the house and moved away in '95."

"Shit!"

"Why?"

"A lot of our girls were viciously killed and left completely naked," Bradshaw said. "We never recovered their clothes."

The room went quiet. The connection was undeniable.

Kennedy turned to the task force, suddenly a wartime commander briskly giving orders.

"Run this guy through our system," he directed. "See if we have Smith in the binders of photos that we showed the girls. If not, let's run his picture past our current women of the evening. And everyone, go grab your files so we can start going through them."

The group dispersed to their respective desks. I could hear metal filing cabinets creaking open and slamming shut. Moment later, they returned to the conference room and dropped thick folders and binders onto the table.

Bradshaw opened a spreadsheet of victims' names, dates, biographical information, and details of death.

"We have 25 girls in all," he began. "Our cases started around 1988 and the last one was 1995 . . ."

". . . the same year Smith moved away," I pointed out. "Causes of death?"

"The majority were manual strangulation combined with vicious stabbing. Serious overkill stuff."

He lined up victim photos on the table, images of young women's bodies gouged from head to toe. Many had defensive wounds so significant the flesh in their forearms and hands were cut to the bone. Others had pieces of fingers missing. I imagined the amount of force and violence it took to inflict this kind of trauma. The killer would have been in an uncontrollable, emotional rage during the attacks.

Dansman cleared his throat. Neither of us had ever seen anything so gruesome.

"Did you come up with any suspects?" Dansman asked.

"A few potentials, but nothing added up," said London. "This guy was smart. We never recovered any DNA. We recovered little to nothing in the way of physical evidence for comparison."

The task force spent months showing mug shots "to every known hooker," but nothing came of it.

"I spent many nights with countless girls," said Mastranardo. "Problem was, most of those girls were so high they didn't even know their own names."

"And," I added, "maybe your killer had no priors."

"That crossed our minds," she said. "We thought he had to be a real unknown to this area. Maybe even an interstate trucker making stops in the city."

I checked my notes for the list of names Janice Miller gave us.

"What can you tell us about a girl named Karla Storer? Janice Miller said she was a friend."

Bradshaw pulled out Karla's file.

"Came from a good family. Went to college. Got a taste for heroin and coke. Karla's family put her in rehab a dozen times, but it didn't take. She began turning tricks to support her habit."

He placed a photo of Karla on the table. Underneath her caked-on makeup and disheveled appearance, she had a baby face.

Storer disappeared in the summer of '92 after getting into a customer's sedan hatchback, Bradshaw continued. Her boyfriend, a fellow addict, was the last person to see her alive.

"He saw her get in the car," said Bradshaw. "A white guy with glasses was behind the wheel."

"Where did you find her body?" I asked.

"It wasn't as easy as that," Bradshaw said, shaking his head. The detectives in the room shifted uncomfortably.

"The next day we were called to the third floor of a public parking deck. It looked like somebody had been slaughtered and their blood was used to paint the walls."

Bradshaw handed me a pile of photos, each one more depraved than the one before. They reminded me of the blood-painted walls in the Manson family murders circa 1969. I handed them to Dansman, who flinched as he scanned them.

"I don't see a body at the scene," I said.

"Exactly," Bradshaw replied, "There wasn't one. We had a scene that looked like *The Amityville Horror* without a body. A few days later, Karla's body turned up in a dumpster in Trumbull near a strip mall. Some worker was taking out trash and noticed a terrible smell. He looked inside and saw a body. Once we figured out it was Karla, we rounded up the most likely suspect."

"The boyfriend."

"You got it. We brought him in and put him through hell. He was crying, yelling, and passing out from heroin withdrawal. The next day, when he was sober enough, we polygraphed him. He passed. I was there. He told us we could put him in jail for the rest of his life if we wanted, but his life was over because the love of his life was killed while having sex with a strange man. He blamed himself for letting her get in that car."

Once he'd been ruled out as a suspect, the boyfriend sat with a sketch artist and gave a description of the customer in the car, said Bradshaw. When the artist finished the sketch, the boyfriend freaked out.

"He cried uncontrollably and pointed at

the picture, saying: 'That's him! That's the guy she got in the car with! That's the guy who killed Karla!' "

"Do you have a copy of the sketch?" I asked.

"Sure," said Bradshaw, as he dug through his files.

"*What the . . . ?* It should be here. Who the hell took the sketch from my case folder?"

Silence.

"I'll call Trumbull and have them fax over a copy," said Kennedy.

Meanwhile, something Bradshaw said stuck in my mind.

I opened my folder and searched, pulling out a motor vehicle record of the car Smith registered after Fran's 1991 disappearance: A sedan hatchback matching the color and description of the car Karla Storer got in the night she disappeared.

I slid the record to Dansman, whose eyes widened.

Next, I pulled out a 1992 mug shot of Smith.

The old fax machine in the corner of the room squealed.

Mugshot in hand, I walked to the fax machine and watched as it slowly spit out the composite sketch, inch by inch.

When it was done, I held up Smith's

mugshot and the sketch, side by side, to the room.

The room fell silent again, this time in shock.

The shape of the head, the almond-shaped eyes, the thin lips depicted in the sketch. It was as if Smith had posed for it.

As I pulled into the driveway at home, I tried to erase the images I'd seen that day of women's faces and bodies slashed and chopped.

I turned the key in the front door and heard Connor on the other side, singing along with a purple dinosaur.

"Daddyyyyyyyyyyyyy!" His face lit up as he ran to me — our brown Chesapeake Bay retriever, Chelsea, and white American bulldog, Rose, close behind. My heart did a somersault.

"Hello, little buddy."

I hoisted him into the air. Alex came downstairs with Caitie, still warm from a bath, and put her in my other arm. Caitie touched my face with her fingers as I kissed the top of her soft head. I held both my children close to me.

Once again, after a day of butchered bodies and lost souls, their sweetness and innocence helped erase some of the torture I'd seen.

"Did you eat?" Alex asked.

"Matt and I grabbed a burger on the way back."

Another missed dinner.

"How did things go today with your lady of the night?" Alex asked.

"Good, good."

Alex hesitated.

"Hey, Bobby, do me a favor. I know how you get with some of these cases. Don't go overboard with this one, okay?"

"What do you mean?"

"I don't want you to get crazy over a case nobody gave a damn about to begin with. Between us and your work in New York, you've got more than enough to take care of. Please don't let this take you away from us more than you already are."

I put my arm around her and kissed her.

"Don't worry. I've got bigger fish to fry than this guy. Besides, I've got local and state cops sharing the work on this one."

"I know you, Bobby. You won't be satisfied unless you do it all yourself."

"Relax, Alex. This is just another case, no different from any others."

But that wasn't true, and Alex was right to be worried.

Even as we sat on the living room couch and she laid her head on my chest and I stroked Caitie's hair and sang the Barney the dinosaur song with Connor, my mind was elsewhere.

It was spinning with the day's events and what I needed to do next:

Smith didn't know we were onto him yet — we'd use that to our advantage and connect all the dots, build a strong case against him, before any arrest. Find Karla's boyfriend and show him a photo of Smith and get a positive ID. Ask him if there's anything else he remembers about that night. Are there any other prostitute homicides that might be related to Karla's? Any of those women still around who haven't burned out or lost their minds and might recognize Smith from a photo? Run the VINs to locate all vehicles registered to Smith and process them forensically. Check for Karla's DNA. Check for semen, blood, hair. Can we find those bags of clothes from Smith's attic? We can't rush this, we gotta do it right. Time is on our side.

What else, what else, what else?

Find Smith, of course.

There are one million John Smiths living in the United States and I've gone through paperwork for half of them.

Where the hell is that son of a bitch?

Connor's tender singing pulled me back to the living room, if only for a moment. He crawled onto my lap.

I love you. You love me. We're a happy family.

The next morning, my Smith strategy was still churning around inside my head as I drove to work in the middle of a rainstorm.

In the middle of the New Jersey Turnpike, traffic came to a crawl. I slowed my Bureau-issued "Bucar" — a 1998 Ford Windsor Minivan — and turned on the radio.

Smith killed his wives and dozens more, I thought.

But I was left with the same problem those cops had years ago: no DNA or hard evidence. If only I could find the bodies of Janice Hartman and Fran.

If only they could speak to me from the . . .

"Okay, ladies and gentlemen, at the top of the hour we are honored to have with us once again, psychic John Edward . . .

"You have got to be kidding me," I said out loud, punching my steering wheel. "I can't get away from this guy!"

"Maria from Hoboken, you're on with John Edward."

"Hello Maria. I'm seeing a young boy, aged five or six. His name has a light J or W sound like Juan, José, or Jesus . . . he's showing me a swimming pool and a ball floating in the pool. He went to get the ball . . . but he didn't know

how to swim. No one saw him going in the water. He drowned. This is your son, isn't it?"

My reaction to Edward's voice this third time was visceral. Like a pair of hands were grabbing my insides and twisting them. Like I wanted to wring this guy's neck with my own bare hands. He was a con man, taking advantage of innocent people, making money on the grief and pain of others.

I wanted to bust this fraud.

"Yes . . . my son, Jesus! We were visiting friends who had a pool. He wandered off and saw a big beach ball floating in the water. Nobody saw him go in . . ."

"Maria, I'm also seeing an older man and woman, they're above you. Who has the G sound like Glenda, Georgia, Gloria?"

"My mother, Gloria."

"The number seven is significant to her, either the seventh of a month or the month of July."

"Her birthday was in July."

"Okay . . . she was sick for some time. She's showing me, you by her bedside at the hospital."

"Yes, that's right."

"She was in some kind of coma, she couldn't communicate for the last few weeks . . . you talked to her. She wants you to know that she heard what you were telling her."

"Oh my God."

"She's showing me . . . I hope I'm getting this right, but did you have a chicken in your house?"

"We had chickens when I was a young girl. There was this one chicken that was too fast for my dad to catch when it came time to eat it. My mother laughed hysterically when dad tried to dive after it. It was so funny she decided to keep the chicken as a family pet. My father hated it. He called it El Diablo."

"Okaaaay, now I've heard everything. Your dad, he's with mom, right?"

"Yes."

"They are showing me a baby, a little girl. Did you just have a baby?"

"No . . ."

"Are you planning on having a baby? Because I definitely see you holding a new baby."

"I'm three months pregnant!"

"Congratulations. I hope I didn't let the cat out of the bag. You might want to paint the nursery pink."

The reading continued, and against my better judgment I kept listening. I became so transfixed I forgot to turn the radio off. By the end, the caller was still sobbing, but they were tears of joy.

This John Edward knew details of how and where her little boy died and information about the mother's past and future. The woman on the radio confirmed it all.

I felt my gut gnaw at me and tried to ignore it. *This is crazy. This is a bunch of crap. He's a fraud.*

When I got to work, I stood by the office window, staring out at the dark sky over Manhattan. I was glad DeStano wasn't there; I needed to be alone to think.

Logic told me what I'd just heard wasn't possible. My soul, my instinct, my need to find Janice and Fran and put away their killer said something else.

I opened my folder and pulled out photos of Janice Hartman and Fran Smith, laying them side by side on my desk. Again, I couldn't tear my eyes away from theirs.

I made a promise to them in Dansman's office that day. I was not a perfect man by any means, but I was a man who kept his promises.

I picked up the phone and dialed.

5

The Chosen

I got the phone number for John Edward's office in Long Island from the radio station and made the call.

This is crazy.

When his assistant answered, I explained that I was working on unsolved homicide cases for the FBI and was hoping to meet with John to get help on a missing person case.

Silence.

"Is this a prank?" she asked. "Are you really with the FBI?"

I assured her it wasn't. And I was.

"John doesn't get involved with police cases," she said, "but I'll talk to him."

She sounded doubtful, but after a few weeks the appointment was set. When I told Dansman about it and suggested he come with me, his face lit up like a kid on Christmas morning. He'd just seen John on Fox News's *The Crier Report* and was all charged up.

"I don't want anyone knowing about this, Matt. No joke."

"Okay, Bob, okay."

On the morning of the appointment, Dansman gathered a bunch of Fran's items from the evidence locker, as per John's assistant's direction — a pair of eyeglasses, a makeup case, a hairbrush, a hair roller set, and a stationary set.

"He uses them to get a feel for the person's energy," the assistant said on the phone. "It will help him connect with the person you're looking for."

Before we left the office, I quickly grabbed a few extras from female colleagues: a bracelet, a compact mirror, a woman's watch, and a necklace.

Control items, I thought. If this guy was legit, he should be able to tell the difference between what belonged to Fran and what didn't, right?

I was still sitting on a fence of extremes when it came to this psychic. Part of me thought he was a fraud, and the lawman in me wanted to take him down. I even researched reasons to arrest him. Wire fraud? Mail fraud?

And yet, my stubborn heart wanted to believe he was the real deal.

We arrived at his office on Long Island as a family was leaving. They were crying and thanking the young man, whom I took to be John, in the center of the room. The mother threw her arms around him and hugged tight.

"You have no idea what you have done for us today."

I could feel my anger rising. This guy was taking advantage of a grieving family.

The young man — he had a boyish face, brown hair, and glasses — approached me.

"Hi, I'm John. Are you Agent Hilland?"

He was not what I expected. From the voice on the radio, I imagined an older man with a grand, theatrical, presence. This guy was younger than me, humble, and unassuming. He looked like someone's kid brother. He looked like *Harry Potter.*

"Yes. Thanks for seeing us," I said, introducing Dansman.

"Glad to help. Oh. You're not FBI," John said to Dansman.

"You're right, I'm not," said Dansman. He shot me an I-told-you-so look. *See?*

Okay, one point for the psychic. But what else will he know? I was prepared for this to be a bust.

We sat at a large, wooden desk in a plain, unadorned room. No candles, no incense, no crystal balls.

"My assistant tells me you need help with a case," John began. "The first thing I need to say is that if I end up helping you, it must stay private between us. I don't want you to mention it to the press, I don't want to be in any paperwork."

"That's not a problem," I told him.

"Good. Have either of you worked with a psychic before?"

"I have," said Dansman. "A few times, in other cases."

"Never," I said.

"Let me explain how I work. The information comes to me from my spirit guides in three different ways: clairvoyance, clairaudience, and clairsentience. That means I see pictures, I hear thoughts, and I get feelings or sensations. I will interpret what I'm seeing, hearing, and feeling using my own frame of reference, and hopefully you'll understand it.

"Some of the information you might understand right away. Some you might not. It's important that you write everything down, even if you don't understand. It could make sense to you later."

We took out our notebooks and pens, ready to go.

"I'll get people above you, to your side, and below you," John continued, "meaning older, the same age, and younger. I might be off by a name, but not by an initial."

And one more thing, he emphasized.

"*Do not* give me any information or try to steer me in any direction. I want to describe to you exactly what I'm getting without interference."

We nodded.

"Before we begin, do you have any questions?"

"Yes," I said. "I want to confirm. This is an active case. It's not our practice to discuss our investigations with the public, so . . ."

"As far as I'm concerned, you were never here." John said, cutting me off. "I prefer it that way. Nothing personal, but I don't like to get involved with law enforcement. My only condition in helping you guys is that you don't mention to anyone that you met with me."

Good. We were on the same page. Though I could see slight disappointment on Dansman's face.

"Let's get started," said John. "Did you bring any belongings of the person you are looking for?" John asked.

Dansman pulled the items from a bag and placed them on John's desk.

John closed his eyes, took a deep breath, cupped his palms together, and focused on them. After a minute, he reached over and moved the "control" items — bracelet, mirror, watch, necklace — from the group and put them in a pile to the side.

I was stunned. He'd figured it out right away.

"I don't know what these things are," said John, "but they have nothing to do with the reason you're here," he said.

Dansman and I glanced at each other. Point two for the psychic.

John returned his focus to Fran's items and picked up her eyeglasses. He looked up, almost past us, as if he was staring at someone behind us.

"I'm seeing a woman. She looks older than her actual age. She's crossed over. She has two names like Mary Anne, Barbara Anne . . . , but people called her by her second name . . . there's an F sound like Fern or Fran . . . wait. It's *Fran.*"

My heart raced. Dansman's eyes were locked on Edward.

The next chunk of information came in a rush of words.

"She was vain about her appearance. She had breast implants — they're showing me serial numbers on them — and dyed blond hair. Blue eyes. She wore a lot of makeup. Fran was a smoker. I smell cigarette smoke and strong perfume, like when a person tries to cover up the smoke scent with a lot of perfume. She's also showing me that she couldn't walk, like she broke her leg? She's showing me crutches. I feel a strong pain in the back of my head. Was she struck in the head? Yes . . . she was hit in the back of the head with something. She didn't see it coming. Weird," John said, still looking beyond us.

"I feel like she was tricked into going somewhere by someone she trusted. A boyfriend or husband. He is still here, he hasn't crossed. He has a simple J name, like John or Jim or Joe. And a second S name, very common, like . . . Smith."

I shivered. This was unreal.

John put down the glasses and picked up the hairbrush.

"After she was hit in the head, the J-S name — let's call him 'Smith' — strangled her to make sure she was dead. Not like a bloodbath or anything. It was like he knocked her out with one blow, then strangled her."

I sat back in my chair, stunned. *What the actual hell?* Was he was seeing all this play out in front of him? I looked over at Dansman, who was equally shocked.

I barely had time to register the horror he

described when another rush of information came.

"He was much younger than her," John continued. "Maybe ten years. She was angry. Was there another woman? She thought there was another woman. But not in the same state where they were living.

"She's showing me stairs. They were upstairs, on a third floor if not higher. There was an argument. She confronted him about a bunch of things, not just one issue. It feels like a whole bunch of different things. Smith was lying to her and she knew it. She called him out on it. He felt like his worlds were crashing together."

John shook his head.

"Man, this guy has major control issues. *Major.* He needs to be in control. Whatever she did or said, she was taking that control away from him, and he didn't like it."

Dansman and I scribbled notes as fast as we could, trying to keep up.

"The woman, F name — Fran — was fed up and demanded Smith take her somewhere. He was lying to her about so many things. I don't understand this. She's showing me furniture. Did he steal her furniture? There's also a second home. Like I said, she was calling him out on all his lies."

Dansman and I kept nodding. John kept

getting hit after hit, like a pinball whacking against the bells in a machine. Tilt, tilt, *tilt.* But not only was John confirming details we already knew, he was giving information we didn't know — details that made sense, information that rang true that we could follow up on.

We kept scribbling. He kept talking.

"So, Smith calms her down, he appeases her somehow. Like, 'Don't worry, Honey, I'll show you everything is okay.' I see them walking out of an apartment building or condo. She's using crutches. It's in the daytime, not at night. Wait, other people saw them leaving — a couple who live in the same building. It feels like they were walking in as she and Smith were leaving . . . *Oh.*"

John looked at Dansman.

"You interviewed these people?"

Dansman nodded.

"And they told you they saw them leaving together. But the timing doesn't line up. It's like he kills her on a Saturday but you guys don't know she's missing until a week later."

Again, Dansman nodded. He was speechless.

"So, he, Smith, helps this woman, Fran, to the car. He drives. She thinks she is going somewhere to see something she believes he is lying about. He's taking her to this place . . . it feels right off a major highway. It's ironic. She was nervous and pissed off, because she knew she was about to expose his lie. And *he* was nervous and pissed off, because he knew she was about to expose his lie. They both knew.

"So, whatever this place is, it has an industrial feel to it, like metal and steel, blacktop, concrete . . . I hear the highway. It's near a major highway with lots of traffic. There are many doors . . . metal garage doors . . ."

I was so charged up I couldn't stay quiet any longer.

"Like a public storage unit?" I asked.

John's eyes lit up.

"Yes. It absolutely feels like that. Definitely New Jersey, not far from where they lived and where he worked."

Again, Dansman and I exchanged a glance. Smith had that public storage facility in New Brunswick, New Jersey, where Fran's furniture was supposed to be.

John continued.

"It was still daylight. I see him pointing to a door and drawing her attention away from what he was about to do. Then he just did it."

John's eyes darted around, as if he was watching it happen.

"For her it was in an instant," he said. "She didn't even know what happened, she was unconscious before she hit the ground. Then, instantaneously, he pulls her inside whatever this thing is, this garage unit, and closes the door so nobody can see what's happening."

John paused, as if trying to process the deluge of images.

I had to ask. He said not to steer him in a direction, but he didn't say not to ask questions.

"What did he do with her body?"

John glanced at me, then gazed again beyond me. He squinted, like he was trying to see or understand something.

"She's not in one piece," he said. "He dismembered her and put the pieces in something. She's encapsulated."

"What do you mean?" I asked.

John's brow furrowed.

"She's encapsulated in something. I keep seeing cylinders . . . I'm not sure what this is. He's very smart. Whatever he put her in, it's got no smell and it's somewhere no one would suspect there was a body . . . or pieces of a body."

"Like what?"

"I don't know. I keep seeing cylinders. Her body is in these cylinders but also in something to keep her preserved, like fluid . . . or concrete."

I'm sure Dansman was thinking what I was thinking. Smith worked at an industrial company called Carborundum, which produced refractory, heat-resistant concrete blocks.

"You know when you see a new development being built, and they have these huge concrete . . . I don't know what you call them . . . storm drains?" John asked.

"Sewer drains?" I asked.

"Yeah. Like that. When you find her, her body parts will be remarkably intact. Well preserved."

My heart was racing now. I was hanging on his every word.

"So, we *will* find her?"

John paused. He looked thoughtfully at whatever invisible presence was behind us.

"I *think* so. But it's not going to be easy," he said. "And it won't be anytime soon."

Suddenly, John's mood shifted. He stared at me, confused and angry.

"I don't understand this. Wait. Why are you really here?"

Shit, I thought. *He knows I wanted to take him down.*

I certainly didn't feel that way anymore.

Now I felt in awe of him and shaken up, disoriented. I wondered if what he was doing was real. How else to explain the information he was getting that he couldn't know? The skeptic in me was reaching for other answers, but I couldn't find them.

John was staring at me, now baffled.

"You already solved this case!" he said. "You already found her. The girl in the box . . . down the side of the road, in a ravine. I can see the newspaper headlines, LADY IN THE BOX. You've already got her!"

Dansman and I looked at each other, confused. We had no idea what he was talking about and told him so.

"I'm seeing a line of police cars along a rural county road and a box on the side of the road."

"We don't know what this is," I told him.

He focused again on images invisible to us — sights and sounds we couldn't hear. A moment later, he relaxed and sat back in his chair — a look of understanding on his face.

"This woman you're looking for is one of many," he explained. "This guy has killed other women. Several, in fact. There are victims you don't know about yet. This 'Lady in the Box' is one of his victims, but not linked to the items you brought. Some of his victims have been recovered but not identified."

That set my pulse racing again.

"Several? How many has he killed?"

John looked into my eyes. His voice sounded angry and sad.

"More than you want to know."

John frowned.

"This guy is creepy," he continued. "He has all kinds of issues. He lives a life of deception with secret relationships and activities. He also has sexual issues. He has sex with some of his victims after he . . . And you're going to find out he has sexual interest in men and . . . kids. He's bad news."

A second later, a look of repulsion filled John's face.

"There is something *very wrong* with this guy. He has issues. Personal and family issues. His mother is important as to why he is the way he is. He is like her in many ways with his storytelling and compartmentalization. He hates her . . . it's a very sick relationship."

John reached for a pencil on his desk and quickly scribbled on a nearby notepad — the letter "M." He stared at the letter, retracing it over and over, then looked up.

"Who is Michael?" he asked.

"John's younger brother."

"Michael is important," John said, his voice growing insistent. "Michael knows what John did. He's the key to breaking this thing wide open for you. *You need to get to Michael.*"

I stopped writing, waiting for what he'd say next.

"Michael warned some women to stay away from Smith," John said. "He was worried Smith would *kill* them."

I held my breath, trying to stay calm.

"Did Michael *see* Smith kill someone?"

"I don't know if he saw John kill. But he saw the results of his brother's rage."

Again, I kept my voice as steady as possible. I could feel sweat running down my back.

"John," I asked. "Are you saying that Michael saw the bodies of women Smith killed?"

John looked off into the distance again.

"Yes."

All three of us were quiet for a minute, then John continued.

"Michael is terrified of his brother. He knows what John is capable of. He's also afraid of the police."

"Why?" Dansman asked.

"He thinks he will go to jail for what he's seen or what he knows."

"So, how do we get to Michael?" I asked.

John shrugged.

"I don't know," he said. "Just do what you do."

John put down Fran's hairbrush and scanned the remaining items on the desk. After a minute, he picked up the stationary set and touched the hair rollers. He looked beyond us again, eyes moving left to right, as if he was trying to find something.

"Smith. You haven't found him yet, have you?"

"No," I said.

John's eyes searched again.

"He's west. Like all the way west. California, the southern part. He's out there reinventing himself like a chameleon. He has a new job, new friends, maybe even a new wife."

I flinched.

"He doesn't know you're looking for him, does he?"

"No."

"He also has a strong connection with someone in the Northeast, north of here. Massachusetts or Connecticut? Maybe farther north."

New Hampshire, I thought. The woman in the Glamour Shots photo.

"Whoever this person is, and I think it's a

woman, he's still in contact with her. This Smith is very smart. Very smart. He covers his tracks. He uses people. He has taken advantage of this person."

I made a note and circled it. *We had to find that woman in the glamour photo.*

Out of the blue, John said:

"They're showing me prostitutes. He's into prostitutes? You really need to look at that."

"What do you mean?" I asked.

"This guy is into some perverted sexual stuff. I mean beyond kids, men, and women. He gets off on being in control. It's more than . . ."

John's face cringed in disgust.

"This guy's had sex with dead people," he says. "People he has killed."

Dansman gasped. A chill ran down my spine. John shook his head.

"Look, I never like to get involved with police because I don't want to be the guy who says, 'he did it.' But this guy . . . your guy is *pure evil.* He has killed and will kill again unless he's stopped.

"And the scary thing is, he's so unassuming. Put us in a room with him and ask someone to pick out the serial killer and we'd be going to jail before him. He has flown under the radar his whole life. But for whatever the reason, he's now on your radar."

John paused, realizing something. He pointed to me.

"Agent Hilland, you have a connection to him."

"Me? But how?

"Things happen for a reason," John said. "Whatever the reason, you were drawn to this case. It feels like you had to fight to get this case going. Like you were first told 'No' but you kept pushing."

I nodded.

"This case will be like that for you. Nothing will come easy. You will have to continue to push. But be careful," John warned.

"Be careful of what?" I asked.

"Forgive me for speaking out of turn," John said. "We're strangers and I really don't know you, but I feel your energy. You are a man of extremes, there's no middle ground in your world. You will make it your mission to get this guy at all costs. That could mean your personal life, your family, your status at work, whatever."

I felt the weight of his words. I knew what he was saying was true.

"So then . . . will it be worth it?" I asked.

"I can't answer that for you."

"Will I get this guy?"

"I'm not sure. My gut tells me yes. But along the way, you will be tested in ways you cannot imagine."

John closed his eyes, as if he was concentrating on new information coming in.

"Who is the J name like Jennifer, Julie or Jan?" he asked.

"Janice," I said. "John's first wife. She disappeared years ago, like Fran. Her body was never found."

John put his hand up. I was saying too much.

He drew the number 5 on his notepad.

"The number five is very significant. That can mean the fifth of a month or the month of May. It has great significance to this case and Janice."

I reached into my bag and took out photographs of Janice and Fran, placing them on the desk in front of John.

"That's Fran, the woman we've been talking about. And this is Janice, she was married to Smith in the seventies."

John studied the pictures without comment. I took out a photo of Smith and put it on the desk next to the women. John picked it up and held it in his hands. He whispered:

"Pure. Evil."

He looked at me. And for the first time during the entire reading, I felt John get uncomfortable. There was an urgency in his voice.

"Look, I don't mean to sound melodramatic. This man, John Smith, knows no bounds. He is very intelligent, unpredictable, and has gotten away with things his entire life because he was smarter than everyone around him. Putting him behind bars will not be easy.

"But if you don't, he will continue to kill. It's going to take everything you've got to make this right. And like I said, it will come at a cost. What that cost is, I don't know."

I sat there, still, letting his words sink in. Dansman looked overwhelmed.

"But don't let my words discourage you," John said. "Smith's energy is very strong. But *yours is stronger.* If he is fire, you are the water that can extinguish his flames."

I shifted in my chair.

"But is it worth it? Is this something I should do?"

John was steady in his response:

"Only you can make that decision," he said. "But I'll tell you this: certain people are called upon, chosen, to do very difficult and special things."

"Chosen by who?" I asked.

"God. The universe. A higher power. Whatever you want to call it. And you've been pulled into this for a reason. This is bigger than a regular case, Bob. This is bigger than the FBI.

"This is a fight between Good and Evil," he said.

Good versus Evil? No pressure or anything.

After all the information he'd given us, I still wasn't sure John was legit. He knew details about the case, yes. But could that be a mind-reading ploy? How do I know he is actually communicating with "the Other Side," like I heard him do on the radio?

What happened next answered my question.

Like the control items I brought that day, I'd also arranged for another kind of "test" for him. The day before, I telephoned Fran's daughter, Deanna, and requested she be on standby in Houston. I explained to her about the meeting with John, and that I would try to get them on the phone together for a reading. If he was for real, I wanted to connect Deanna with her mother.

If he could really communicate with the dead, I wanted to reach Fran.

We got Deanna on the phone, and a torrent of information immediately poured out of John. But it had nothing to do with Fran.

John started getting details about a

grandfather who died from lung cancer, someone who loved the sea and was a sailor, fisherman, or merchant marine. John saw glimpses of old ships and a man with white hair and glasses, born in a northern European country, in the Scandinavia area.

None of it made sense to Deanna. John looked at Dansman and me.

"Do either of you know the person I am describing?"

Dansman had a grandfather who passed from cancer, he said, and began listing details that might fit John's description. John listened intently, until . . .

"Wait a minute," he said, abruptly. "Stop."

He raised his hand like a traffic cop, bringing cars to a halt. John put Deanna on hold and pointed at me.

"You," he said. "Your grandfather's name was Carl or Charles?"

"Carl. But . . ."

There were no buts. John immediately got my father's name next.

"Whose name is Robert besides yourself?"

"I'm junior."

"And Robert is Carl's son?"

"Yes."

John ended the call with Deanna — he knew the energies coming through were going to be for me, not for her. He did that thing where he stares through and beyond you. His next question shattered any remaining skepticism I held onto.

"And who has the drinking problem, you or your father?"

"My dad," I whispered.

After that, John was on fire. The information came blasting out like a blowtorch.

My grandfather was a sailor from Norway, John said, who came to this country as a young man. He loved my father but didn't know how to show his affection. He wasn't the kind of man to tell his son he loved him.

"Your relationship with your father is similar," said John. "Your dad doesn't know how to tell you he loves you or that he's proud of you. If you heard him say it, you probably wouldn't know how to handle it."

I felt a lump in my throat. He was right about everything so far.

John described how my father's drinking hurt the family and that, as the eldest of five, I took on a lot of responsibilities. Right again.

"There's a message you need to tell your father from his dad," he said.

"What?"

"Your grandfather wants your dad to know he is proud of him and loves him. He couldn't say it while he was here. Tell your dad that his father knows he did the best he could."

I nodded. I could barely breathe.

The next message from my grandfather was for me, to learn from both my father and my grandfather's mistakes.

"Tell your kids that you love them every day," said John.

I was barely containing my emotions when a third message came through, this time for my mother.

John paused, as if an invisible entity spoke softly in his ear.

John heard my mother's name, then my grandmother's. She died when my mother was a child. The only photo I have of her is a yellowing black-and-white snapped on Coney Island in 1954. She's leaning out a window, the sun on her face, her arms folded across the sill.

"Your grandmother is holding a young boy, her son," John continued. "He passed from an injury to the head. Something internal, like bleeding in the brain or an aneurysm. His name has a G or J sound like Jimmy, Joey, Georgie, Johnny . . ."

He must be mistaken, I told him. My grandmother had only two children; my mother and her sister.

"No," said John, with absolute confidence.

"She had only two children that you *know* of. This boy is her son."

He went on to say that my mother never grieved properly for her mother's passing and blamed herself, believing she hadn't been a good daughter.

"You need to tell her that her mother read the letter she put in the casket and wants her to know it wasn't her fault. She was a perfect daughter. Her mom wouldn't have changed a thing. It was just her time to go."

My head was spinning. I felt like I was in a free fall. Dansman was choked up, too.

All those listeners I'd heard on the radio who cried, whom I thought were actors — this must be how they felt. I was now one of them.

John could see how discombobulated I was. He dragged his chair over from his side of the desk until it was directly across from me. He sat and leaned forward, close to me, to get my full attention.

"Bob, I know you came here for help with this case, and I hope something I said will help," he said.

"But do not doubt that everything happens for a reason. You were pulled to this case for a reason. And you came to see me for a reason. And your grandparents came through for a reason.

"It's very important that you share what happened here with your parents. The messages are for them, they need to hear them."

I had so much to say, so many questions to ask, but I didn't know where to start. I was never at a loss for words, but this had silenced me.

As I thanked John at the door and shook his hand, he had one last parting message.

"Everyone has their own journey, Bob," he said, "and yours is just beginning."

My first meeting with John Edward in 1998 led to an unlikely, secret, decades-long collaboration.

6

VALIDATIONS

NEW WITNESSES

Robert Farr, *owner of Milford house*

NEW FBI AND POLICE

Gerry Downes, *special agent, FBI's Child Abduction Serial Killer Unit*

Marie Dyson, *profiler, Behavioral Analysis Unit (BAU)*

Mary Gallinger, *coordinator, the National Center for the Analysis of Violent Crime (NCAVC)*

The meeting with John Edward lasted four hours. When we left his office, I was in a daze.

Dansman and I drove back to Jersey together and the whole way, he kept saying over and over:

"See! *See?* I told you! He was amazing!"

I was so stunned; I barely remember getting into my car at Dansman's office. I don't remember driving home, either. After the meeting, I walked around in a fog for days, replaying every word John said, analyzing every detail.

I tried to describe the experience to Alex. She was as diehard a skeptic as I'd always been and thought psychics were charlatans. But whether she believed in John's abilities and my recounting of them or not, she couldn't deny she saw a profound change in me.

I walked into John Edward's office that day a cynic and walked out with my belief system rattled, turned upside down, like one of those snow globes after a vigorous shake.

Was any of this possible?

I was an evidence man, a man of facts. But this stranger, this psychic, put black-and-white, hard facts right in my face. Information he couldn't have known, that couldn't be denied.

I'd heard people talk about the veil that separates this world and the next, but I never seriously considered we mere mortals could pierce it.

Could we? Did John?

And what about this fight between Good and Evil. What was that all about?

John's very insistent final words to me that afternoon were about my parents. He urged me to pass along the messages he received from my grandparents, meant for my mother and father. He was passionate about this, but I debated whether I should.

Just mentioning the word "psychic" would start my father on a tirade, calling me crazy. And my mother was so sensitive, so emotionally vulnerable, she cried at Hallmark commercials. I worried that bringing up what John said would hurt them in some way or discredit me in their eyes. My father was already judgmental. I didn't need to give him another reason to roll his eyes or sit in silent condescension.

But after four days of no sleep, I had no choice. I still wasn't sure what exactly happened in John's office that day or what I now believed, but I knew withholding these "messages" from my parents was eating away at me.

I got my father on the phone and started off with the usual chatter — sports, politics, the weather. Then I told him about the Smith case, warily mentioning I'd gone to a psychic for help. Testing the waters.

"A psychic!" he sneered, as expected. I cut off his rant before he could go further.

"Yes. John Edward. I heard him on the radio. He claims to communicate with family members who've passed on."

Silence.

"I went to his office and arranged for him to talk to someone involved with the case, the daughter of one of the victims. I was hoping her deceased mother would come through in the session with information."

More silence.

"So, what happened?" he asked.

"Well. When John started talking to the daughter . . ." — I paused, nervous — ". . . your father, Carl, came through."

"My *father*?"

"Yes. And Dad, there's something I'm supposed to tell you."

Pause.

"Go ahead."

I was surprised he wanted to hear it. With a lump in my throat and knot in my stomach, I read the details I'd jotted down in my notebook.

"Your father wants you to know that he is sorry for what you've gone through, he's proud of you, and he loves you . . . he couldn't say it while he was here. He knows you did the best you could under the circumstances."

I stopped and waited, in case my father wanted to respond. Silence. I could hear his steady breathing.

"Your father wants to apologize for being

so cold and distant," I continued. "He saw how the family dysfunction fractured relationships. He wants you to know he's sorry for his apathy."

Again, only silence.

"Dad, are you still there?"

In my thirty-plus years, I'd never seen or heard my father express emotion other than anger. As far as I was concerned, he didn't have any others.

"Yes," he said, in a whisper. His voice was quivering. "Thank you."

The Rock of Gibraltar had emotions!

A second later, my mother was on the line.

"Bobby, what's wrong? Why is Dad upset? Is everybody okay?"

I assured her all was fine and explained what I'd told him. Then I kept going.

"After Dad's father came through, mom, the psychic told me he saw a woman who'd passed. She was holding a very young boy, her son. He insisted it was your mother and the boy had a J or G sounding name, like Joey or Georgie. I told him he was wrong because I knew your mother only had you and Aunt Jackie . . ."

My mother began to cry.

"Georgie," she said, through sobs.

My heart skipped.

"What? Who?"

It took a few minutes before she was able to speak again.

"His name was Georgie," she said, softly.

"*Whose* name, Mom?"

"My brother."

And for the first time, I heard a long-held family secret. My mother explained that before she and her sister were born, her mother gave birth to a son they called Georgie, who died suddenly as an infant. Georgie's father was not my grandfather, that's why he'd been kept a secret.

"The doctors said something ruptured in his head," she continued. "I remember seeing a picture of a baby but nobody ever spoke of him. The city buried him in a potter's field. My mother's heart was broken."

I was stunned. *How did John know about this boy when I never did?*

Again, I kept going.

"Mom, there's more I'm supposed to tell you."

I described how John saw the letter she'd written to her own mother, the one she'd placed in her mother's casket. And that her mother wanted her to know that her passing wasn't my mother's fault, that she should not feel guilty about it.

My mother was 12 years old when her mother passed. She was so devastated she couldn't attend the funeral and sat outside crying.

"Your mom wants you to know that you were the perfect daughter and that she wouldn't have changed anything. It was just her time to go."

My mother took a deep, healing, breath.

"Thank you, Bobby," she said, her voice filled with emotion. "You don't know how much this means to me."

When we ended the call, my head and heart were spinning. I felt like I'd shared the most intimate moments of my parents' lives with them, unheard of before this moment. And, what I told my mother and father gave them some degree of emotional closure, that was obvious. It also validated for me more of the details John had given.

Again, I asked myself . . . *is John for real?*

And if he was, could this Long Island psychic help me find Fran and prevent Smith from hurting other women?

A few weeks later, I was surrounded by the Child Abduction Serial Killer Unit (CASKU) and a team of FBI profilers in a conference room in Quantico, Virginia, tucked away at a clandestine location near the FBI Academy.

"What do you think this is, *The Silence*

of the Lambs?" DeStano teased before I left New York.

"Let me tell you about these 'profilers,'" he continued. "They're a bunch of wannabe agents who never made a case in their life. They run around telling everybody else how to solve cases, putting a psychological spin on why these assholes kill people."

DeStano downed his umpteenth coffee of the day and crushed the paper cup.

"Utter bullshit, a waste of time. You'd be better off calling Miss Cleo on the Psychic Friends Network."

Ha. *If he only knew.*

It was true, the FBI was known as a land of egos, power plays, and careerists, as I was learning. I'd already had an angry encounter with the coordinator for the National Center for the Analysis of Violent Crime (NCAVC), Special Agent Mary Gallinger. She was well-known around FBI offices for her confrontational personality.

She stormed into my office days before the Quantico meeting — scowl on her face, FBI badge prominently displayed on her gun holster — and demanded to know, "Who the hell do you think you are?!"

She accused me of trying to usurp her position because I'd set up the meeting myself. Moving forward, I was to call her to coordinate such gatherings. "Keep me informed about any operation associated with this case," she insisted.

Oh, boy. This was going to be fun.

But we had great, humble, unflappable minds at the FBI, too. And I wanted to pick the brains of our highly trained and experienced agents and use their knowledge of criminal behavior and psychology to get inside Smith's head.

As well as profilers, we rounded up agents, sheriffs, and any police officers who'd had the slightest involvement with the Smith case, plus anyone with unsolved prostitute cases, like Bridgeport, that might be linked.

I hadn't located Smith yet, and that was an issue. John told us he was out west, like California. Our last intel was that he returned to Ohio from Connecticut in 1995.

Another dead end was Karla Storer's boyfriend, the one who saw her getting into a car the night she disappeared. We found him, but he was zero help. Still an addict, he could barely communicate. Also, I had giant gaps in Smith's timeline spanning the eighties, where I had no idea what he was doing, where, and with whom.

And who was the woman in the wallet photo? Still had no idea.

But in the months since taking over the

case, I'd also found new leads. The biggest piece of evidence sounded like a playing card from that murder mystery board game, Clue: the killer in the attic with a bloody knife.

Weeks before the Quantico meeting, I tracked down the current resident of Smith's house in Milford, Connecticut. At first, our phone chat didn't yield anything too surprising.

Robert Farr bought the house in 1995, four years after Fran went missing. He described Smith as "a wack job, a real weirdo," who told Farr he was moving back to Ohio to run the family real estate business.

"He never looked me in the eye," said Farr. "He had this whiny voice and a handshake like a dead fish. My wife felt uncomfortable with the way he looked at her, like a cold stare. He freaked her out. You didn't want to let your guard down around him."

Farr reminded me of Joe Pesci's character, Leo Getz, in the film *Lethal Weapon 2.* He reported the details like a wannabe cop.

Smith was "in a hurry to get rid" of the house, said Farr, who described seeing an unknown woman help him pack up: Long dark hair, brown eyes, stocky. A dead ringer for the woman in the wallet Glamour Shot.

The bank was in the process of foreclosing on the house because Smith had defaulted on the mortgage. When Farr bought it, it was in disrepair.

What came next, though, was a shocker. I asked Farr if he ever came across anything unusual on the property.

"Yeah," he said, "I found a bloody knife hidden in the attic."

I was taking notes and held my pen midair, thinking I'd heard wrong.

"You . . . what? What did you say?"

Farr recounted the time he installed a fan in the attic during his first summer at the house. As he buried wires in the rafters, "I picked up a piece of insulation and found a kitchen knife, the big kind you find in a butcher block set, with a 12-inch stainless steel blade. It had little red and brown spots on it. The last time I checked, stainless steel doesn't rust."

His discovery was so alarming, he said, that he intended to call the police about it but never did.

"Mr. Farr," I said, holding my breath. *"Do you still have the knife?"*

He most certainly did, he assured me. It's been sitting in a coffee can on a shelf in his garage for years.

The next day Dansman, DeStano, Barre, and I drove to Smith's old house in Milford, Connecticut, to get that bloody knife.

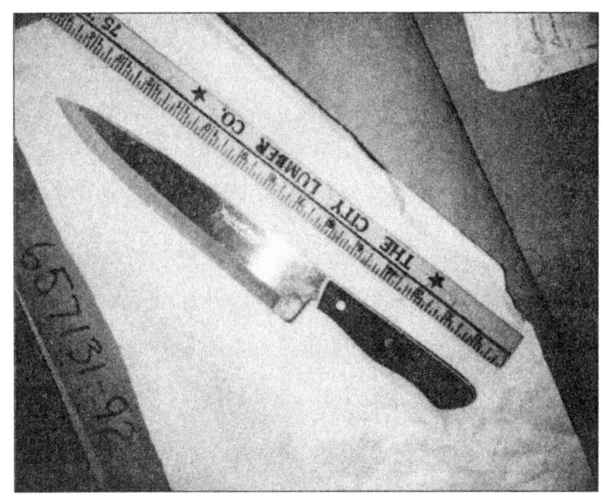

The knife found in the attic of Smith's Milford, CT, home
(COURTESY OF THE FBI)

We took a comprehensive walk through the house to see if anything else caught our attention. While the others were inside, I went out to the back of the property and gazed out at the choppy waters of the Long Island Sound.

The house had an unstable, spooky energy. I imagined imprisoned prostitute Janice Miller at this house, hearing Smith's anguished yells, afraid for her life.

A cold breeze off the water made me shiver.

"Let's bring in forensics to process the entire house," I said to the group, when I got back inside. "And a cadaver dog."

* * *

In the conference room at Quantico, two dozen of us from various agencies brainstormed. Included in the group were Potts, Gallinger, Dansman, and Barre. And coffee. Boatloads of mediocre java. FBI agents drank it like vampires sucked blood.

A 20-foot timeline spanned one wall, and the table was stacked with folders, photos, maps, and police reports.

"With our knowledge and experience concerning serial killer investigations," Special Agent Gerry Downes, of the Child Abduction Serial Killer Unit, told the group, "We hope to offer ideas and successful strategies we've used in the past."

Over the next three days, we reviewed 30 unsolved murder cases of prostitutes and drug addicts. As we went around the room and described cases potentially related to Smith, the air became dark and heavy.

I remembered John Edward's presentiment. *This is a fight between Good and Evil.*

"The more we know about the victims," said Downes, "the more we know about their killers."

Janice and Fran weren't prostitutes or drug addicts, but their personality profiles and dysfunctional histories put them in the same "high risk" category. Other commonalities among the victims included:

- The majority were found partially or completely nude, their clothing never located.
- The initial attacks were blows to the head or manual strangulation attempts.
- They were completely or partially subdued before an onslaught of blows from a knife that eviscerated their bodies.
- They had significant defensive wounds — several victims lost pieces of fingers as they raised hands to protect themselves.

"We've studied hundreds of serial cases over the years," said Marie Dyson, a profiler in the Behavioral Analysis Unit (BAU). "And I can tell you, there is incredible rage in these attacks. But it's almost like . . ."

". . . like someone lost control," Downes finished her sentence. "And that loss of control shifted to rage."

"Right," said Dyson. "The manner and causes of death used by offenders almost always stays the same. One guy will kill simply by strangulation, others by beating or slashing their victims. But in these cases, we're seeing hybrid assaults in which the killer attacks his victims in different ways. To my colleagues here at BAU, does anyone recall seeing anything like this before?"

The profilers shook their heads.

"What does this mean?" I asked.

"It means *if* these victims were killed by the same guy," said Dyson, "this is new territory for us. We've never seen such hybrid assaults involving different attack signatures. Killers may become more efficient over time but they don't typically change their MO. These attacks seem schizophrenic . . . dysfunctional."

Dyson rose from her seat and walked around the table, stopping by each investigator to pick up the crime photos they'd brought. At the front of the room, she clipped the photos to a large whiteboard.

"When you look at these photos, what jumps out at you?" she asked.

"Extreme violence," said Potts.

With a red marker, Dyson wrote the phrase on the board in capital letters.

"Overkill," said Gallinger.

"Anger," yelled Dansman.

"Rage," said Barre.

"Fury," shouted someone else.

Dyson added each word to the list. When no more came, she wrote across the top: "Complete loss of control!" She circled the word "control" and stood back.

"I see a guy who goes out and picks up women. He might intend to kill them from the inception, but I'm not so sure. His initial motivation might be sexual, psychological, companionship, who knows? Then, something goes wrong. It could be as simple as the victims don't want to do what he asks. Or a smirk or look he thinks they give him. I can envision dozens of scenarios. Whatever takes place, *the killer feels emasculation or a loss of control.* And when this guy loses control, he really loses it."

Dyson pointed to the pictures.

"Whatever strategies he might've used to subdue his victims go out the window and he attacks by any means necessary. Striking them on the head to knock them out. Strangling them to gain control."

Dyson pointed to the most gruesome photo of the bunch.

"Here's the kicker. The more this guy tries to regain control, the more he loses it, as his own insecurities and rage take over. It creates its own momentum."

She summarized what we had so far: dead prostitutes, two missing wives, a bloody knife in the attic, bags of women's clothes, a photo of an unidentified girlfriend, and secret girlfriends.

"Overwhelming circumstantial evidence," said Dyson, "but nothing physical that connects Smith to a single one of these cases.

Most importantly, we have no idea where Smith is right now."

All eyes went to me.

"I've gone through about 65 percent of the records so far," I told them, "and am narrowing it down. Soon as I find him, we'll put surveillance on him."

After we found him, outfoxing him would be the next hurdle.

"Smith gave the illusion of being cooperative in the past," Downes said, "but in reality, he never provided any substantive information. He sat with many of you for lengthy interviews and agreed to searches and did just enough to make you believe he was being cooperative when he was steering you away from the facts."

The group of investigators nodded in agreement.

"It's like he's playing poker," I said. "And he wants to know everyone's cards before he makes his next bet. We need to figure a way to take him out of his element, a way to change the game. We've got to take the control away from him."

Dyson leaned forward on the table.

"We need to screw with this guy," she said. "He wants to play games? We'll bring plenty."

Dyson fired off a list of questions. Where

was Smith? What is his current pattern-of-life? Has he remarried? Where does he work? Who are his friends? How does he spend his money and time? Who in his past might know these answers?

"We need to identify everyone in Smith's life who may hold a piece of this puzzle. Identify opportunities and vulnerabilities to gain cooperation and develop evidence. Someone knows something, it's just a matter of finding that one person," Dyson insisted. "We need to operate covertly. And when the time is right, show Smith we are now the ones holding the cards."

We went around the table, throwing out ideas.

Potts worried friends and family wouldn't be helpful. "They wouldn't talk in the past," he said. "And the ones who did played dumb. If we go back to them, be prepared they'll tell us to pound sand."

Gallinger seized the opportunity to inject herself into the dialogue.

"I say we interview everyone around him first and slowly turn up the heat. We conduct an overt investigation and surveil Smith while we do it but keep him on the outside. When the pressure is high and the time is right, we go to Smith."

Gallinger confidently sat back in her chair.

I sat up.

"I'm not so sure about pressuring him like that," I said. "He might react in a way we don't want and can't control."

Another idea, kind of radical, was forming in my mind.

"What if we interviewed everyone at the same time?"

Everyone looked at me, confused.

I stood up and paced in front of the white-board. I could see the entire scenario, playing out in my head.

"We find Smith and take him to a hotel room. The room will be wired and we'll have the profilers next door observing," I said.

"Once the interview with Smith starts, we'll have interview teams throughout the country with Smith's family, friends, and associates, ready to initiate simultaneous interviews. We let everyone know that we're talking to everyone else to increase the pressure. As the teams get information from the subjects, we feed it to the profilers, who feed it to whomever is interrogating Smith in real time. If we do it this way, we have the advantage of surprise on Smith. And total control."

The majority around the table nodded in agreement, except Gallinger, who glared and shook her head.

"Too many variables," she said. "We'll never be able to pull it off. A lot could go wrong. With my way, we can take our time and strategically control the pressure."

It was the land of egos, I reminded myself, and I needed to tread carefully.

"I'm not saying your way is wrong, Mary," I said. "I just think slowly screwing with Smith over a period of time has a greater potential to go sideways on us."

Insulted, Gallinger pushed away from the table and looked over to Dyson.

"Marie, back me up here? Bob's idea is not realistic."

Dyson didn't worry about egos — not ours, anyway. Just the narcissistic, dangerous ones of killers like Smith.

"I *like* it," said Dyson. "It gives us a strategic advantage over Smith. He thrives on control and order. This completely incapacitates him, pulling his legs right out from under him. We'll show him we know every aspect of his life, make it a 'this is your life' type of interview. Either he'll confess or someone will come forward with information. Maybe both. Brilliant idea, Bob."

Back home a few days later, I was fighting traffic on my way to John Edward's office when my pager buzzed nonstop from a number I didn't recognize. I pulled over to a payphone.

"Who the fuck do you think you are?!" a woman I didn't know yelled over the phone. "What gives you the right to hang my picture in the shopping mall?!"

"Excuse me?"

It took a few minutes to sort out. Apparently, the manager of the Glamour Shots studio in Nashua, New Hampshire — one of the locations I'd sent Smith's wallet photo — enlarged it to poster size and stuck it in his window, with my pager number, and the message:

DO YOU KNOW THE WOMAN IN THIS PICTURE? IS SHE ALIVE? IS SHE MISSING? IS SHE HIDING? ANYONE WITH ANY INFORMATION IS ASKED TO CALL SPECIAL AGENT ROBERT HILLAND OF THE FBI NEW YORK OFFICE.

Jesus. On the phone was the woman in the wallet photo.

"Look ma'am, I'm sorry. I didn't ask anyone to put your picture . . ."

"Do not bullshit me!" she screamed. "Do you really think I'm that fucking stupid? Do you really think there is anything you could possibly tell me that I don't know about John Smith? You've got some set of fucking balls!"

"Ma'am, I know you're upset but . . ."

"Don't you even pretend to think you know how upset I am! You don't understand shit! You're all a bunch of ass clowns. He hasn't done anything. He couldn't hurt a fly. Those whores he married took everything they could from him and left him high and dry. They got what they needed and now his life is a nightmare because of them. Stay the hell away from John and me!"

She hung up. And this was back in the day when you could slam a phone so hard, it hurt the listener's ear.

Well, this is great, I thought. My next thought a fraction of a second later was: *Holy shit she's still in touch with him!*

Just like John Edward had said.

I redialed.

"Which part of leave me the fuck alone don't you understand?" she screamed.

"Now you listen to me," I said, "and make no mistake about what I'm about to tell you. I had nothing to do with your picture in any store front. All I know is Smith was somehow connected to your picture and I needed to find you and talk with you. You've got every right to be upset. But I *promise* you, as much as you might *think* you know about Smith, you have no idea who he really is."

"That's exactly what he said you would say."

"Look. I need to meet with you as soon as possible."

"Go to hell!"

"What is your name?"

"Kiss my ass!"

"Well, Ms. Kiss-My-Ass, let me explain the situation. I have your phone number. With one phone call and a subpoena, I'll have your name and address. Then I'll be at your house knocking on your door. We need to talk. You can either speak with me at a time and location of your choosing or we'll subpoena you before a grand jury. But make no mistake, we will meet. The only question is whether it's under your terms or mine."

"Go fuck yourself!" she screamed again and slammed the phone a second time.

When I arrived at John's office, I was in a mood.

I'd gone to ask him follow-up questions from our first meeting, and . . . I don't know. I needed to see him again to make sure what had happened before was real. And I wanted to ask him about this woman who just yelled my ear off.

In what I'd soon learn was typical John fashion, I'd barely sat down when he started churning out messages from the Other Side. He spoke fast, as if he was being bombarded with words and images and was trying to keep up.

"Who is the T name like Tara or Terry?" he asked me.

"I don't know."

"You're about to get an unexpected call from someone who will help you. It's a female energy. But be careful, she is or was close to Smith."

"Which is it?"

"I'm not sure. I feel a break or separation between them. Be careful though. Whoever this is, she doesn't trust you."

John seemed focused on something, or someone, in the room.

"Wait!" he said. "Did your guy get married again?"

"Again, I don't know."

"He's about to. Oh, you haven't found him yet."

"No,"

"I'm getting pulled west. I mean all the way west, like California. Southern California to be more specific. That's where he is. You're about to find him. Really soon."

"That's a relief, because . . ."

"Don't forget about Michael," John cut me off, his tone was urgent. "He knows what happened. He'll be afraid to talk. Don't intimidate him. Become his friend. Gain his trust."

"I'll try . . ."

"And don't forget you already have one of the bodies. It was found in a box down a ravine next to a road. I keep seeing the newspaper headline, LADY IN THE BOX."

I still had no idea what John was talking about.

"Any idea who it might be or where it was found?" I asked.

"It feels west of wherever he killed her. Not close but driving distance. Maybe another state or two away. Concerning who she is . . . not sure. She's definitely connected to him. She died by his hands."

It was like John was staring at a dead body in the room, but only he could see it. I sighed in frustration.

"They want me to tell you to look right in front of you," he said.

"Who are they? And what does that mean?"

"*They* are my guides . . . my spirit guides."

Oh yeah. He had explained all that at our first meeting, but I was too stunned to remember it all.

"We all have them," he continued. "They give me the information I see. They want you to pay attention to what's right in front of you."

"But . . . what do they mean by that?" I asked. I was impatient. *If they are spirit guides, couldn't they be more specific?* "It's kind of ambiguous," I added.

"No. Not really," said John. "When we focus solely on the destination, there's a tendency to lose sight of the actual journey. It's important to focus on the steps right in front of us that will ultimately lead to the destination. You need to try and be more in the moment. Don't stress so much about getting to the destination. Relax and take in what's all around you, here and now. Meditate. By learning how to let go, you will grow. And I promise, you will reach your goal with greater clarity. Pay attention to what's in front of you."

Meditating, letting go, relaxing, and going on a "journey"? Those New Agey things were as far away from me as you could get.

"They want me to tell you one other thing," John said.

"Alright."

"Whether or not you realize it, you are very intuitive. Trust your instincts. They will serve you well."

John repeated what he said before, and my thoughts during the Quantico meeting.

"This is not any other case," he said. "It's a battle between Good and Evil. And Agent Hilland, you're on the front line."

The battle he described needed an army, I thought.

"Don't you mean *we're* on the front line?" I asked.

I looked at John. We were still relative strangers, but I felt an unexplainable connection to him. I think I liked the guy. I *trusted* him, and I didn't trust too many people.

"Look at you and look at me," John replied, with a smile. "One of us talks to spirit guides and the other one walks around with a big badge and gun. One of us is a teacher and the other is a fighter. You figure it out."

A few days later, I was driving through the Holland Tunnel when my pager went off like a machine gun. This time, I recognized the number. It was the angry woman from the wallet photo. I pulled over at the next gas station.

"Agent Hilland? I'm sure you remember me from a few days ago . . ."

"I remember."

Her tone was a complete 180 from before.

"I've done some thinking since we spoke and," she paused, "you might be right. We should get together and talk."

"I'm glad you changed your mind," I said. "Let's arrange it. But we have a problem."

“What?”

“When we meet, do I refer to you as ‘Ms. Kiss-My-Ass’ or do you have a name?”

She laughed. That was a good sign.

“My name is Terry. Terry Poszier.”

John’s words from our second meeting a few days earlier echoed in my mind:

A “T” name like Tara or Terry . . . someone who will help you . . . a female energy . . . close to Smith.

Chalk up another validation for the psychic.

7

Portrait of a Killer

NEW WITNESSES

Terry Poszier, the woman in the wallet

NEW FBI AGENTS

Agent Carol Vykas, *New Hampshire*
Agent Roy Speer, *Cleveland*
Agent Raelene York, *California*

A loud shot rang out, and the car jerked violently to the right.

My colleague, Special Agent Carol Vykas, slammed on the brakes.

We were on our way to New Hampshire to meet Terry Poszier, the woman in the wallet photo, and deep in conversation about Smith and the concept of evil when the car slid into a tailspin.

The vehicle skidded on its side, and I was sure we'd flip over. Thankfully, we came to an abrupt stop. We climbed out of the car to find the front tire on my side blown out.

As I changed the tire on the side of the road, I couldn't help but relate the accident to our dark topic.

"I'm not superstitious or into the occult," I told her as I spun the jack and watched the tire lift. "But I swear, it feels like an evil shadow has been trying to work against us in this case."

It was crazy talk, but what if John Edward was right and the fight was real and the Dark Side was trying to stop me?

Like, I finally found Terry, but then I'm in a car accident when I'm on my way to see her. Or, I get sent a zillion boxes of papers to sort, blocking my path to finding Smith. Or, the Dark Side pits my colleagues against me.

I didn't mention John Edward to Agent Vykas, keeping my promise to the psychic that he'd remain secret. Dansman was sworn to secrecy, too. I didn't want anyone knowing, anyway. Last thing I needed was merciless teasing by my fellow agents and a crystal ball plopped on my desk.

John had cracked my belief system wide open, that was true. But I was struggling with the pieces left behind.

At the Marriott Hotel in Nashua, I recognized Terry immediately — she looked just like the wallet photo I'd examined a hundred times.

Her demeanor was guarded, not as receptive as she was during our phone chat. She sat in the lobby restaurant with arms and legs tightly folded as I placed a stack of files on the table. Vykas took out a pen to take notes.

I spent some time building rapport with Terry, trying to gain her trust, before placing a photo on the table — the one with the fluffy blonde hair and mischievous smile.

"This is Fran," I said. "She was Smith's second wife that we know of. They met in Florida and later moved to New Jersey. On October 4, 1991, Smith reported her missing to the West Windsor Township Police Department."

I took out a photo of Janice Hartman and placed it next to Fran.

"While investigating Fran's disappearance, the police discovered Smith had also been married to this woman, Janice. Smith reported her missing to local authorities in Ohio in 1974. Neither Fran nor Janice have ever been located. Smith remains the lead suspect in both disappearances."

Terry seemed annoyed.

"I know all about his missing wives," she said, weary, and explained her history with

Smith. She'd known him for six years, she said. They met at work at a printing company and began an affair when Terry was having marriage problems. One day, a package arrived at work with a bunch of newspaper clippings about Fran and Janice.

"I'm pretty sure it was sent by Fran's family," she said. "I confronted him. He assured me it was all bullshit and that his wives abandoned him without notice and ran off. He said the police had no evidence against him or he would have been arrested and charged with their murders."

"And what do you think?" I asked.

"I believed him. You don't know him the way I do. He is a sensitive, quiet, and brilliant man. He treated me like a queen. I knew he could never have done anything like that. There's no way."

The way she spoke about Smith reminded me of the way brainwashed cult members talked about their sinister leaders.

"So then . . . why are you here talking with me?" I asked.

Terry's certainty drained from her face.

"Agent Hilland, do *you* believe he killed these women?"

I leaned forward to make sure I had her full attention.

"Not only do I think he killed them, and

others," I told her, "but I'm amazed you're alive, sitting here talking to me. And I think somewhere deep inside, you know he has killed. And that he will kill again."

She fumbled through her purse for a cigarette. Her hands shook as she slid one between her lips.

"Do you know where John Smith is right now?" she asked.

The question felt like a gut punch. If I told her I didn't know, she could storm off thinking I was using her to get to him. If I told her I did know, she could call me out as a liar.

"I can't answer that. This is an active investigation, so I can't discuss certain details."

She grabbed her purse and shot up from her seat.

"Go to hell!" she said, suddenly angry. Or was it hurt? I couldn't tell. Her emotions involving Smith were understandably complicated. "You have the nerve to stroll in here with your New York attitude to ask me a ton of personal, probably embarrassing questions . . . and you don't have the decency to answer a simple question from me? I'll ask you one more time, Agent Hilland, do you . . ."

I needed to build her trust again.

"Yes," I lied. "I know where Smith is."

She collapsed in her chair and began to sob.

"That son of a bitch," she cried. "I never should have trusted him. That lying, manipulative prick."

The rest of the story poured out of her, with the tears. She and Smith were engaged to be married, she explained. In 1995, after his stepfather died, he moved back to Ohio to help run the family business, but they continued their romance long-distance.

"He sold his house in Milford. I helped him pack," she said. "Then early last year he told me he had come into some money. He invested a quarter of a million dollars in a high-end custom SUV business called Laforza in Escondido, California. You know, that's the place he's working now . . ."

Bingo, I thought. *Nailed down his location. And John Edward was right about Southern California. And about Smith potentially remarrying.*

"Right, right," I said to Terry, glancing at Vykas to make sure she was taking down every word.

Smith and Terry were looking at houses to buy, she said. Until she got a call from a friend a few days earlier, telling her about the poster of her in the window at the Nashua Mall.

"I was horrified," she said. "I called John and asked him if he knew who you were."

"What did he say?"

"He told me again that it was all a bunch of crap and not to worry. That nobody could prove anything and he was the real victim. He told me not to talk with any cops or FBI agents that might show up and try to talk to me."

When Smith's daily calls stopped after that and he wasn't answering her calls, Terry got worried and reached out to a colleague at his work.

"She told me, 'He's been busy. He and Diane have been out shopping for their wedding.' I was shocked," she said. "I thought . . . who is *Diane*?!"

When she finally got Smith on the phone, he assured Terry she was the one he truly loved and he was marrying Diane "to make it look good when the FBI come to talk with me," said Terry.

"He said he wanted to have the appearance of 'normalcy' . . . to put forth an image that he's a normal middle-aged man — happily married, working hard at a job he loves, surrounded by friends, family, and loved ones. He wanted to create this image that there is no way he could have killed anyone."

Terry was so incensed about his lies and

the other woman that she decided to call me back. *Hell hath no fury like a woman scorned,* I thought.

"I gave him everything I had," Terry cried. "My love, my patience, my support, and my loyalty."

I nodded. She was obviously heartbroken. But it was time to ask some difficult, sensitive questions, I told her. One reason I'd brought Agent Vykas with me was so Terry would have a female present as emotional support as I broached more personal topics.

"I understand," she said.

"Terry, I need to ask you about your sexual relationship with Smith. Was there anything strange or unusual about it?"

She shook her head, and then paused.

"There was this one thing that was strange, now that I think about it."

"What was that?"

"When we went to hotels, he would pour a bucket of ice into the sink and fill it with water. Once the water got freezing cold, he'd soak a couple of wash cloths and wring them out and have me put them inside my vagina to make it cold. Then, he'd remove them and ask me to lie face down and hold my breath while we had sex."

Vykas and I tried not to react.

"Like . . . you were dead?" I asked.

Terry raised her hand to her mouth in disgust.

"Oh my God! Is that what that was? I thought he was trying to do something kinky. What a sick fuck! How could I have been so stupid?"

"I don't think you were stupid," I reassured her. I thought of the "high risk" category of women Smith pulled into his lair. They each seemed damaged and vulnerable in their own way.

"You were going through a difficult time in your life and he took advantage of it," I said. "You were looking for something that was missing."

Terry dabbed her eyes with a napkin.

"I know he isn't much to look at, but when he came into my life, it was like God himself heard my prayers and sent him to me. He was exactly what I needed."

I later learned that Terry was trying to find her faith during this troubled time in her life and Smith latched onto that. He bought her a bible and highlighted passages that justified their affair as ordained by God.

"Maybe he *became* what you needed," I proposed.

Now I was thinking of our Quantico meeting, and the dozens of hours the team spent deconstructing Smith's psychology and MO.

"Smith's a chameleon," I explained. "He

studies people around him at work, at social gatherings, or even the supermarket. He'll hang out at the periphery at first and study women like a wolf stalks its prey, and he'll identify that one woman who seems stressed, upset, or alone. When the time is right, he'll engage that woman in conversation and identify what she feels is lacking in her life, and he will become that very thing."

I felt like I knew this guy to his evil core.

"For women struggling financially, he became a wealthy benefactor," I told her. "For women in need of physical or emotional love, he was Casanova. For women in need of salvation, he was a religious prophet. But he was none of these things. He was a predator playing upon the weakness of others."

Tears streamed down Terry's face.

"Agent Hilland, I'll do whatever I can to help you. He needs to be stopped. I need to fix this and make things right."

She looked down at her hands. She was tearing her paper napkin into little pieces.

"Something that you said earlier is weighing heavily on me."

"What's that, Terry?"

"That I'm still alive."

As the sun rose, I jogged along Manhattan's West Side Highway. Bruce Springsteen's raspy voice pounded into my eardrums through my head phones. He was singing his heart out about heroes and saviors, making things good and finding redemption.

"Thunder Road" was a good jogging tune. Gritty, but hopeful. Melodic, but with enough of a beat to pace myself to.

The lyrics made me think about Smith's victims, looking for saviors. And about heroes, which I did not consider myself to be. I wanted to help these women. Terry was alive, and maybe it was because that do-gooder manager at the photo studio stuck her poster in the window. She might have been his next victim. And what about this Diane he was about to marry?

I had to get this guy.

I looked to my right, across the Hudson River toward New Jersey, then made my way through the streets back to Federal Plaza.

Back at the office, new intel was coming in.

I got a call from our FBI offices in Cleveland with a surveillance update on Smith's brother, Michael, the one John Edward keeps asking me about.

He was now a forklift operator in the area, but like Smith he previously worked in the family business, Pleasant Hill Management, where they owned apartment buildings and townhouses. Mike was the maintenance man handling repairs on the properties before the business went into bankruptcy and foreclosure. He currently lived a quiet life in Medina County with his wife and son and rented a piece of land nearby with a pond and vegetable garden.

Smith's mother, Grace, lived nearby. Her husband, Sam Maltz, the original entrepreneur of the business, died suddenly and unexpectedly in 1995.

"After Sam died," said FBI agent Roy Speer, on the phone from Cleveland, "a bunch of the more attractive, younger female tenants received an unannounced visit from Smith and Mike." Speer had a languid Midwestern accent that reminded me of a country singer.

"Mike introduced his brother and explained that in light of Sam's death, Smith would be taking over management responsibilities, and he was the one they should send rent to or contact in case of emergency, etcetera, etcetera.

"But listen to this! The very next day, Mike went back to these women by himself. He told them to stay away from Smith, that he was 'bad news.' Mike referenced Smith having wives who disappeared. He warned them that if Smith ever showed up at their apartments and their husband, boyfriend, or brother wasn't home, not to let him in. Mike said he and his family lied to police in the past to cover for Smith. Each woman I spoke with described Mike as very nervous when talking to them about this."

I remembered something John Edward said in our first meeting.

Michael warned women to stay away from Smith . . . he was worried Smith would kill them. Michael is terrified of his brother. He knows what he is capable of . . .

"So, if we believe these women . . ."

"And I do," Speer interjected.

"Then Mike clearly knows something."

Don't forget about Michael. He knows what happened.

My pager beeped. It was John.

"I've got to run, Roy. I really appreciate your great work."

"Happy to help. This is a righteous case brother! I've got you covered out here."

I dialed my new psychic hotline friend.

"John."

"Bob, I called to pass on some information."

"Okay."

"Smith knows you're looking at him. He's trying to cover his tracks in anticipation for when you arrive."

"Arrive for what?"

"I don't know. To interview him? Arrest him? Whatever it is you're going to do, Smith is preparing for it. He wants things to appear 'normal.' Whatever you do, don't telegraph when you're going. Use surprise to your advantage."

John's words confirmed what Terry said: *He wanted to have the appearance of "normalcy."*

"Understood," I said. "Any specific strategies coming to your mind?"

"Nope. Just do what you do. Take away his strengths and attack his weaknesses."

"Can your guides be more specific?"

John Edward paused, as if he was checking in with them.

"Smith uses deceit like a house of mirrors," said John. "You can't directly confront him with the truth. He'll shut down. But as good and effective as he is at using deceit, he's also bad at it. He can never keep any of his stories straight. He simultaneously plays the roles of superhero and victim. He's the hero in all his stories and is consumed by his own ego. You're going to have a tough time with him. But my cards are on you."

"Okay. By the way, remember you said that Michael knew something?"

"Yes. He absolutely does."

"I corroborated that."

"Good. But now you have to get him to talk to you."

"No doubt. Do you have any other thoughts or impressions that would help?"

"That's it for now. But we'll talk again before you leave."

"Leave?" I asked. "Where am I going?"

"California."

A few weeks later, on a bright sunny afternoon in Escondido, California, Special Agent Raelene York sat in her Bucar, covertly parked in a busy industrial complex.

The chaos of the commercial complex allowed her to hide in plain sight. No one noticed when she raised a 35mm camera with a zoom lens and aimed it toward the custom car manufacturing company across the street, Laforza Automobiles.

She focused on a moving target and, with the whirr of the camera's motor drive, snapped a series of pictures. Then she hid her camera on the passenger seat and grabbed her FBI radio, holding it below window level.

"Heads up, guys. Subject is on the move. He's walking out of the building and entering a green Ford Explorer. As a marker, there is a miniature Mickey Mouse hat attached to the radio antenna on the passenger side of the Explorer. A white female with blond hair is seated in the front passenger seat."

The camera's target — John Smith — climbed into the driver's seat of the SUV.

"Copy," one agent replied, "I'm on Mission Road at Enterprise. I'll take the eye if he moves this way."

"I'm set up across the street at the corner of Auto Park Way," another agent responded. "I've got this side covered."

Smith exited Laforza's parking lot and headed east on West Mission Road.

"Alright, the Explorer turned right on Mission and will cross your bow in a few seconds."

"Copy," the first agent replied.

Neither Smith nor (by this time) his new wife, Diane, had any idea they were being followed by a team of highly trained FBI agents.

Smith unwittingly led his invisible entourage to a quaint seaside restaurant where he and Diane were escorted to a table with a brilliant view of the Pacific Ocean. Moments later, Special Agent Raelene York and a male agent casually made their way to a table a few feet away.

Smith was elusive and bright, we knew this. And according to Terry and John Edward, he already knew the FBI was sniffing around.

Still, he was oblivious that evening that his entire dinner conversation was being closely monitored by two intrepid FBI agents wolfing down expensive calamari at the next table.

They were on the job.

A few hours later, my pager buzzed to life.

I was on my way home, late as usual, fighting traffic, and pulled over to a payphone.

"Guess who I just had dinner with, in a beautiful restaurant, overlooking the ocean?" asked agent York.

"Brad Pitt."

"Nope."

"Leo DiCaprio."

"Nope."

"Okay, you've got me. Who?"

"Smith and his wife, Diane."

I nearly dropped the phone as York described sitting so close to the elusive object of my waking hours she could practically touch him.

"Boy is he strange," she said, and immediately noted the high-pitched, nasally voice. "Really creepy. For two hours he bragged to Diane about all these ridiculous things he's done and places he's been. It was so obvious he was full of crap."

"What was your impression of Diane?"

"Not the sharpest knife in the drawer. I'm not sure whether she believed him as much as she didn't care. She kept bringing up money and some Ferrari Smith bought her. Like she was with him for financial reasons. They're a very odd couple. We can't figure out Smith's angle."

"What do you mean?"

"There doesn't seem to be anything between them, no chemistry. They acted more like distant acquaintances than newlyweds. They didn't hold hands, hug, or kiss. My partner who sat at the table with me swears Smith is gay."

"Why?"

"Based on how he carries himself. It crossed my mind, too."

"What else did you find out?"

"We've got his pattern down. He's the first one in the shop in the morning and the last one to leave at night. Sometimes he'll leave during the day to run to a local parts store or visit Diane. She's a receptionist at a nearby business. This past weekend they went shopping and ate at a few restaurants. Typical weekend stuff."

"Any luck identifying any friends or associates?"

"We know most of his business associates and colleagues at Laforza. He doesn't have much happening outside work other than Diane. Looks like he's leading a pretty normal life."

"That's what he wants us to think," I said.

"What do you mean?"

"Nothing is what it seems with Smith. He's Jekyll and Hyde. Terry says he's expecting us and creating a superficial false reality."

"What can we do out here to help?"

"You've established the pattern of life for Dr. Jekyll. Now we need to do it for Mr. Hyde."

"I don't understand."

"Smith will do everything he can to maintain this 'normal' boring life, but he cannot contain his impulses. He cannot maintain this. His need for sexual deviance, prostitutes, and darkness will surface.

"And when it does, we need to be there."

When I finally arrived home that night, my children were rays of bright against the dark. They were Jedi lightsabers in a world populated by Darth Vaders.

"Daddy!" Connor yelled, as he and Caitie — scrubbed pink and pajamaed — and our two dogs ran to greet me at the door like a traveling carnival.

I picked Connor up and threw him in the air.

"Hello, big boy! How are you?"

Caitie grabbed onto my leg and hugged it like a tree. I reached down and tickled under her chin until she squealed.

Alex appeared from the kitchen, surprised to see me.

"Oh! You're home earlier than I thought you'd be. Sorry, but I put dinner in the fridge."

"That's okay," I said, leaning in to kiss her. "I'll grab it in a minute."

I carried the kids into the living room, blowing raspberries on their necks, and pulled them onto the floor for an epic tickle fight.

Alex sat down and sighed with relief. It was probably her first break of the day.

"How was work?" she asked.

"Good. Fine. How was your day?"

"Well," she began, "Caitie was running a low fever, maybe from teething? I gave her children's Tylenol which put her to sleep for a while. She seems better now. And I think Connor is still fighting that ear infection. We should think about getting those tubes the doctor talked about . . ."

As she spoke, the kids climbed all over me like I was a set of monkey bars. I listened to Alex while lifting and twirling them.

A minute later, my family balancing act

was interrupted by the shrill ring of my new work cell phone. I grabbed it.

"Hello?"

I spoke a few minutes with a colleague, then closed the flip phone and put it on the table nearby. When I looked up, Alex was glaring.

"What's wrong?" I asked.

"You're kidding me, right?" she said, frustrated. "You can't pay attention to me for five minutes? I'm talking to you about our kids and the family's welfare, and you couldn't care less. But the minute work calls, everything stops and they have your full attention. I wish for one minute you cared about us half as much as you did that damn job!"

She got up and stormed away.

"Wait, Alex . . ."

She stopped and turned.

"New rule, Bobby. I don't want to hear the name 'John Smith' spoken in this house ever again. Do you hear me?"

As she left the room, my cell phone rang again.

She didn't even bother to turn around this time as she said her next words:

"I hate your work!"

8

Don't Worry, She's Dead

NEW WITNESSES

Scott and Ellen Mintier, *Smith's former boss and his wife*
Dick Gromlovich, *Smith's former supervisor*
Dee Hartman, *Janice Hartman's sister*
Kathleen McDonald, *Smith's teenage crush*
Kelly Perdoni, *Janice Hartman's friend*

Alex was right, that bastard Smith was monopolizing my mind.

But I believed that to be a good FBI agent you had to have passion and focus. You had to care and feel it in your soul. And as I would experience, some cases grabbed you at your core. The Smith case was the first like that for me.

"Hey Bobby, you look like hell," DeStano said the next morning, lowering his newspaper and staring at me over the brim of his glasses.

"I didn't sleep," I said, and told him about my quarrel with Alex.

"Aw, don't let it get to you. We've all been through it with our wives at one point or another. If you get involved in a big case, it can take on a life of its own. But Bobby," he said, putting his paper down. "If you're not careful, it can consume you."

"Is that what you think this case is doing to me, DeStano?"

He got up, came over, and sat on the edge of my desk.

"You talk about this case every day. You want to put this son of a bitch in jail. You want to find his victims. You're pissed off at this guy. That's good stuff because it drives you to turn over every stone."

"So, what's the problem?" I asked.

"The problem is, I can't remember the last time you talked about any of your other cases or," he pointed to a framed family photo on my desk, "your family."

I listened quietly.

"Being passionate about a case is great, but it can also eat you up. And there's one thing you can't forget."

"What?"

"Like I said before, no matter how good you are or how hard you work, you might not be able to bring a case against this guy."

"If I felt that way, DeStano, I never would have taken it on."

"Let me say it another way," he said, walking back to his desk. "You played a lot of sports, right? Well, when two teams take the field, only one can win. As talented as you might be and as hard as you play, sometimes you lose, and it's just the way the ball bounces."

I pondered his speech.

"Yeah. But you know what, DeStano? The guy who says, 'That's the way the ball bounces' is usually the guy who dropped it."

I wasn't planning on dropping any balls.

I had dozens at play, in motion, all over the country.

We had surveillance teams observing Smith in California, his brother Michael in Ohio, girlfriend Sheila Sautter in Connecticut, and more. If all went as planned, we would have 16 simultaneous interviews of friends, family, and coworkers for the hotel interrogation extravaganza I was organizing.

I scanned Smith's old résumés from the files and looked for new, untapped leads. A momentum was building. By early 1999 I was filling in gaps of Smith's life that the previous investigations missed.

I delved into his dark past and the people who populated it, putting together pieces of the enigma that was Smith.

May 1999 — Surveillance photo of Smith days before the marathon hotel interrogation (COURTESY OF THE FBI)

* * *

SCOTT MINTIER, Smith's former supervisor
EILEEN MINTIER, Scott's wife
Seneca Falls, New York

"We never knew the real John Smith."

Rumor had it, the small town of Seneca Falls, New York, was the inspiration for the fictitious Bedford Falls in Frank Capra's heartwarming film, *It's a Wonderful Life.* I could see why. As a soft snow fell, I drove by quaint homes with picket fences and a bridge that looked like the one George Bailey stood on for his final plea: "I want to live again, Clarence! Please, let me live again!"

Too bad Smith's wives and whoever else died at Smith's hands couldn't make that same plea for a movie magic ending. I aimed to give them a legal one instead — justice.

Scott Mintier and his wife, Eileen, were a sweet couple in their sixties.

"It's not every day the FBI is in our home," said Scott, as Eileen poured coffee. "This business with Smith must be pretty serious."

I couldn't give him details, I explained. But I asked if he could shed any light on Smith's history and the inner workings of his mind.

"Smith first worked for me in the '70s in Delaware, Ohio," Mintier began. "He was in his mid-twenties. I was a production supervisor and he was an engineer. He was very intelligent and had remarkable ability, like a gift. He could study how things worked, it didn't matter what it was — an engine, a hydraulic system, a circuit board, you name it.

"Once he figured out the system design and function, he could reverse engineer the thing and reassemble it better than before. He could design and manufacture parts, improve production capacities, and was an exceptional problem solver during system failures.

"He was one of the best engineers who ever worked for me — a tremendous worker."

When Mintier got a new job in Indiana, Smith soon followed and worked under him there, too. He was the first one in to work every morning and the last to leave at night.

"He loved his job. A supervisor's dream. But he was a very strange guy. He had this other side."

"Other side?" I asked.

Mintier leaned forward in his chair.

"He had no interpersonal skills. And frankly, most of the guys at the plant thought he was gay. Keep in mind, the late seventies and early eighties weren't the politically correct times of today, so the guys were rough on him about it."

Mintier mentioned the high-pitched voice, and that Smith's mannerisms were "effeminate" — a detail Agent York also observed.

But here was the new kicker.

"He wore women's clothes to work."

"What?"

"You heard me right. He wore women's blouses, sweaters, and sometimes jewelry to the plant. To the point where it became a problem. I worried a few of our guys were going to do a number on him."

"Did he dress in women's clothing every day?"

"Not every day. It came and went," he said.

"Was this a transgender thing?"

"I don't think so. It was more a weird disturbing thing. He even started wearing a woman's watch, and another worker threatened Smith about it. That's when I thought the guys were going to rough him up."

"Tell me about the watch."

"It had a narrow silver herringbone band and a green face. There were little emeralds and diamond chips around the bezel. It was definitely a woman's watch. He wore it for several days until I called him into the office. The guys on the production floor were calling him 'faggot,' 'queer,' 'Queen John,' you name it."

"How did he respond?"

"He acted like none of it bothered him. He ignored them or laughed along. The whole nonsense became too much of a distraction, though, so I finally told him to get rid of the watch and start dressing more appropriately. He shrugged his shoulders and said 'Okay.' "

"You know, Scott," Eileen interrupted, "that's the watch he gave Kathleen."

Kathleen was their daughter, Eileen explained, who was in high school at the time.

"He had a strange affection for Kathleen," she said. "He'd come to our house after work to help her with homework. He was a good tutor. And they'd go to a local roller-skating rink. He even took her to a David Cassidy concert, which was a big deal for her."

"Did you have any concerns about Kathleen

spending so much time with him?" I asked.

"None whatsoever," said Eileen. "We were under the impression he was gay and enjoyed spending time with girls. He seemed harmless. Like a big brother, or even a big sister. He was this young, very slight man with the mannerisms of a woman — an *older* woman," she said. "I never met his mother, but I always suspected he may have been very much like her."

I envisioned the murderous Norman Bates in Hitchcock's *Psycho,* dressed up in his dead mother's clothes, wig, and makeup.

As I left their picturesque home, Mintier had a parting, somber thought.

"This is going to sound strange seeing how we trusted him with our daughter," he said, "but something else about Smith never sat well with me."

"What do you mean?" I asked.

"I never felt we knew the *real* John Smith."

* * *

DICK GROMLOVICH, Smith's former boss
Indiana

"What did the son of a bitch
do now, kill somebody?"

"I knew I'd be getting a call about Smith one day," said Dick Gromlovich over the phone, with a hearty laugh. "What did the son of a bitch do now, kill somebody?"

My silence was deafening.

"Jesus Christ! You've got to be kidding me!" he said, with exasperation.

"What can you tell me about him?" I asked.

Gromlovich took a deep breath and collected his thoughts.

Smith worked for him as an engineer, he said, and was a "a decent worker" and "smart," but "I never cared for him."

"Why not?" I asked.

"He was damn strange! I had a bad feeling about him. I always had my guard up around this guy."

"Were you afraid of him?"

"Hell no," Gromlovich replied, defiantly. "He wasn't scary like that. In fact, we all thought he was queer."

He repeated Mintier's description of women's clothes and jewelry.

"He traipsed around the plant like he was Liberace. The guy was a flamboyant nut who got under everyone's skin. The guys were going to kick the shit out of him."

"Because of the clothes?"

"It was everything. His prima donna attitude, his constant bullshit."

Gromlovich agreed that Smith was fixated on Scott Mintier's daughter, Kathleen, back in Ohio.

"Oh, yeah. Obsessed. He couldn't get enough of Kathleen. He worshipped her. Wanted to control her like he owned her or something. Sometimes we even wondered whether he was wearing Kathleen's clothes. Those two were inseparable."

"You said you had a bad feeling about Smith."

"I'm not sure how to explain it," he said. "But . . . there was something *evil* about him. You know how you meet people who have a strange darkness about them that's just below the surface? I always felt there was another side of him, and it wasn't good."

Yeah, I knew. Looking into Smith's eyes for one minute, years ago, revealed that to me.

"As feminine and goofy as he was, sometimes one of the guys would say something that went too far, and Smith would stop what he was doing and stare at them, with a look that would chill you to your soul. His entire face and demeanor changed, like he became someone else. Then, as soon as that evil face appeared, it vanished."

"What else can you tell me?"

"The guy was a pathological liar. He lied about everything. You name it. No matter what the conversation, he was an expert on everything. He had seen it all and done it all."

"Can you give me an example?"

"How many do you want?" Gromlovich said, with a laugh. "One time he told us he installed the turbocharger on Andy Granatelli's Indy car that won the Indy 500 in 1967. Hell, he would have been 16 years old at the time! Another time he bragged about working for a university interpreting the Dead Sea Scrolls. The guy was so full of shit."

I asked if he recalled any other moment that stood out as unusual.

He did.

"It happened in late spring or early summer of 1979. He took a call at work from family in Ohio. That itself was strange because he never got calls at work. He told me he had an emergency back in his hometown of Seville, Ohio, and he had to leave right away to take care of things. It was so out of the norm because he practically lived at the plant. We often joked that he lived in a secret room somewhere at the facility. For him to take off like that meant something must have really been wrong."

"What was it?"

"Hell, if I know. But whatever it was, he looked like he'd seen a ghost."

"So, he left?"

"He left. When he came back a few days later, he told us the emergency involved his family's business and repairs to a house. Agent Hilland, there is one thing I know without any doubt."

"What's that?"

"That phone call, it shook him to his core. He looked like a penned-in animal, ready to claw someone's eyes out to get away."

* * *

KATHLEEN MCDONALD, Scott and Eileen Mintier's daughter
Stratford, Connecticut

"He lives in a world of fantasy."

Kathleen McDonald, tall and athletic, burst through a set of heavy industrial doors at the manufacturing plant, Sikorsky Aircraft, armed with safety gear to give me.

After I donned a hard hat, reflective vest, eye goggles, and ear protection, she led me through a plant as big as a football stadium. Welders climbed in and out of helicopters in various stages of development as sparks shot out.

Once we reached Kathleen's office, she wasted no time making one thing perfectly clear about her and Smith.

"He liked me . . . I mean *liked me.* But I didn't feel the same way about him."

Kathleen described what the others said — the feminine mannerisms, the women's clothing, the jewelry. The belief that he was gay.

"He was weird. Don't get me wrong, he was nice and treated me well. He helped me with homework and went to all my basket-ball games. I poked fun at him and called him a dweeb and even asked him why he wore women's clothes."

"What did he say?"

"Like everything else he didn't want to talk about, he would deny it and change the subject. He would stare at me with that gummy, toothy smile."

One rainy afternoon, around the time of Kathleen's 16th birthday, Smith picked her up in his Corvette to take her out.

"We were sitting in his car and out of no-where, he handed me this watch."

Kathleen reached inside a desk drawer and pulled out a purple velvet bag. From the bag, she retrieved a woman's watch — it had a silver herringbone band and a green face surrounded by emeralds and diamond chips, like her father described.

She handed the watch to me.

"He said it was a special gift for my birthday. I was blown away. As you can see, it's very distinctive and pretty. I could see right away that it wasn't new though. It didn't have a box or anything. I asked him where he got it."

Kathleen looked down and wrung her hands together.

"What did he tell you?"

"He said it belonged to his wife. I was shocked. I couldn't believe he was married, let alone to a *woman.* I said, 'I didn't know you were married!' "

Kathleen halted.

"What did he reply?"

She halted again, trying to keep her voice steady.

"He said: 'Don't worry about it . . . she's dead.' I remember a cold chill running through my body when he said that. I can feel it now," she shivered. "The way he said it was so ominous."

Kathleen repeated what her parents and Gromlovich said — that she felt she never knew the *real* Smith.

"He wore a mask, but I never got to see

what was behind it. He lived in a fantasy world. He was the center of the universe, the hero in all the stories he told, and we were supporting characters."

"Do you think he believes the stories he tells?" I asked.

"I'm not sure. Maybe he just wants everyone else to believe them."

I looked at the watch closely, studying it.

"Please keep it," she said. "After what he said to me in the car that day, I never even put it on my wrist. It holds a terrible energy. I want nothing to do with that watch, or John Smith."

* * *

LODEMA "DEE" HARTMAN
Janice Hartman's younger sister
Ohio

"He looked possessed. With this crazed smile on his face."

As I walked to the Sikorsky Aircraft parking lot, I got a call from Sergeant Potts at the Sheriff's Office Wayne County, Ohio. He'd just got off the phone with Janice Hartman's younger sister, Dee.

"She gave good background for the period

when Janice and Smith first eloped and lived in Columbus," he said. "Dee spent weekends with them and weeks during the summer."

Dee told Potts about a disturbing incident that happened in 1972, when she was 12 years old.

"Smith tried to force her to have sex with him," he said.

"Dee, Smith, and Janice were hanging out in the bedroom. Dee was on the floor watching cartoons. Smith and Janice were on the bed. At some point, Smith asked Dee if she'd ever seen a man's penis. She was scared and didn't answer. Janice told him to knock it off, but he didn't stop. He walked over to Dee, grabbed her hand, and started to unzip his pants. Dee was terrified. She began to cry and tried to pull her hand away. She said Smith 'looked possessed, with this crazed smile on his face.'

"Then Janice jumped off the bed," Potts continued, "and smacked Smith across the face. Smith let go of Dee's hand, and she ran away crying. He told Janice he was just screwing around."

I shook my head and tried to stay calm.

"We've got to get this guy," I said to Potts, through clenched teeth. "Anything else?"

"Just that she believes Janice is dead and

that Smith killed her. Dee was the last to see Janice alive when Janice drove off with him."

"Wait. I thought they were divorced at that point?"

"Yeah, they were divorced. But Dee remembers Janice driving away in her new 1974 Mustang with Smith in the passenger seat."

"Did Janice tell her where they were going?"

"No. But Dee was very bothered by the fact that Smith had Janice's car after she disappeared and kept driving it."

"Did you ask her if she remembers a watch?"

"Oh, yes. Dee remembered going shopping with Smith to get a birthday gift for Janice. He specifically wanted to buy a watch and asked Dee to help him pick it out."

I tucked the phone under my chin and reached into the purple bag in my pocket, pulling out the watch.

"They went to the jewelry counter," Potts continued, "and Dee saw one she knew Janice would love it, and . . ."

"Potts, what did the watch look like?"

Potts read from his notes.

"Dee said it had a silver herringbone band, a green face, and was encrusted with diamonds and emeralds around it. They gave it to Janice for her birthday."

I held the watch in my hand and pressed it to my forehead, closing my eyes.

Janice.

* * *

KELLY PERDONI, Janice's friend
Ohio

"John Smith is pure evil."

The suburban neighborhood was permeated with backyard barbecue smoke and the sound of children playing. As Potts and I walked up the driveway toward a modest split-level home, a woman walked out of the garage and intercepted us.

She was pretty, but what struck me most about the first time I saw Kelly Perdoni was how much she resembled Smith's first wife, Janice Hartman.

Kelly recognized Potts right away.

"I told you not to come back," she said.

Potts had been there a few weeks before to get Perdoni to talk about Smith, but she refused. She was terrified to speak to him.

But we needed her. When Smith filed the

initial missing person report about Janice, he gave officers the information for the report from Kelly's house.

"There's a reason she's so scared," I said to Potts. "We need to figure out what it is."

So now Potts was back . . . and I was with him. Kelly was not happy.

Potts attempted to introduce me.

"I don't care who he is," she shot back.

I stepped forward and extended my hand.

"Hello Kelly. I'm Bob. I've come all the way from New York to speak with you."

She shook my hand quickly, then pulled back, folding her arms together.

"I understand if you don't want to talk," I said. "But please understand I'm here because someone sent me. Someone very special to you."

"Who?" she asked.

"Janice."

Kelly gasped and covered her mouth with her hand. She began to shake, her eyes filling with tears.

"Would it be alright if we went inside to talk?" I asked.

Although in her mid-forties, Kelly looked older. And yet, her presence and mannerisms were childlike. We sat in her '70s-style living room — shag carpeting, ornate wallpaper. As if time had stood still for Kelly Perdoni after Janice disappeared.

Kelly's nervousness was evident. I tried to put her at ease.

"I've spoken with a lot of people who knew Janice," I began. "Everyone described her as a beautiful girl. Full of life, always happy, always willing to help others."

Kelly's face lit up.

"That was Janice for sure. She was always so positive and happy, even when things were bad. Janice was very special. Everyone loved her."

"Tell me about your friendship," I asked, with a smile.

"Janice was the big sister I never had. She looked out for me, protected me, and kept me safe. I really looked up to her. We were best friends. I've never been closer with anyone in my entire life. We shared everything together . . . our hopes, our dreams, and our fears . . ."

I paused, giving her a moment.

"Janice kept you safe, you said. From what or who?"

Kelly looked down.

"Oh, you know . . . mostly from boys who were trying to take advantage, or sometimes it was preventing me from making bad decisions, that kind of stuff. Janice and I didn't have much in the way of close families. We were on our own. We took care of each other. We were sisters . . . our own little family."

"She sounds very special," I said, then softened my voice to a near-whisper.

"Kelly, who else did Janice keep you safe from?"

She looked up quickly, afraid.

"Where is Smith?" she asked, panicked. "Does he know you're here talking to me?"

"No, no," I said, reassuring her. "He is far away. He has no idea I'm here with you. There is absolutely no reason to be afraid. I won't let anyone hurt you. I promise."

She began to cry, wiping tears with the back of her hand.

"You don't understand. He was stalking us in the end. The divorce was final and Jan just wanted to get away."

She described how she and Janice liked to go dancing, but they stayed away from local clubs to avoid bumping into Smith.

"But no matter where we went or how far, he always showed up. He was obsessed with her. Janice was afraid of him but kept trying to appease him to keep things cool."

One night at a club out of town, the two girls were having a great time dancing, talking to boys, flirting.

"Then late into the night, as I came out of

the bathroom, Jan came over to me like she'd seen a ghost. She grabbed me with both arms and said, 'Oh my God, he's here!' I looked across the bar and there he was, leaning against the wall staring at us. We were scared to death. Janice freaked out because she had been kissing a guy and dancing a slow dance with her arms around him. She looked across the dance floor and there was Smith, glaring at her, with a look of fury."

"What happened next?"

"We ran out of there, got in Janice's Mustang, and drove like hell. He followed us. We drove so fast on those dark back roads. He stayed right behind us the whole time. I will never forget that night."

"Kelly," I said, more insistent now. "What happened to Janice. *What did Smith do to her?"*

She covered her face with her hands.

"Please, don't do this," she cried. "Please . . ."

Kelly leaned forward in her seat, facing the floor.

"You know what," I said. "Janice is with us, right here, right now. And she wants you to talk with me, Kelly. She wants you to help us make sure that what happened to her will never happen to anyone else."

Even before meeting John, I believed in

this; that our loved ones went to heaven after they passed, but were still with us, wanting us to do well.

Kelly remained still, looking down at the floor.

"Let me ask you something. If Janice walked through that door right now, what would you say to her?"

She hid her face again like a frightened child.

"I'd tell her I was sorry," she said, voice trembling. "That I did the best I could."

"Why are you sorry?"

Kelly doubled over again, in a fetal position, with elbows on her knees. She was afraid to look up at me.

I reached into a folder and pulled out an 8 x 10 portrait of Janice — a high school yearbook picture — and placed it on the floor, between Kelly's feet, so she was looking directly at it.

"You know Kelly, when I first met you in the driveway, I was struck by how much you look like Janice. If I didn't know any better, I'd swear you were sisters. Now, there's one thing I know for certain. Whatever happened back then, whatever he did to Janice, it wasn't your fault."

Kelly's tears fell, landing on Janice's photo. As if Janice was crying with her.

"You had no control over what happened. Janice isn't mad at you. She loves you like you love her."

She was in anguish. She wrapped her arms around herself.

"I understand you're afraid. But like so many years ago, Janice is still protecting you. That's why she sent me here. She's here with us right now and wants you to be strong."

I sounded like John now — his reading style had infiltrated my interview style.

Kelly reached down and picked up Janice's picture. She sat back in her chair and hugged it.

"I'm sorry Jannie. I'm so sorry."

Kelly was nearly in hysterics.

"Agent Hilland, I'm afraid for me and my children. I beg you to keep him away from us. John Smith is . . . *pure evil.*"

"Kelly, what happened back then?" I asked, softly.

She suddenly sat upright and turned away from me and Potts. The only thing greater than her grief was her fear.

"I can't help you," she said, with finality. "But Janice will lead you to her. You can't kill a spirit like that. She's with me all the time. I feel Jan and talk with her every day. When I lost her, I lost everything."

She turned to me and grabbed my hands.

"Jan picked you for a reason. She will help you. Believe me she will help you. But I can't. I wish I could, but I can't. I remember things in pieces. I'm not sure what was real and what wasn't. Some things should be left alone," she pleaded.

"Kelly, the only way to move forward is to acknowledge what happened and let go of the past. I worry for you, for Janice, for her family, and for all the other women . . ."

Kelly dropped my hands.

"Other women? What other women?"

"The other women who knew Smith, who also disappeared."

Kelly let out a cry, "Oh my God!"

She dissolved into sobs; there would be no more talking that day.

When we left Kelly's house, she stood in the driveway clutching Janice's yearbook photo to her heart. I left it for her.

She didn't tell us much on the surface, but Kelly Perdoni told us plenty without saying a word.

There was a reason Janice was dead and Kelly was not, I thought, as we drove away.

She knows something. She saw something. She's terrified to talk about it.

She knows Smith killed Janice.

* * *

JOHN EDWARD'S OFFICE, Long Island
April 1999

John's office was filled with the lingering scent of burning sage.

"It's called smudging," he explained, as he waved a thick stick of the herb in the corners of the room and behind the door.

"It's a Native American tradition used in prayer and healing practices and a method of psychic protection. It cleans the energy around a place, object, or person."

"How does it do that?" I asked.

"The smoke attaches to negative energy, and as it clears out, it takes the negative energy with it. Like when you dust and clean cobwebs. But this is for *energetic* cobwebs, to clean up your energetic house."

I watched, wondering to myself where the heck one gets a giant stick of sage.

"You can use the sage from your spice rack in the kitchen cupboard," he said, with a smile. "Very practical. Sprinkle some in an ashtray and burn it."

"I'll get right on it," I said. *Alex would love that,* I thought.

Little did I know that in the years to come . . . yeah, I was going to need this smudging. And I was going to believe in it. And I was going to do it.

This was my third time seeing John Edward in person, though we'd kept in touch on the phone since our first meeting. But now I was preparing to go to California to pick up Smith and was having pregame jitters.

The work I'd done all year led up to this epic moment, this Super Bowl event, where we would hopefully nab Smith and get him to a hotel and pull off this vision of more than a dozen interviews at once — the brainstorm idea I had that day at Quantico.

John had become my psychic "coach" on the Smith case, so a pregame pep talk was in order. Plus, I wanted to know if his "guides" had any . . . well, guidance.

"Be patient," he said, of the upcoming interrogation. "Be persistent, but don't rush things."

"Right, right."

On his desk, I fanned out pictures — Smith, his victims, and the dozen or so people we planned to interview. John studied the photographs. I knew the drill by now: don't give him any details or lead him or do anything that will give him *any* hint of information unless he asks for it.

"You're close," he said, and paused — a

slight frown on his face. "But I don't know if he's going to tell you what you need. It's going to be long . . . a long interview. Be patient."

"I'll be patient."

I waited — *patiently* — for John's guides to be more specific.

(I thought of that film, *Field of Dreams,* when Amy Madigan's character, Annie, says to her husband, Ray, played by Kevin Costner, "Ray, this is a very nonspecific voice you have out there, and he's starting to piss me off!")

John had a look of frustration on his face. He shook his head, as if he was watching a scene unfold in his mind.

"I don't see Smith opening up," he said. "I see him trying to play the victim. A 'poor me' thing. Like this is a big misunderstanding. He'll try to tell you that his wives left him."

John paused and focused, as if trying to understand a foreign language.

"He may give you something though. If he does it will be completely unintentional. I see a break in him. Something will happen during the interview. You will know it when it happens. Be ready."

"What should I do when it happens?"

"Not sure. Trust your instinct. It feels like

he will lose himself at some point during the interview."

John suddenly got very certain.

"I hate to sound like a broken record, but I have to say this again: Michael knows . . . *Michael absolutely knows.* You need to get Michael to talk. But remember, Smith is smart, he won't fall for traps easily."

"Any suggestions?"

"I don't know what this means but they — my guides — are telling me 'Grandma.' Mention his grandmother."

I jotted down "Michael" and "Grandma" on my notepad.

"So . . . overall?"

John was silent. He looked immersed in deep conversation only he could hear.

"There are a lot of energies at work here," he said. "More than you can possibly imagine. Don't get discouraged or frustrated. This may not be solved as quickly as you want. Persistence is the key."

"I know how to persist."

I reached into my pocket, taking out Janice's watch.

"I'd like you to hold something and give me your impressions."

I extended my hand and John put his under mine, palm up.

"Wait!" he said. "Before I take it . . . did this come from a dead woman?"

"Possibly. I'm not sure."

John explained that there were two types of psychometry ("reading" an object by touching it). One was objective, to get information about the object and its history. The second was subjective, to get information about the person linked to the object. He liked to clarify which before touching the object.

He nodded. I placed the watch in his hand.

He took a deep breath and focused. A minute later, information rushed out.

"I'm getting a J name like Jen or Jan. She's connected to Smith. It's funny, I don't know how to say this but it's like Smith gave this watch twice, to two different people. But the J name . . . somebody close to her picked it out specifically for her. It's like whoever saw this watch instantly said, 'Oh she would love this' or somehow instantly connected it to her. It's strange though . . . hold on a minute . . . where did you get this?"

"From another person."

John gazed into the abyss.

"Smith gave this watch to someone else . . . another woman. He really liked her! Did he tell this other girl . . . I see her as younger, a teenager maybe . . . did he mention or hint that the watch had belonged to a wife and that she was dead?"

"Yes," I said. Talk about specific.

"Who was the wife?"

"That's the J name," I reminded him. "Smith's first wife, Janice Hartman. Her sister picked out the watch as a birthday present."

"Is that the D sounding name, like Dee or Deirdre?"

"Her name is Lodema but she goes by Dee."

"And the sister Dee, she's still here with us?" John asked. "She's alive?"

"Yes."

"It's funny. I see Smith giving the watch to Janice but she turns to Dee to thank her. It pissed Smith off. Like the sister was getting the credit for the gift he paid for. And the woman who gave it to you, she told you a story connected to the watch?"

"Yes. She said Smith gave it to her as a birthday present and told her it belonged to his first wife who was dead. Like you said."

"Is that the hard C or K name like Cathy or Katherine?"

"Kathleen."

"And she had no idea he was even married and was shocked when he told her."

"Right."

John looked off into the distance for a minute.

"You're definitely getting closer."

"Closer to what?"

"To the answers. They keep showing me that headline, LADY IN THE BOX."

"A victim who's already been found, right? By a ravine."

"Right," said John. "But not identified."

'Wait a minute . . . it's not Fran in the box, right?"

"Right."

"So . . . could it be Janice in the box?"

John thought for a moment.

"Possibly."

* * *

LAFORZA AUTOMOBILES
Escondido, California
May 2, 1999

Agent Raelene York and I sat in her Bucar across the street from Smith's work.

We could see his black Mazda Miata — with wide suspension and oversized rims — parked in the company lot.

York and I raised our binoculars.

"See the receptionist at the desk, in the large window to the left?" York asked. "Her name is Linda Drury. She's talking with Smith right now. He's standing in the doorway to her right. I can just make him out. Watch, he'll show himself."

The bright California sun hit my binoculars. I could only make out his silhouette at first. Then he stepped into the room, coming into full view.

I felt a surge of energy rush over me. The way a hunter feels when he's laid eyes on the prey he's been waiting for, an elusive trophy.

"Hello, John," I whispered out loud, as I focused my binocular lenses on his face. "It's been a long time."

* * *

LAFORZA AUTOMOBILES
Escondido, California.
May 5, 1999

As the sun rose, Agent Mary Gallinger and I sat in a nondescript Buick sedan in the same place across from Smith's workplace. Three FBI SWAT SUVs with blacked-out windows were parked nearby, and dozens of agents in unmarked police cars were positioned along the driving route from Smith's home to Laforza.

I felt like a football coach about to lead

his team onto the field for the biggest game of their lives. But this was no ordinary opponent.

Soon, I thought, I would stand face to face with pure evil.

I remembered what John said at our first meeting: *The number five is very significant. That can mean the fifth of a month or the month of May. It has great significance to this case.*

And here we were, on May 5, about to nab Smith.

"Eagle 5 has the eye," said a voice over the radio, an agent from the FBI surveillance team. "The subject entered a black Mazda Miata and is headed west toward the expressway. Eagle 3 he should be crossing your bow in 30 seconds."

"Copy," a second voice, Eagle 3, answered. "I've got him. He's turning right onto the expressway and is merging into traffic. We're headed your way Eagle 2."

"Copy," a third voice, Eagle 2, replied.

As Smith made his way closer and closer, my adrenaline rose.

"Subject is getting off at the Escondido exit ramp," one of the Eagles reported. "Now we're stopped at the red light at the bottom of the ramp."

I looked toward the nearest intersection and saw Smith's Mazda.

"There he is!"

Smith pulled into Laforza's entrance lane for the parking lot, got out of his car, and walked to a front gate to unlock it.

Gallinger and I swung our car up behind him, got out and walked over to Smith.

"Good morning, Mr. Smith," I said.

"Hello," Smith said, cautiously.

"I'm Special Agent Bob Hilland of the FBI and this is my partner, Special Agent Mary Gallinger."

We held up our credentials. Smith took a quick look.

"We're working out of the Holiday Inn down the street and were wondering if you might have some time to speak with us?"

"Speak with you about what?" Smith asked.

He looked like a caged animal, contemplating escape routes.

"Your missing wives."

9

Pure Evil

LAW ENFORCEMENT

Gerry Downes, *special agent, FBI's Child Abduction Serial Killer Unit Agent*

Marie Dyson, *profiler, Behavioral Analysis Unit (BAU)*

INTERVIEW SUBJECT

John Smith

I called Agents Gerry Downes and Marie Dyson at the Holiday Inn to let them know we were on our way and Smith was in tow.

They immediately paged the interview teams across the country, in California, Ohio, Connecticut, New Hampshire, and Indiana — to signal that the game was on, the interviews were about to begin.

At the Holiday Inn in Escondido, Gallinger and I took Smith up to a suite on the third floor. We were to be his lead interrogators. Downes and Dyson were set up in a "monitoring room" next door to observe us on closed-circuit television (CCTV) and funnel critical information between us and the agents spread out in other cities and states.

After a year of reading about him, studying him, thinking about him day and night, talking about him, looking for him, cursing and loathing him . . . I was finally in a room with Smith.

And when you're in an enclosed space with somebody like that, you find out what Evil tastes like, sounds like, and feels like.

Hour One

The suite had a living room with couches and chairs, a kitchen and dining area, and two bedrooms with bathrooms. The walls were covered with surveillance photographs, diagrams, charts, and reports — giving the impression of a covert investigative command center.

As we entered, Smith casually glanced around, seemingly unfazed by the overwhelming display.

"Make yourself comfortable, Mr. Smith," I said, pointing to a living room chair behind a coffee table.

"I apologize for the mess, but we've been very busy. You can understand why we didn't want the cleaning staff coming through here."

I was calm and cool. *Don't rush,* said John Edward. *Be patient.*

Smith sat in the chair. Gallinger took a seat on the couch next to him and I sat on a chair on Smith's other side, putting him in the middle.

"California is nice," I said, like an old friend shooting the breeze. "Now I understand why so many people live out here. Beautiful weather, great beaches, and everybody is so health conscious. It sure is a long way from our part of the country."

"Yes," said Smith, with a strained smile. "It's nice out here."

"What made you come out here?"

"I guess it was Laforza."

"I see. We were noticing the SUVs in the area. Pretty sharp. I wish I could afford one."

Smith sipped on a coffee we got at the hotel's breakfast buffet before coming up. He held on to the cup like it was a life preserver.

"They are very nice," he agreed. That was all the small talk Smith could muster. He cleared his throat.

"You wanted to talk?"

He was trying to act calm, but I could see he was afraid.

"That's right. We've been working with some other agencies concerning the disappearances of your wives, Fran and Janice. We were hoping you could fill in some of the blanks and clear up some questions."

"I don't know how much I can tell you. They took off and left me. I haven't seen them since."

"I appreciate that, Mr. Smith. But it's important we go through some details and share some of our findings with you."

"Okay," he said, with little affect.

Gallinger launched in: "Mr. Smith, what can you tell us about Fran?"

"There's not much to tell," he said. I could hear some of the nasally, high-pitched tone everyone talked about. "I came home from work one day and she was gone."

"Let's go a little further back in time, then," I said. "How did you and Fran first meet?"

"We worked together in Florida. Fran was a receptionist, and I was a contractor. She was very nice, and we struck up a relationship. We started dating and married a short time later."

"How long did you date before you were married?"

"I don't know," he shrugged. "A few weeks?"

"Wow, that's a pretty quick courtship," I

said, with a smile. "Sounds like a real, 'love at first sight' story. You must be a man who knows what he wants. You see it and go after it."

"Not exactly."

"So, tell me, after you and Fran married, how long did you stay in Florida?"

Smith shifted in his seat. "That was one of the things that upset Fran. She didn't want to leave Florida. But when my contract ran out, I found work in New Jersey. Fran didn't like it much up there."

"Why didn't she like New Jersey?"

"Well, it was a few things. She missed her mother, her friends, and her job. In Florida we bought a new house right next door to her mother. Fran liked the convenience and privacy. She picked out new furniture for the house and was very upset we had to leave it behind."

"I can understand why Fran wouldn't want to move," said Gallinger.

Smith nodded. "When we moved to Jersey, she was mad at me all the time."

"Oh? Why is that?" I asked, keeping my tone light.

"Well for one, I spent a lot of time at work. I was the project manager at Carborundum and usually worked 12- to 14-hour days. I had to work weekends sometimes."

Gallinger jumped on that: "What about your house in Connecticut?"

Smith paused and glared at her.

"What about it?"

Gallinger tossed a picture onto the coffee table in front of him. It was a photo of Smith with his arm around Sheila. The tension in the room shot up.

"How long had you lived there with Sheila when you married Fran?"

Smith tightened his lips. I could see the carotid artery in his neck pulse.

"Sheila and I were just friends," he said. "We bought that house together as a joint financial investment. Sometimes I went up there on weekends to take care of house repairs or maintenance. You know, those kinds of things. Sheila was a tenant."

"Did Sheila pay you rent?" Gallinger pressed.

Smith glared at her again and didn't answer.

"Mr. Smith, let's stop for a moment," I said. "It's important that we're on the same page. I mean no disrespect, but it's not by accident or coincidence that we're here with you. We've done our homework. We know the answers to the questions we're asking. We know what you've told investigators in the past. We know what's true and what's not. We're not here to rehash old stories but to set things right. Sheila was your friend, that's true. She was also a girlfriend you once proposed to. You shared a close relationship for years. You even had two miniature collies named Christopher and Amanda."

As I spoke, I placed photos of Sheila with the dogs on the coffee table. Smith glanced at them uncomfortably.

"We're not here to waste time," I continued. "We want to work with you to make things right for you, Janice, Fran, and others."

Smith flinched ever so slightly at the word "others."

"Did Fran know about Sheila?" Gallinger asked, diving in once again.

"There was nothing to know," he said, annoyed at her persistence. "Like I said, Sheila and I weren't a couple. We were friends."

"Alright, then. Let's go back to Fran being upset," I said. "Why was she upset?"

Smith fidgeted with his coffee cup.

"Well, for one, her crazy sister and daughter were filling her head with all kinds of things. Fran started questioning everything I did. When I left for work, when I came home, where I went on weekends."

"That must have been stressful," I said.

"It was," Smith replied. "Plus, Fran was

upset because she couldn't find a job. She had no friends in Jersey and was always going on and on about her mother and how great Florida was. Add to all of that, her hip. Fran fractured it at a hotel in the Poconos. She was getting out of the tub and slipped. The recovery was taking a long time because Fran had osteoporosis. She relied on me for everything, and she was always complaining."

"That sounds like a lot to deal with," I said, supportively.

Smith cautiously relished the sympathy.

"How did you handle it all?" I asked.

"What do you mean?"

"You had a new wife struggling with a lot of issues. Certainly, that would affect your relationship and create a lot of stress for you as well?"

"Not really. I was too busy with work. Fran was so dramatic about everything. I can only imagine the stories she must have told her family."

"Did you ever think of leaving Fran?" I asked.

"No."

Gallinger handed me a document. I glanced at it, then handed it to Smith.

"This is a copy of the divorce paperwork you initiated when you still lived in Florida.

According to the deputies who served Fran, she was shocked and furious. When she called you at work, you came home early, told her it was all a big mistake, and withdrew the divorce petition."

I paused.

"So, I'll ask you again. How did Fran's stress, anxiety, and frustration affect you?"

Smith's pale, waxen face turned red. He shrugged his shoulders and out came that high-pitched voice again.

"There's not much to say. I just tried to help Fran."

"How?" I pressed.

"By letting her vent and talk through her issues."

"But you were at work or in Milford. When did you talk through these issues with her? She was like a steam kettle ready to blow. What happened when she got angry with you?"

"Fran was a good woman. She never attacked me."

"Attacked you?" Gallinger said.

She was like a dog with a bone now.

"Is that what happened?" she pressed. "Did Fran lose it because she had enough of your stories and excuses? She suspected you had a girlfriend in Connecticut. She wanted to see her Florida furniture that you said was in storage. But you'd put it all in the Milford house with Sheila. Come on, Mr. Smith, Fran wasn't stupid. She didn't trust you. You told her too many stories and she got sick of it. On top of all of that, her sister Sherrie was on the sidelines whispering in her ear and spinning things up."

Smith's face was crimson with anger as Gallinger chipped away at him.

"None of this would have happened if it weren't for Sherrie," he said.

"I agree," I said. "If it weren't for Sherrie, Fran would be alive today. Sherrie was a problem. She got inside Fran's head and turned her against you. Fran was listening to Sherrie instead of you."

Smith's jaw tightened.

"What happened when Fran confronted you?" I asked, hoping his anger would make him slip up and say something incriminating.

Smith took a deep breath, closed his eyes, and regained composure.

"There was no confrontation," he said. "I left for work one morning, and she was gone when I came home."

I glanced at Gallinger. We needed to shift strategies. I moved to another line of questioning.

"John, do you think Fran is alive or dead?"

Smith sat back in his chair, took a breath,

and centered himself. "I'd have to say she's probably dead."

"Why?"

"Because I guess she would have surfaced by now after all this time."

"Do you feel any sort of guilt about what happened to Fran?" I asked.

"I feel somewhat responsible."

"How so?" Gallinger asked.

He paused, carefully measuring his words.

"Well, suppose two people have a fight. More of an argument or disagreement. And after the argument one person is so upset that they run out of the house and get hit by a bus and die. It was an accident. But the person they argued with would feel guilty or responsible."

"Is that what happened?" Gallinger pushed. "Was Fran's death an accident? Was it simply a loss of control and then Fran was dead?"

Smith sat straighter in his chair.

"I *never* lose control."

I leaned forward.

"We all have a breaking point, John. We all have the potential to lose control. The person who says they never lose control is often the first to lose it. But I'm going to guess that Janice and Fran tried to control everything, that they were far too demanding."

Smith looked like a volcano about to erupt.

* * *

In the room next door, Downes and Dyson were watching on a TV screen, analyzing every word and shift in Smith's demeanor.

"Ease back Bob," Dyson said aloud to the monitor. "We've got a long road here. You're doing great. Pull back a little. You're not there yet."

"Smith is still very guarded and restrained," Downes added. "He needs time to loosen up. His nonverbals are clearly deceptive."

"I think Bob sees that," Dyson added. "He just needs to be patient. It will come."

The phone rang. Downes grabbed a pen and picked up, marking the time on his notepad.

"Hey Gerry. This is Brian Potts from Wayne County." Potts was in Ohio with Smith's brother, Michael.

"Michael is nervous as hell and clearly knows something."

"Has he given you anything?" Downes asked.

"Kind of. He's talking about a rumor about Janice being buried at an address on Grace Lane, under the garage floor."

"What has he said about Smith?"

"Nothing. He told us about this story he heard about Grace Lane. It's one of the townhouse complexes Sam Maltz built years ago. But it's obvious Mike knows more than he's letting on. We'll keep talking to him," Potts said.

"Got it," Downes said.

Hour Three

Gallinger and I continued to prod and poke Smith.

By hour three I'd removed my suit coat, loosened my tie, and rolled up my sleeves.

Gallinger had also removed her jacket and, as always, her gun and badge were prominently displayed on her belt.

Smith sat ramrod straight but showed telltale signs of stress. Underneath his armpits, growing stains of sweat were moving down his shirt. The putrid scent of his body odor became more pronounced.

Gallinger and I kept tossing more photos and police reports onto the table in front of Smith. He remained stoic. Almost robotic.

"John, do you remember that day back in March of 1992, when the West Windsor Police brought you in and questioned you for hours?" I asked. "It was the day they impounded your cars, searched your condo, your work, and the house in Milford."

"Yes," Smith answered.

"Do you remember later that evening

talking with Sheila? She was quite upset because detectives and search dogs had torn apart the Milford house."

"I remember."

"Do you remember Sheila told you that she loved you and would stand by you no matter what? That she would work with you to get through it all?"

Smith remained silent.

"Sheila read the search warrant affidavit to you over the phone, and the section about you failing a polygraph examination concerning Fran's disappearance. She asked what you lied about, and you admitted you lied but wouldn't elaborate."

"I never said that," Smith challenged.

"You told Sheila that when the police finished conducting their investigation, they would find no physical evidence. That the lack of physical evidence was going to save your butt."

"I never said that," Smith repeated.

"And Sheila asked you, no . . . she *begged* you . . . to help Janice and Fran. And you told her it was too late to help them."

"I don't know why Sheila would say that," Smith said, unmoved. "I never said any of those things."

I removed a tape recorder from a briefcase, put it on the table, and pressed PLAY.

A recording from that 1991 phone call between Sheila and Smith began to play.

I lied to the police . . .

They won't find any physical evidence . . .

It's too late to help them . . .

Smith stared at the tape recorder, looked at me, and shrugged.

"Okay," he said, in a whiny, nasally pitch.

"Okay what?" I asked.

He shrugged again.

"Perhaps that recording refreshed your memory. Why was it too late to help Janice and Fran?" I asked.

He shrugged again, and several minutes of silence followed.

I stared at him, waiting.

"What do you want me to say?" he asked, lifting both hands in an "I-don't-know" gesture.

"I want you to tell me what happened to Fran and Janice."

"I've told you a dozen times already. They left me. I have no idea what happened to them."

I got up from my chair — the first time in three hours.

"Come with me," I said to Smith. "I want to show you something."

He got up and I led him to the dining room, which had an entire wall covered with posters, photographs, charts, and reports. I pointed to a large chart in the middle. It contained photos of Smith surrounded by pictures of his friends, family, and coworkers. Each photo was connected to Smith by a line, like a spoke on a wheel.

"Do you recognize any of the people in this chart?" I asked.

Smith nodded. "Some of them. I guess."

"Here, let me help."

I pointed at the photos, one by one.

"Starting at the top, we have your brother Michael; his wife Tawnya; your other brother, Stephen; your present wife, Diane; Dave Hops, the owner at Laforza; Trevor Haywood; Susan Haywood; Sheila Sautter; James Ventrillo; Joan Ventrillo; Nancy Seneco; Terry Poszier; your mother, Grace; and finally your Uncle Don.

"Each one of them has a small piece of information about what happened to Janice and Fran. Do you know what else they have in common?"

Smith shrugged his shoulders. "What?"

"At this very moment, every one of them is being interviewed by FBI agents throughout the country."

Smith looked shell-shocked. He could feel the control slipping away.

"We didn't choose them by accident," I

explained. "Everyone here is a piece of the puzzle, and some are providing information to our agents as we stand here."

As if on cue, there was a loud knock on the door. The knock was followed by a folded slip of paper, slid underneath.

Gallinger walked over and picked it up. She read it and brought it to me in the bedroom. Smith watched, worried, as I read it:

MICHAEL MENTIONED A RUMOR ABOUT JANICE BEING BURIED AT 2019 GRACE LANE, UNDER THE GARAGE FLOOR.

I folded up the piece of paper and stared Smith down for a long, penetrating minute.

Could this have something to do with the box John keeps talking about?

"We better go back to the other room," I told him, ominously. "There's been a new development."

10

Rope-A-Dope

We returned to our original positions by the living room coffee table, and I placed the folded bit of paper on the table.

I turned to Smith. He looked like he was preparing to take a punch.

"Michael knows everything," I told him.

Smith froze.

"When Sam died," I began, "you sold your house in Milford at a loss to avoid foreclosure. You quit your job unexpectedly and moved in with your mother to help run Pleasant Hill Management, the real estate business Sam had built. Shortly after returning to Ohio, you had Michael take you around to the apartments and townhouses to introduce you to the women in those properties. Do you remember that?"

Smith sat still like a wax figure.

I continued.

"So, Michael does as he's told. He

introduces you to these pretty young ladies and tells them you are the man they need to contact should they need anything. But here's the funny thing. Do you know what Michael did after that? He went back to every one of those ladies by himself and warned them to stay away from you. He told them that your wives disappeared and he and the family had to lie to the police to cover for you."

I paused and took a sip of water from a bottle on the table, not taking my eyes off Smith.

"Now," I went on, "I can only imagine. What did Michael know that was so horrific that he needed to warn these young women? What would make your own brother so worried that you would hurt these women?"

Smith was barely breathing.

"I don't know why Mike would say that," he said. "It's simply not true."

I reached into a brown accordion file on the floor, took out a thick stack of papers, and plopped them onto the coffee table with a thud.

"Here are 18 sworn affidavits from different women who all tell the exact same story. What is it that Michael saw, John? What does he know?"

For the umpteenth time, Smith shrugged: "I have no idea."

I grabbed the folded piece of paper on the table, opened it, and held it up to him.

"Tell me about 2019 Grace Lane."

Smith swallowed hard. The nasally voice returned.

"I don't know what to tell you. That's a townhouse development Sam built in the seventies. He named the street after my mother. I don't know anything particular about unit 2019."

"Apparently Michael does," I said. "He just told our agents in Ohio we might want to check under the garage floor. Something about a box under the concrete."

Smith looked ashen.

"I don't know what he's talking about," Smith insisted.

"Sure, you do," I said. "Why would Michael give us such specific information? Why would he warn those women?"

"I don't know," Smith repeated.

"I do," I said.

In the hotel room next door, Downes and Dyson continued to field calls from the interview teams, make notes, and monitor our progress on the CCTV screen.

"Hey Gerr, I think we should compare notes," Dyson said.

"Sure," said Downes. "What have you got?"

Dyson adjusted her glasses and looked over her notepad.

"Smith's new wife, Diane, and his work colleagues all tell the same story. Smith told them he was married once, to Fran, and that she died of cancer. Diane said Smith carries a picture of Fran with him. Lots of inconsistencies about his background, education, and financial situation. What did you get from the other teams?"

"As expected, Michael was the big one," Downes began. "He's making reference to stories he's heard and keeps bringing up this 2019 Grace Lane. The guys are convinced there's more but he's not giving it up yet."

Downes flipped a couple of pages and continued. "Let's see . . . Grace, the mother, is not cooperative. They're having a hard time getting a good read on her. They think she's playing the crazy old lady role but knows more. Nothing from the uncle. Oh, the guys in Connecticut are getting a strange vibe from Sheila Sautter in Connecticut. They think she's holding back but are having a hard time reading her."

Downes and Dyson checked the CCTV monitors.

"Smith is one tough nut to crack," said

Dyson. "Evasive as hell. It's like trying to nail Jell-O to the wall."

Back in the suite, I took the interrogation up a notch.

"One thing I've learned after years as a cop and an FBI agent is there truly is no such thing as the perfect crime," I told Smith.

"When a crime is committed, particularly a violent, emotion-evoking one like yours, mistakes are always made."

I signaled to Gallinger.

"May I have the Connecticut files please?"

Gallinger handed me another accordion folder. I flipped through it and kept talking.

"Remember when you sold your house in Milford and rushed out to Ohio after Sam died?"

No response.

"You were in such a rush to sell that house you took a $60,000 loss and owed the bank money after closing. I've been to that house. Nice little place on the water. But in your haste to pack up all those garbage bags filled with women's clothes in your attic, you forgot something important."

Smith looked over at the files with apprehensive interest.

"Ah! Here it is," I said, pulling out an 8

x 10 glossy and laying it on the table. The knife from the attic.

"You left behind this knife, John. The guy you sold the house to found it. Guess where?"

I paused. No answer.

"That's right. You left it in the attic under the insulation."

I handed the picture to Smith, who took it with a trembling hand. His colorless face grew even more colorless if that was possible.

"I don't know anything about this," he said.

"Of course not," I said. "Let me share something else. I interviewed Janice Miller. Remember her? She was the prostitute who moved in with you. What did you keep in the attic that was so important that you told her never to go up there?"

Smith smirked.

"So now you're going to believe some whore?" he said, sharply.

"Whoa, that's not very nice," I said. "I don't think you would have brought a whore to visit your family in Ohio, would you? Oh, that reminds me, did you know that there were a bunch of prostitutes who were killed back then? Many were cut up, cut to hell. Some of the most vicious defensive wounds I've ever seen. And guess what? Most of the women were found completely naked, their clothes were never recovered. In one case, a witness got a close look at the guy who drove off with one of the victims."

Gallinger produced a picture of Karla Storer, one of the prostitutes from Bridgeport and Janice Miller's friend.

"Yes, sir, that's her." I continued. I was on a roll.

"Karla was a real pretty girl. As I understand it, some guy drove off with her in a sedan hatchback. She was found naked in a dumpster three days later."

Gallinger dropped pictures of the crime scene onto the coffee table. Smith looked, still expressionless.

"For God's sake, this poor girl looks like she was attacked by a shark," I said, dramatically. "It just so happens that Karla's boyfriend watched her get into the guy's car. He gave a description to a sketch artist."

Gallinger handed the composite sketch to Smith, who took it with an outstretched, shaking hand.

"I might be wrong," I said, "but I suspect a jury would say you look an awful lot like that guy. By the way, what type of a car were you driving back then?"

Smith was mute, transfixed by the sketch that looked like him.

I lowered and softened my voice.

"You see, John, we need to figure out a way to help you. How we can work together to bring an end to all of this. We're passed the point of debating with you. You can't debate the truth, it's bigger than that."

Smith feigned obliviousness.

"I don't know what to say," he repeated. "You think I'm some kind of monster. That because of these circumstantial things, I must have something to do with all of this. I don't know what to tell you."

"Tell us what happened to Fran and Janice."

"I keep telling you, I don't know."

HOUR SEVEN

Like nailing Jell-O to the wall, Dyson said.

That's exactly how it felt.

It was now late afternoon, seven hours into our arduous psychological journey with two-time-wife-killer Smith.

In the profiler's room, Downes and Dyson were joined by several FBI agents and local investigators who'd finished their own interviews and come to the hotel room to watch the main event.

The profiler's room was strewn with pizza boxes, soda cans, and coffee cups. Dyson rubbed her eyes to relieve the strain of staring at the CCTV monitors for so many hours. Downes stood up, stretched, and rubbed his neck.

"What do you think, Marie? How much longer?"

"They've covered everything. Bob's run through every theme and is repeating himself now. I think Smith is numb to it at this point. I don't see any cracks. I give it another hour, tops."

Back in the hotel suite, the room was thick with tension.

The three of us looked like fighters in a boxing ring, swinging exhausted punches in the last rounds of a fight no one could call.

Smith sat quietly, waiting for the next round to begin. Gallinger studied files and photos, looking for a new plan of attack.

I leaned back in my chair, weary, contemplating a miraculous, inspirational Hail Mary pass to save the day.

And then I remembered John Edward's advice: *Mention his grandmother.*

A rush of energy hit me. I leaned toward Smith.

"You know what, John? I feel sorry for a lot of people involved in this case. I feel sorry for the women you've killed. I feel bad for their families and friends. I also feel sorry for you. I honestly believe you need help because you can't control what's happening and don't understand what causes you to do these things. You're also a victim of your own fantasies and psychoses."

Smith looked interested. He loved playing the victim, after all.

"But the people I feel most sorry for," I continued, "the people I wake up thinking about in the middle of the night are your grandparents, Ethel and Chester. They had to go to their graves knowing the terrible things you did."

Smith looked wounded. I'd hit a chink in his armor. He slowly slumped forward, dropping his shoulders. I moved closer.

"Your grandparents loved you; you could do no wrong in their eyes. Ethel loved you like a son. There was nothing she wouldn't do for you. For years, they both knew your secrets. They knew what you did.

"Ethel hid the pain but carried the guilt every day of her life. It must have been a terrible thing for her to draw her last breath plagued by the horror and guilt you caused. She must have felt like her soul was carrying the evil you caused.

"Ethel passed three months ago," I continued. "I'm very sorry for your loss, John. I'm sure you wanted to be there for her at the end but couldn't."

I looked at Smith's face; actual tears were streaming down his cheeks. Gallinger was astonished. Smith stared straight ahead, hypnotized by my words.

It was working.

In the hotel room next door, the group of agents, detectives, and profilers were glued to the CCTV monitors, transfixed by the sudden break in Smith's demeanor.

"Oh my God!" Dyson whispered. "Here it is. Tread carefully, Bob."

* * *

Smith was in a trancelike state.

I inched closer, gently invading his personal space. I spoke in a low, comforting tone.

The grandmother.

"You were the apple of Ethel's eye," I cooed. "When she talked about you, she lit up with pride. I'm sure you loved her dearly, too. You both shared a very special bond, that's evident. But we both know the things you couldn't control, the things that weren't your fault, they caused Ethel terrible pain.

"Now, I don't know what's waiting for

us on the Other Side. But I have to believe what we did here matters. I would hope that your grandmother is not judged because she covered for your actions, John. And I believe she is here with us, in this very room. And she needs to make sure things are set straight to have peace. She loves you, John, and she needs your help."

It was surprising how often this tactic worked, bringing up people's dead loved ones. Smith's cheeks were wet, but he didn't wipe his tears; he didn't even acknowledge them.

But he began to speak. This time, he used a deeper, more natural voice — not the high-pitched whine from before.

He spoke as if he was under a spell, as if he had no control over what he was saying.

"I don't know how to begin talking about it," he said. "I don't know how to begin to confess. My life has become a living nightmare and I don't know how to make it stop."

The hairs on the back of my neck stood up. This was the "break" John talked about!

Smith was about to confess!

"I feel responsible for what's happened to those women," Smith continued. "Perception has become reality and I need this to stop. I can't control it."

He stopped talking and sat in deep thought

for a moment. It looked like he was allowing himself, for the first time, to accept the ugly truth of what he'd done.

I placed my hand on his shoulder as a gesture of support.

"You're not the first person who's struggled with these problems," I said. "We're here to help you. It's going to be okay."

Smith flinched.

His face changed from genuine pain, sorrow, and truth, to one of fear, recognition, and shock. Before my eyes, he changed from a man on the verge of confessing to someone who recognized his own jeopardy.

My touch and voice had broken him from his trance!

He pulled back, shaking my hand off his shoulder. I watched his confession slip through my fingers.

"It's okay, John. No one is going to hurt you," I said, trying to get back to where we were. "We're all in this together," I said, comforting. "I know this is difficult but it's going to be okay."

But it was over, I could see that. So could Gallinger. Nothing I said now was working.

Smith covered his face with his hands and feigned emotion.

"I miss my grandmother so much!" he whined, dramatically. "I wish I was with her during her last days. I'm sorry, Grandma. Please forgive me!"

I had completely lost control, and Smith was in the driver's seat. I glanced over at Gallinger, who ran her fingers through her hair in frustration.

Inside the monitoring room next door, Downes threw his clipboard in frustration.

"Dammit! He had him!"

Dyson stood up, hands on hips. "The physical contact broke Smith out of it. He'll never get it back. Smith will shift his game and try to get out of there ASAP. Now this will be about Smith's exit strategy. He lost control once. He won't let it happen a second time."

Back in the suite, Smith lifted a hand to his forehead.

"I have a terrible headache coming on. Could I trouble you for aspirin?"

I stared at him in frustration, as Gallinger went to the kitchen to investigate the first-aid kit.

"Let's go back to where we were before, John," I said.

"I'm sorry, Agent Hilland, but I can't help you. I keep saying the same thing over and over but you won't believe me."

Gallinger returned and handed Smith aspirin and a glass of water. Smith gulped them down, then placed his hand on his chest.

"Do you think we could shut the lights off in this room?" he asked. "They're giving me the headache . . ."

I got up and shut off the overhead lights, switching on two lamps.

Great. Now Smith had us running around for him.

"That's worse," he said, recoiling from the lamp light.

"This isn't bedtime, John," I said. "What we do in the dark will be revealed in the light."

Smith smirked. He was enjoying my frustration.

But at least I knew what he was up to. He'd continue making small requests that would shift to large demands, and I had to stop him before it escalated.

Smith closed his eyes and rubbed his chest and shoulder area.

"Agent Hilland, I'm having pain and tightness in my chest. It's spreading down my arm."

Shit. Too late.

"Stop the bullshit!" I shot back.

Smith moaned in pain.

"I think I'm having a heart attack."

He stood up and threw himself across the couch, curling up in a fetal position, and moaned louder.

"Leave me alone. Just let me lie here and die."

"No way, John," I said. "This is not happening!"

I tried again to pull him back in time, to the place on the cusp of a breakthrough.

"I understand you're stressed and this is difficult," I said, switching back to my comforting voice. "But I'm here to help you."

"If you really want to help," he moaned, "call an ambulance. I need to go to the hospital!"

Forty-five minutes later, we heard a knock at the door.

Agent Gerry Downes stood in the hallway with a group of paramedics, firefighters, and emergency responders. I stepped into the hallway and closed the door.

"What the hell is this?" I asked.

"Bob, Smith has been asking for an ambulance for nearly an hour. If something happens and he dies, we've got a problem."

I sighed and introduced myself to the ranking paramedic.

"Captain, here's what we've got. The guy

in there is being interviewed for the disappearances of his wives. He is 48, no known medical history. We've been interviewing him for the past . . ."

I looked at my watch.

". . . *nine* hours. It's my opinion that he's faking this medical emergency as a ruse to get out of here."

The captain nodded.

"Go ahead and check him out and if there's anything wrong with him, take him to the hospital. Don't hesitate. But if you determine there's nothing wrong with him, I wouldn't have any heartburn if you left him here with us."

"Got it," the captain said.

I opened the hotel room door and led them inside.

As soon as Smith saw the emergency responders, he started groaning dramatically again, grabbing his left arm and chest.

"Thank God you're here," he cried. "I'm having a heart attack. I have pains in my chest that are radiating down my arm. I need to go to the hospital."

One of the paramedics whipped out a pair of scissors and sliced Smith's shirt up the middle.

"What are you doing?" Smith protested.

"We're conducting an electrocardiogram,

Sir," the paramedic replied, as he taped stickers across Smith's chest and ribs.

"Is all of this really necessary?" he asked.

"It is if you're having chest pains," said another paramedic. "Standard operating procedure. Could I get your name and date of birth?"

"John Smith."

The paramedic jotted down the information.

"Date of birth?"

"April 2, 1951," I answered, before Smith had a chance. "Blood type A negative. No history of heart issues or high blood pressure in the past. Mother and father both alive and well. Neither suffer from heart disease. No medications other than Valtrex. His medical insurance card is in his wallet located in the glove box of the black Mazda Miata parked outside of the hotel."

I was an encyclopedia of John Smith facts and trivia.

Smith looked startled by it.

The paramedic readied the equipment.

"Sir, if I could ask you to lie still and remain silent for a few seconds."

"Oh, don't worry," I said, dripping with sarcasm. "He's good at lying, and he's good at remaining silent."

The ECG monitor beeped and the

paramedic examined the scroll of paper it spit out. He handed it to the captain, who also examined it.

"Mr. Smith," said the captain. "The results of your electrocardiogram clearly show you are *not* having a heart attack. You have a slightly elevated pulse rate but your cardiac functions are perfectly normal. There is no need for you to go to the hospital."

Smith clutched his chest.

"There must be something wrong with your machine," he whimpered. "This crushing pain in my chest is unbearable. I need to go to the hospital where a *real* doctor can check me."

The captain loomed over the couch.

"Mr. Smith, I have been a Level III trauma paramedic for over twenty years. My wife is a cardiothoracic surgeon at San Diego General Hospital. I have saved people's lives during my service in the military by literally cracking open their chests and massaging their hearts with my bare hands. There is no one in the county who knows more about the heart than I do. So, it is from that experience that I can tell you with absolute certainty you are not having a heart attack. There is nothing wrong with you."

I was impressed. And grateful.

Smith was livid.

"Captain, are you denying me medical attention? Are you refusing to take me to the hospital?"

The captain turned to me with a look of apology and exasperation.

That son of a bitch won — this round, anyway.

I nodded to the captain, giving him the go ahead.

"Alright folks, we need to put the patient on a saline solution stat," the captain directed his team. "Let's get him properly hydrated. I need a two-line port in his arm. Be sure to get a good vein. I need his blood pressure checked every three to five minutes. Let's ensure we've stabilized his vitals and strap him down to a stair chair."

A clamor of paramedics and equipment surrounded Smith like bees around a beehive. They knew what their boss was telling them to do: screw with Smith as much as possible. The more they pricked and prodded, the more theatrical Smith's response got.

I watched, arms folded, furious at Smith.

As the paramedics began wheeling him out, Smith looked at me and . . . winked.

"Hold on, guys," I said. "Before you take Mr. Smith out, can I speak with him privately for a minute?"

The emergency team filed out, leaving Downes and me alone with Smith. His smarmy victory turned to panic. I leaned down, inches from his face.

"Let's set the record straight before they roll you out of here," I said.

"We both know this little ploy is complete bullshit. It's a good play, though, I give you that. But here's the important thing you need to understand and remember."

I leaned in even closer. I could see every pore on his pale face.

"This isn't over by a long shot. From this moment onward, your life will not be your own. When you wake up in the morning, I will know it. When you lay your head down to sleep, I will know it. I will know every time you talk on the phone, drive a car, and take a piss."

I reached into my pocket and pulled out the watch with the green face. Janice Hartman's birthday watch.

I held it in front of Smith's eyes.

He winced, recognizing it instantly.

"What's the matter, John. You see a ghost?"

He looked like he might have a heart attack for real this time.

"You see, we're not some local sheriff's office. And I'm not Barney-fucking-Fife," I said, standing up straight, stretching my

6'8" frame after nine hours of hell with this monster.

"We're the FBI," I told him. "And if it takes my last, dying breath, I will make sure you spend the rest of your life in jail.

"Make no mistake. The next time you see my face, you'll be behind bars."

11

Clowns and Rainbows

SMITH'S FAMILY
Grace, *Smith's mother*
Sam Maltz, *Grace's husband*
Ethel, *Smith's grandmother*
Chester, *Smith's grandfather*
Michael, *Smith's brother*
Tawnya, *Michael's wife*

NEW LOCATIONS
Seville, Ohio
Townhouse development on Grace Lane
Grace's house
Ethel's house and the family garage on Pleasant Street
Michael's house on Pleasant Street

Back in New York, I returned to John Edward's office frustrated and discouraged.

His first book, *One Last Time,* had hit bookstores a few months earlier, and his popularity was on the rise. He was in demand on all the top morning breakfast radio shows. But in the year since we met, he was always a phone call away when I needed to ask him about Smith — and in dire moments like this, to meet in person.

We had formed a brotherly connection, I felt. He was relaxed enough to feel comfortable calling me by my first name. For a cop's son, that's major.

"We spoke with Smith for *nine* hours," I told him, "and then . . ."

"Wait!" he said, looking off into the distance.

"They're showing me Smith crying. I mean *real, genuine emotion.* Did he break down?"

"Yes."

"And when he got to the edge, something happened and it pulled him back. It was like . . . one second he was there and the next he wasn't."

"Right again," I sighed in frustration. "I don't know. Maybe I need to walk away from this one."

"No way!" said John, adamant. "That's not your nature. To the contrary, you're even more focused now than you were before. Now you've felt his energy. You know what he's like. Use that knowledge against him."

I shook my head.

"Look Bob, you're knocked down right now. But you'll get back up. Everything happens for a reason. You planted a lot of seeds, now give them time to germinate and take root. I'm going to tell you again, be patient. This is not over — not by a long shot."

"I know. Be patient. Your guides have anything else they want to say?"

John paused and listened.

"Yes. They're saying again: 'Michael. *Michael!*' What did Michael tell you?"

"Not a lot. He mentioned a rumor that Janice may be buried under a garage floor in Ohio."

John paused and squinted. "Nah, I'm not feeling that."

"What are you feeling?"

"Just . . . patience. Let things happen in their own time."

I sighed again.

"I'm trying. But I hope Smith doesn't kill anyone else in the meantime."

"He won't," John said, with confidence. "Whatever you said to him in California scared the living hell out of him. He's paranoid now, looking over his shoulder."

I rubbed my temples. I thought about the precious time Smith was taking away from my wife and children, the strain it was causing at home.

"What would happen if I did walk away from this?"

"You won't," said John. "You can't. But if you did, it's absolutely your free will to make that decision."

"What would the outcome be?"

John paused. A sadness passed across his face.

"For you? Regret. For Smith? Freedom. For other women? *Death.*"

To know John is to know his spirit guides — "the Boys," he sometimes called them — they were his wise team on the Other Side.

And like other higher powers embraced by people in this mortal world, they were in charge, and they worked in mysterious ways.

"I'm not a Magic 8 Ball," John told me once. "My guides give information we are meant to have when we are meant to have it. The spirit world works on their timeline, not ours."

For someone like me who was a doer, a front-line fighter, a guy who set his sights on the goal line and made the touchdown, that meant they could be frustratingly vague. Other times, though, they could be mind-bendingly accurate.

Perhaps the most important quality to remember about John's guides is that they are always 100 percent accurate. John's interpretation may mess things up, but his guides will not.

Case in point: Michael Smith.

A few days after John's guides insisted for the third time: *Michael, Michael, Michael . . .* I received a call from attorney Ron Speer, Michael Smith's lawyer, to arrange a follow-up meeting.

"My client might be able to provide information that may assist in your investigation concerning his brother," said Speer.

I hung up the phone with new confidence. I'd returned to New York with egg on my face among my colleagues, and now here was an opportunity for me to redeem myself, to win the game again. I had no idea what Michael was going to say, but I was filled with anticipation.

The following week I sat in a conference room with Speer, Michael Smith, and Michael's wife Tawnya. I slid several documents across the table — immunity contracts that gave Michael full protection from prosecution so long as he did not directly contribute to the deaths of any of the victims in our investigation.

"It takes a lot of courage for you to be

here," I told him. "I'm very grateful to you for that."

"I want this to be over," he said, signing the paperwork and sliding it back to me.

Michael took a deep breath.

"I don't think you're going to believe what I'm about to tell you," he began, "but I promise you, everything I'm about to say is the truth."

Michael's story began on Thanksgiving Day, 1974. He; Smith; their mother, Grace; grandmother, Ethel; and other family members were at Ethel's house readying for dinner. Michael took a break from watching college football — the rivaling Ohio State versus Michigan — and went for a stroll outside.

The family owned a small gas station and repair shop next door, which was closed for the holiday. It was a two-bay garage with a small office attached and two gas pumps out front. Michael noticed one of the bay doors open, walked over, and found Smith inside.

"He had the lift raised and was wrestling with some plywood and a saw," Michael described. "He was building a box, he explained, to put Jan's belongings in. Jan had taken off and left some of her stuff behind."

The box. Finally, John's BOX!

Michael thought it strange his brother

wasn't using regular moving boxes and told him so. Smith explained he wanted something stronger, "so her stuff wouldn't get messed up." When Michael began suggesting he use oak or cherry for the box, Smith snapped back, so he left.

An hour later, Michael returned and saw the bay door now closed.

"I pressed my face against the window," he said, "and I saw John standing next to the box he built. It was resting on top of the lift. A pile of Jan's clothes and stuff were on the floor by his feet. He was picking up one or two things at a time," Michael gestured with his hands, "rolling them up, and placing them in the box."

Michael paused.

"One thing really struck me," he said.

"What was that?" I asked.

"All my life I never saw my brother cry. He never showed any emotion. That day when he was putting Jan's stuff in the box, he was crying."

The following week, Michael passed through the garage again by chance and saw the plywood box still there, pushed against a wall, with other things on top of it.

"I didn't pay it much mind," he said. "The box stayed in that exact spot from November of 1974 until May or June of 1979."

"What happened in 1979?" I asked.

At that time, Smith was living and working in Hammond, Indiana. The family had closed the gas station, and the grandfather, Chester, was cleaning it out one day.

"I lived a couple of houses away from Grandad's on Pleasant Street. I was at work when I got a call from Grandad to get over to the garage right away. Something was wrong."

When Michael arrived, Chester was nervous and he pointed to the plywood box.

"That's John's box," he said. "Do you know what is inside?"

Chester had tried to pry it open. It stank like an old, dead turtle. Michael knelt, pulled a piece off one end of the box, and peered inside.

"I saw what looked like dirty rags and what I thought were two cylinders. At first, I thought they were the bottoms of a scuba tank. I had a bad feeling. I picked up the box, put it on my shoulder, and carried it to my backyard. Then I got a crowbar and pried the top of the box open."

Michael swelled with emotion.

"What was in the box?" I asked.

Michael closed his eyes and took a deep breath.

"The first thing I saw was a bunch of

clothes and stuff. They were discolored and smelled bad. I didn't want to touch anything with my hands, so I broke off a tree branch and used it to poke around in the box. I moved some of the clothes around and then I saw a pewter crucifix and rainbow-colored hair."

"Rainbow-colored?"

"Yep. It was red, yellow, blue, green, and orange. I thought it was a clown's wig. Then I moved the hair out of the way and that's when I saw her face."

"Who's face?"

Michael exhaled.

"Janice."

"Janice?!" I asked.

"Yes. I touched her face with the stick. It was hard, like wood. It was Janice in the box."

"What did you do then?"

"I ran back to the garage and got Grandad. He came to the backyard. I told him Janice's body was in the box. He panicked. I told him we needed to call the sheriff. Grandad said we couldn't call the sheriff because it would kill Grandma, she was still recovering from a heart attack."

Instead, Michael made a rare call to Smith at work.

Two pieces of the puzzle snapped into

place. *This must be the phone call Smith's former boss, Dick Gromlovich, told me about.*

Michael continued.

"I told John that Grandad and I found his box in the garage. 'Did you open it?' he asked. I said yes. He said, 'I'll be right there,' and hung up."

I glanced at DeStano, who was taking notes fast and furiously.

"Are you okay Michael? Do you want to take a break?" Speer asked his client. Michael shook his head, "No. I need to get through this."

Tawnya rubbed her husband's back.

"What happened after you got off the phone?" I asked.

"I went inside and got drunk!" he said. "I couldn't believe what was happening. Grandad went inside to be with Grandma. Eight hours later to the minute, John came screeching into Grandad's driveway with his brand-new Corvette that Grandma bought for him. I was on my porch when he pulled in. He went inside Grandma and Grandad's house and spent fifteen or twenty minutes in there. Then I watched him come out and walk toward my house. I had a knot in my stomach. I didn't want him in my house, so I walked out to meet him."

"What did he say to you?"

"He told me some story that Janice was a narc working for the police and drug dealers killed her and dropped her body off to him. He panicked and didn't know how to handle it because he was worried the cops would think *he* killed her. That's why he built that box and put her in it."

"What happened to the box, Michael?"

"That week the masons were coming to pour the garage floors at a new townhouse development on Grace Lane. I told John he could take the box there and put it in a shallow grave. When the concrete was poured, nobody would ever know the difference. I told him to put her at unit 2019," Michael explained.

"Why that unit?"

"It was farthest away from the road and had the most privacy for him to dig without being seen. I even offered to take him over there to help."

"Did you?"

"No. John said it was his problem and he'd take care of it. The last time I saw the box, I helped him load it into the passenger seat of his Corvette and he drove off with it."

"Did he ever tell you what he did with it?"

Michael shook his head.

"No. A few days later he called and said

that he had taken care of it and told me not to worry about it."

I took a deep breath.

"Where do you think the box is, Michael?"

"I would check 2019 Grace Lane," he said. "Or anywhere between here and Indiana."

I leaned back in my chair, exasperated.

"You see! I said you wouldn't believe me!" said Michael.

I wanted to. But a dead woman stays in a garage for five years in a box and her body doesn't decompose? Her face remains intact? Nobody noticed an unusual putrid smell?

"I'm telling you the truth," Michael said. "I recognized her clear as day. She looked like she was sleeping."

"And the hair . . ."

"Like I said, it looked like a clown's wig. I never saw Janice's hair like that. Normally it was dirty blond."

I struggled to make sense of everything he was telling me.

"Michael, you said that when you initially looked in the box you thought were looking at two cylinders. Like scuba tanks, you said."

"Yes," he said, his voice cracking.

"What were they?"

Michael's face went dark at the memory.

"They were cross sections of Jan's legs,"

he said. "John cut her legs off just below the knees."

I closed my eyes for a second. Images of the murdered Bridgeport prostitutes flashed in my mind . . . forearms and hands cut to the bone, pieces of fingers missing.

"Were the rest of her legs in the box?" I asked.

"No. We never found them."

That night at Walker's bar in Tribeca, DeStano and I tried to drown out the visual of Janice Hartman's severed legs. I was trying with bourbon.

"I don't know, Bobby. Parts of it make sense, but a lot of the details don't add up if you ask me."

"Can't say I disagree," I said, throwing back a shot.

"We can't just start looking for a magic box that secretly preserves a body and turns it into a clown," he said.

I motioned to the bartender for another round.

"Take my advice for the hundredth time," DeStano said. "Close this godforsaken bullshit case that nobody cares about and move on! It's not an FBI problem, it's a local problem!"

"I can't."

"You stubborn, giant bastard!"

I sloshed the bourbon around in my glass.

"You know what, DeStano? I thought the FBI was better than this," I said, slamming my drink down onto the bar. "Is this how it works? We hit dead ends, a case gets hard, and we walk away?"

DeStano turned on his bar stool to face me.

"There's a difference between hitting dead ends and knocking that thick head of yours against a brick wall," he said.

"What are you going to do now big shot? Walk into Buckbee's office tomorrow and say, 'Hey boss, I'm headed to the Cleveland Division with a metal detector and a shovel to look for a magic box that doesn't exist?' He'll shove that shovel right up your ass and throw you out of his office. You'll be reassigned to a rubber gun squad.

"C'mon, Bobby," DeStano said, for the hundredth time. "Let it go."

* * *

John Edward sat cross-legged across from me on the couch in his office. Except for his boyish face, he reminded me of a calm, insightful Buddhist monk.

Grasshopper . . .

I was well-trained by now. I didn't give him any details about my meeting with Michael and did my best to keep answers to yes and no unless otherwise directed.

John's take on my meeting with Michael was the complete opposite of DeStano-No-Cases.

"Whatever just happened is huge," he said. "There's a significant shift in the energy around this case."

"Energy?"

He paused as if trying to decipher invisible clues.

"Did Michael come to New York?"

"Yes," I said.

"They're showing me the city and your office. He was nervous."

I nodded.

"No. You don't understand. He almost didn't come. Michael was plagued with second thoughts."

John paused. "And his wife . . . is she the 'T' name like 'Tina' or 'Toni?' "

"Tawnya."

"You need to thank her. If it wasn't for her, Michael wouldn't have come. I feel like she had to convince him. And whatever Michael told you . . . it's like now, you have a lot more questions than answers."

"You could say that," I deadpanned.

John broke his gaze from the world beyond and looked at me, sober as a judge.

"He's telling you the truth, Bob."

"He can't be," I said, forgetting the cardinal rule: John's guides are never wrong. "What he told me doesn't make sense."

John looked off into the distance again.

"Don't worry," he said. "It will."

He squinted, confused.

"I'm seeing a rainbow and a clown. What does that mean?"

I shook my head in awe. *Wow. How the heck . . .*

"Michael said he saw Janice's body five years after she disappeared and that her hair was rainbow colored, like a clown's wig."

John looked just as perplexed as me.

"Rainbow-colored hair?" he asked.

"That's what I mean. Doesn't make sense."

John continued trying to interpret the images his guides were sending.

"Did Michael say she looked like she was sleeping? Five years after she died?"

"Yup. Makes no sense."

John looked at me with a sense of urgency.

"Have you been to the place where he said this body was?"

"Not yet."

John got excited.

"You need to go there! Is this some kind of garage?"

"Yes."

"They're pulling me to the right. I'm standing in front of this, this garage . . . I want to go to the right. They're showing me an arrow, like a flashing Las Vegas sign, pointing me to the right of the garage. There's someone there you need to talk to."

"Who?"

John sniffs the air.

"I don't know. But I smell pipe tobacco. Like a cherry pipe tobacco."

"What's that mean?"

"I don't know but remember 'pipe tobacco.' "

"Okay," I said, scribbling notes.

John shuddered, as if a cold wind blew across his face.

"What's wrong?" I asked.

He broke his distant gaze and looked at me directly.

"Are you planning to talk with Smith's mother?"

"Yes."

"Her name is opposite her personality and energy," John said. "You know how sometimes people will call a fat guy 'Slim' or a big guy 'Tiny'?" Like that. It's a hard 'G' name like . . ."

"Grace," I said. *Oops.*

"Yup. That would be it," said John. "You need to protect yourself from her energy."

"I don't understand."

"She's Smith's mother, and we agree he's a serial killer, the embodiment of pure evil, right?"

"Right."

"His mother Grace is the energy source he came from. They're showing me the movie *Aliens*."

"Aliens?"

"Yeah. Remember when Ripley comes face to face with this ominous, powerful, scary-as-hell mother alien?"

"Um, it's been years since . . ."

"When the mother alien finally appears," John describes, totally into the scene, "there's this 'Oh shit!' moment. That's what I felt just now when I saw Smith's mother."

"That doesn't sound good," I said.

"Protect yourself. You'll be fine. The thing is, she doesn't have this monster like outward appearance. To the contrary, she'll come off as an innocent old lady. Very disarming but sly as a fox. That's what makes her so dangerous. And that's what she has in common with Smith."

"Will Grace even talk with me?"

John Edward paused.

"Yes," he answered. "But only on a cursory

level. If you make her feel as though it's in her best interest to help you, then she will. She will play head games with you. She's great at manipulating people with lies, trickery, and deceit. She's like her son but stronger in some ways."

"Is she . . . nuts?" I asked.

"Not at all," said John, shaking his head. "She may want people to think she is, but she's sharp as a knife."

John paused. "Bad analogy. Sorry."

"No worries. Does Grace know what Smith did?"

"Yes, but she'll deny it."

John's brow furrowed. He looked alarmed.

"Whatever she tries to give you, don't take it!" he warned.

"Huh?"

"I don't know what this is, but I'm seeing her giving something to you. Her hand is outstretched with something in it for you. I feel like smacking it down, knocking it out of her hand."

I wrote in my notepad: TAKE NOTHING FROM GRACE.

"Nope. I don't like her energy," John continued, arms folded. "There's a lot going on there."

"Anything else I should do? Or *not* do?" I asked.

"Follow your instincts," he said.

John leaned forward, grabbed a sage smudge stick from a table, and handed it to me.

"And the night before you meet with Grace, light this and let the smoke surround you. Then repeat, 'I surround myself in the white light of God's love and divine protection.'

"Say that a few times, clear your head, meditate, say whatever prayers you like. Ask your guides to surround and protect you as you interact with negative forces and energies."

"My guides? I have my own guides?" I almost laughed. "And I should talk to them?"

I took the smudge stick, unsure. Still the skeptic.

"Really?"

John nodded with conviction.

"Absolutely."

12

The Mothership

SMITH'S FAMILY
Grace, *Smith's mother*

NEW WITNESSES
Dick Armstrong, *funeral home owner*

LOCATIONS
Seville, Ohio
Ethel's house and the family garage on Pleasant Street
Armstrong Funeral Home on Pleasant Street

The county roads of Wayne County, Ohio, twisted and turned like serpents.

Sergeant Brian Potts negotiated the curves and dips as I took in the scenery from the passenger window — open fields, rural pastures, and little towns like Andy Griffith's Mayberry.

It was July 1999, and we were on our way to pay a surprise visit to Smith's mother, Grace, to try to get her to talk.

Fat chance, Potts said. He'd tried to interview her during our nine-hour hotel fiasco and, like John Edward, had words of warning for me.

"Talking to her is like dealing with the devil," said Potts. "She was like a caged animal. She wouldn't talk at first. When she finally let us in her house, the furniture was covered with sheets and plastic. There were rows and rows of filing cabinets containing business records for Pleasant Hill Management. She's squirrely. Evasive as hell. She almost wouldn't even acknowledge Smith."

"What did she say about him?"

"Something about him taking money from her and wanting to talk about Pleasant Hill Management."

Grace, it seemed, was a compulsive liar who told stories of great fancy and grandeur, like her son. Also, like Smith, she was incredibly manipulative, angry, and evil.

It was going to be a challenge to get Grace to do what we wanted that day, the purpose of our trip, which was to gain her consent to search her mother's home and garage on Pleasant Street, where Michael says he saw Janice's body 25 years earlier.

Michael's story was so old, there was no way a judge would support a search warrant. We needed Grace's consent to conduct the search. She was now the legal owner of the house and garage after her mother, Ethel, passed away months earlier.

We had to convince this she-devil to let us into Smith's Little Shop of Horrors.

Potts swung into the gravel driveway in Seville, Ohio, that led to Grace's modest split-level home.

It was an unseasonably cold and windy spring morning. We shivered on the front porch as Potts knocked and I hung back a few steps, looking for any movement in the house. Potts knocked a second time, more forcefully this time.

A gust of wind hit us as I noticed the silhouette of an older woman standing motionless behind the curtains of a bay window. I gestured to Potts, pointing out the figure.

Potts leaned toward the bay window and knocked on the glass.

"Hello Grace? It's Sergeant Potts from the Wayne County Sheriff's Office. I'm here with an FBI agent from New York. Would you please let us in? It's cold out here."

The silhouette moved to the front door. After the click of two deadbolts, the door opened a few inches. A small, older woman appeared behind a chain.

"You again?" she said to Potts, sternly. "I

thought I got rid of you and those other FBI agents a few days ago!"

Potts stepped back and gestured toward me. "Hello Grace. This is Special Agent Bob Hilland from the FBI office in New York," he said.

I stepped closer to the door. "Hello Grace, it's nice to meet you. I'm sorry to bother you, but I was wondering if I could have a few minutes of your time."

The cold wind kicked up. Grace clutched her sweater and tightened her jaw.

"It sure is windy this morning," I continued. "Would it be all right if we spoke inside?"

"What's this about?" she demanded.

"I'd like to speak with you about your son, John."

"I've already told your men everything I know," Grace said, slamming the door shut.

Along with Grace's icy reception, another forceful gust of wind pummeled us. Grace's silhouette was back behind the bay window curtains, watching.

I thought of John Edward's advice: *Make her feel as though it's in her best interest to help you.*

I turned to Potts and held up the four-inch binder and accordion folder I'd brought.

"Oh well,'" I said, loud enough for Grace

to hear. “At least I can document that we tried. Let’s head back to Akron and meet with the bank auditors and IRS with these Pleasant Hill Management Records.”

As we walked toward our car, Grace quickly opened the door.

“I’m sorry. Did I hear you say you had some records concerning Pleasant Hill Management?” she asked, coyly.

Grace looked and sounded eerily like Smith. In her seventies with gray hair and a thick pair of glasses, she had that same high-pitched nasally voice, those same hollow eyes.

She came out onto the porch, smiled like a Cheshire cat, and flung the front door wide open for us.

“Won’t you please come in?”

As she led us to the living room, we passed dozens of old filing cabinets and a copy machine until we reached a sheet-covered couch. I sat and placed the binder and folder next to me. Grace’s eyes stayed locked on my props. With an exaggerated smile, she pointed to them.

“My, my, what have we got there?”

I waved, dismissively. “Nothing important. Just financial records.”

“May I ask why the New York FBI is interested in the Pleasant Hill Management Company?”

"We're not. Not directly anyway," I said. "We stumbled onto it. Your son, John, went out to California with an awful lot of cash. We were trying to figure out where he got all that money. Prior to that, John relocated from Connecticut to Ohio and assumed control of Pleasant Hill Management operations. Next thing you know, there were a series of bank foreclosures while Pleasant Hill Management was still collecting rent from tenants but not paying the loans," I said.

I looked at her with a smile so fake, I'd give television evangelists worldwide a run for their ill-gotten money.

"To be honest Grace, we're not quite sure where this will take us or how far we want to look into it."

I gave the binder and files a pat.

"I guess it depends on how we make out with our present investigation concerning your son and his missing wives."

Grace sat back in her chair, holding back fury.

"Did I hear you say that John went to California with a lot of cash?" she asked.

"You did."

"Do you have any idea how much?"

"Roughly $200,000. Or more."

Grace maintained a cool smile.

"We could look through your records

together," she said, "to make sure they're accurate."

My smile was still frozen on my face, rivaling hers.

"At some point. But today I'd like to talk with you about John."

Grace's posture stiffened.

"Agent Hilland, I've got bank investigators crawling down my neck claiming I'm sitting on a pile of money somewhere. The last thing I need is for some FBI agent to come snooping around here causing me more problems."

Translation: You rub my back and I'll rub yours.

"I think we're on the same page and have an understanding, Grace."

She nodded but struggled to hide her anger. "What is it you think I know?" she asked defiantly.

I didn't mince words.

"I think you know that John killed Janice, Fran, and others."

Grace pressed a hand to her chest.

"I'm shocked that you would say such a thing!" she protested. "I know nothing of the sort. I never even knew of Fran until the day police from New Jersey showed up asking questions about her being missing."

I would find out later that she was telling the truth about never knowing her son had married Fran. While Smith had brought Sheila Sautter (his Milford girlfriend), Terry Poszier (his recent fiancée), and Janice Miller (the prostitute who moved in with him) to Ohio to meet his family . . . he'd never brought Fran. He hadn't even told them about her. When Smith's family was first interviewed about Fran's disappearance, they assumed police officers were talking about Sheila.

"What about his wife, Janice?" I pressed.

Grace shifted in her chair and hesitated.

"Janice was a nice girl. I liked her. She took off one day and we never saw her again."

I fixed my eyes onto hers.

"Grace, tell me about John's box in your parents' garage."

Her body moved away from me ever so slightly.

"I'm not sure which box you're talking about," she said, nonchalantly. "I remember John had a wooden box full of old rags."

I could hear John Edward's words in my mind:

Grace will play head games. Sly as a fox. Great at manipulating people with lies, trickery, and deceit. Like her son but stronger.

Well, I could play games, too.

We knew she was involved in some unethical and likely illegal business dealings. I picked up the binder next to me and leafed through the pages, stopping on a particular document. With great deliberation, I glanced over at the filing cabinets across the room, then back down at the document. After an intentionally long silence, I snapped the binder shut and stood up.

"All right Grace. Thank you for your time. You have a lovely home." I looked at Potts. "Let's go Brian. We're done here."

Grace got up from her chair and tried to regain control.

"No, please," she said. "There's no need for this. I vaguely remember something about a box and my parents getting upset with John over it being in the garage. He came from Indiana to pick it up."

I shook my head.

"Come on, Grace. You're his mother. How can you sit there and pretend you don't know what I'm talking about?"

"I keep telling you I don't know anything, but you won't believe me!" she said.

I gave her a cold stare that let her know that I knew she was full of shit.

"John said the same thing in California a few weeks ago. He also told me he didn't steal money from you. But we both know the truth, don't we?"

Grace started to panic.

"What do I have to do to make you believe me?" she pleaded. "What can I do to prove that I want to help?"

I paused for dramatic effect.

"I understand you control the home and garage once owned by your parents."

"That's right," she said, confused.

"Tomorrow I'd like to bring a few agents and detectives to the property to conduct a search."

"The property is on the market. Nobody lives there."

"All the better then. We won't be in anybody's way."

Grace dropped her shoulders and sighed. "It's been so many years. What could you possibly expect to find?"

A gust of wind blew through a crack in the window. I didn't flinch.

"A plywood box."

The next day, a team of police officers and FBI agents stood in the infamous garage on Pleasant Street, guzzling hot coffee and sheltering from the continuing storm.

Along with me and Potts, I'd corralled members of the Cleveland Division's Evidence Response Team (ERT), the Wayne County Sheriff's Office, and the Ohio Bureau of Criminal Investigation.

Senior Special Agent Roy Cavan divvied up the areas we needed to search — the garage and office, the interior of the house, and the surrounding area using metal detectors. As we disbursed, I heard a now-familiar, nasally whine.

"Wait! Wait! Hold on!"

Grace walked into the garage with an umbrella in one hand and a tray of muffins in the other.

"You can't start the day on empty stomachs" she said, with a bright smile. "I made these muffins from scratch this morning just for you!"

With her spindly fingers, Grace picked out the largest one and held it out to me.

"I made this one special for the boss. Here you are, Bob!"

I reached out to take it, then froze.

What does this remind me of, I asked myself. *What the hell does this remind me of?*

Oh yeah! The evil witch offering the apple to Snow White.

John Edward's warning kicked in.

Whatever she tries to give you, don't take it!

I pulled my hand back, smiled politely, and patted my stomach.

"Oh, I appreciate it, Grace, I really do. But I just ate a huge breakfast. I'll be sure to have one in a little while."

The smile evaporated from her face. She stepped closer.

"I insist, Bob. One little bite so I can see if you like it or not. I got up so early to make them for you. Can't you do an old lady a small favor and at least taste it? After all, I *am* letting you search my property."

There was a *quid pro quo* if I ever heard one. The team stood behind her, all eyes on me, motioning to me not to eat it.

I took the muffin from her hand and took a bite, chewing and pretending to swallow.

"Wow, this is one of the best muffins I've ever tasted!"

A big, satisfying smile came across Grace's face. "Well thank you," she replied. "I'll leave you fellas to your work then."

Grace raised her umbrella and walked out. Once she was safely out of sight, I spit the muffin to the ground and pointed to the rest of them.

"Somebody . . . bag those for the lab!" I said, only half-joking.

As the search was underway, I wandered about the property and into the house, ending up in a bedroom on the second floor. It had faded paint and old, musty furniture. Everything smelled damp.

I scanned the framed photos on the wall — Smith as a teenager, Smith as a young man. A high school cross-country running trophy wrapped in a blue ribbon sat on a bureau. As I stood in the bedroom John Smith grew up in, I could feel his energy. I could feel him. It was not a good feeling.

I picked up a picture from the bedside table: Smith wearing a leather jacket in front of a motorcycle. Standing off to the side, away from him, was Janice. She looked lost and scared. Smith was staring at her in the photo, but she was looking into the camera.

Janice was reaching through the lens, from the past, asking me for help.

The photo was still in my hand as I looked out the bedroom window. I could see the garage next door.

How many times did Smith look out this very window knowing his murdered wife's dismembered body was entombed inside that garage?

From my perch, I watched the investigators below comb the yard with metal detectors and cadaver dogs.

Then something caught my eye. I moved closer to the window, blinked, and looked again.

What the . . . ?

I put the photo down and ran out of the room.

I stood in front of the garage as the rain pelted down and soaked me.

To the right of the garage, John said. *There's someone you need to talk to.*

Potts ran over.

"What are you doing?" he asked.

"Look!" I said, pointing to the large, well-maintained colonial home to the right of the garage.

"Have we spoken to the people in that house?" I asked.

Potts looked confused. "No. Why?"

"Michael said Janice's face looked like was she was sleeping. And when he touched it with a stick, it was hard like wood."

"So?" Potts said.

I pointed again. Dug into the front lawn, a prominent white sign read: ARMSTRONG FUNERAL HOME.

"For Michael's story to make sense, there must be an explanation. Janice's body couldn't remain so well preserved unless Smith did something to it. And coincidentally, we have a funeral parlor next door."

He nodded with understanding.

I headed for the funeral home with Potts in tow.

Dick Armstrong was in his mid-sixties, with white hair and a perfectly trimmed handlebar mustache. But the first thing that hit me when he answered the door wasn't the way he looked. It was the waft of cherry tobacco smoke, smacking me in the face.

I smell pipe tobacco, John Edward said. *Cherry pipe tobacco.*

Armstrong was smoking a briar wood pipe, suffusing the air around us with the aroma of sweet cherry.

Potts and I introduced ourselves and flashed our credentials. Armstrong puffed on his pipe and studied my badge.

"FBI, huh?"

"Yes sir," I said.

"It's about time you fellas came to talk with me," he said, opening his door and beckoning us in. He led us to a beautiful, old-fashioned, parlor.

"I suppose you're here to ask me about John Smith?"

"Why do you say that?" I asked, only a little surprised.

"A couple of weeks ago I read an article about him being married to two women and they both were missing. One was the Hartman girl and the other . . . I think from New Jersey. And today I look out my window and see a bunch of FBI agents searching the Smith property."

I nodded. "What can you tell us about him?"

Armstrong took another puff of his pipe.

The funeral home, which was also the Armstrong family residence, had been there for decades. He'd known Smith and his brother, Michael, since they were born.

"He was an unusual boy, you might say. A loner. Didn't hang out with the other kids, which was odd for these parts. In a small town like this everybody knows everybody. We interact at church, in schools, or at community events. John never took to other kids his age. Kept to himself."

"What about his family life or upbringing?"

"I don't know what went on in that house. I do know that Ethel and Chester were more parents to him than his own were."

"Why do you say that?"

"It was obvious in their daily interactions with those boys. Grace treated John more like an adult husband than a son. And John seemed angry any time Grace brought a man around the house, and eventually married Sam. I remember how John stared at Sam. I got the impression that boy really hated him.

"When Grace was pregnant with Sam's

child (John's half brother, Stephen Maltz) John was a pot of water about to boil. I don't think he could live with the thought of his mother being with another man . . . besides himself of course."

Potts and I exchanged glances. The more we heard about Smith, the darker the stories got.

"Did you know his wife, Janice?" I asked.

"I met her a few times," Armstrong said. "Cute little girl. Always laughing and smiling. I often wondered how a guy like him wound up with a nice girl like her. I guess it must be that thing about opposites attracting."

"Maybe," I said. "Do you remember anything about when she disappeared?"

"I couldn't tell you anything about that. To be honest, I didn't even know she was missing until I read that newspaper article. I assumed she smartened up, left him, and moved away."

Armstrong guided his lighter flame to the pipe and inhaled. The tobacco glowed red.

"Mr. Armstrong, I'd like to ask you a sensitive question," I said.

"Go right ahead."

"It's a hypothetical," I said. "What if I told you a young woman was killed. Strangled to death. And the person who killed her built a plywood box and lined it with a bunch of clothes. Before putting the body in the box, her legs were cut off just below the knees. Are you with me so far?"

"Yes," Armstrong replied.

"So, let's say this box was nailed shut and placed in that garage next door. It sat on the floor for five years until one day it was discovered. When the box was opened, the face and body were completely intact and recognizable. The face was hard, like wood. And the hair . . . well the hair had turned from dirty blond to multicolored, like a rainbow. Based upon your professional experience, is there any way that could occur naturally?"

Armstrong lowered his pipe. "Not under the conditions you described. It would be impossible."

"That leads me to my next question," I said. "While I understand the process of how a body is embalmed, I've never seen it done. I imagine it must take extensive training and experience."

"Of course," Armstrong said. "Nowadays young folks get degrees in mortuary sciences. It's not something you learn overnight."

"Agreed. So, let me ask you then. Is there a 'shortcut' to embalming a body?"

"What do you mean?"

"Well, if I didn't know how to embalm a body, is there a simpler way to do it?"

A look of understanding came over Armstrong's face. He puffed on his pipe some more. "Do you hunt, Agent Hilland?"

"Hunt? I'm not sure what you mean."

"You know, hunt . . . like deer, turkey, ducks, that kind of thing."

"Oh. No. I hunt *people,*" I said.

Potts nodded vigorously in agreement.

"Fair enough," said Armstrong, as he stood up. "Follow me. I have something that might answer your question."

We followed Armstrong to the rear of the house, into a kitchen.

"If I could ask you gentlemen to stay here for a moment? I'll be right back."

Armstrong disappeared through a door that led to the basement and returned a few minutes later carrying a large Tupperware container.

"My sons and I are avid hunters," he explained. "Deer, fox, ducks, turkey. You name it, we hunt it. Turkey season started about a week ago. We shot the most beautiful, prized turkey we've ever bagged in over 35 years of hunting. It was so beautiful, we decided to take it to a taxidermist to be mounted. The problem with turkeys, though, is the taxidermist does a beautiful job on the body and feathers, but because of the cellular structure of the head, they can't really preserve it."

Something solid was sloshing around in the Tupperware.

"They cut it off and mount a fake rubber or plastic head on the top of the body. So, when we shot this bird, I cut the head off and placed it in this container filled with 50 percent water and 50 percent formaldehyde. It's been sitting in this solution for four days."

Armstrong put on a pair of rubber gloves and took the container to the sink.

He slowly removed the lid and poured the solution down the drain while keeping the turkey head inside. Then he pulled the head out of the Tupperware, rinsed it under tap water, and grabbed a nearby towel to dry it off.

Tap, tap, tap.

He banged the turkey head against the countertop.

"Hard as wood," he said, and handed me the head.

I studied the face of the turkey; its features were intact.

"So, the answer to your question, Agent Hilland," said Armstrong, as he stowed the head back in the Tupperware, "is yes.

There is a simpler way. All you'd need is a few gallons of formaldehyde, a tub, and some regular tap water from any kitchen sink."

13

Digging

LAW ENFORCEMENT

Roy Speer, *FBI, Cleveland*
Roy Cavan, *senior special agent*
Sergeant Brian Potts, *Wayne County Sheriff's Office, Ohio*
Jane Fisher, *special agent of the FBI's Ground Penetrating Radar Team*

HELPERS

The dog handler
Duke, *cadaver dog*

NEIGHBORS

Patricia Donnolly, *neighbor*
Margaret Boone, *neighbor*

Grace Lane, Day One

Hammer drills bore through the thick layer of concrete.

Plumes of smoke and dust billowed from the garage, drifting over to me and the other agents and detectives on site at the townhouse complex on Grace Lane — the location Michael thought Janice's body might be buried.

I was with Potts, Cavan, and Special Agent Roy Speer — the one who sounded like a country singer over the phone to my East Coast ears — who was joining us from the Cleveland division.

We stood in front of Unit 2019, arms crossed, watching the garage floor get ripped apart.

Our exhaustive search at Ethel's a few days earlier yielded zilch — so far. The cadaver dog locked onto an area on Ethel's garage floor — the spot where Michael first saw the box and body. We removed bricks and soil samples, sending them to the lab for testing. After 25 years, I wasn't betting on finding any definitive results in that respect.

I'd also sent out a teletype alert to all law enforcement agencies in the country — local, state, and federal — asking if anyone had information on the plywood box:

> A SOURCE WAS RECENTLY DEVELOPED WHO PROVIDED INFORMATION CONCERNING THE DISAPPEARANCE OF JANICE HARTMAN SMITH.
>
> THE SOURCE REPORTED JANICE HARTMAN'S REMAINS WERE DISMEMBERED AND DISPOSED

OF IN A PLYWOOD BOX. THE BOX WAS DESCRIBED AS APPROXIMATELY 48" LONG, 20" WIDE, AND 20" TALL.

ALSO CONTAINED IN THE PLYWOOD BOX WERE SEVERAL ARTICLES OF THE VICTIM'S CLOTHING AS WELL AS SOME INEXPENSIVE JEWELRY SUCH AS A PEWTER CRUCIFIX.

THE BOX WAS LAST SEEN IN THE WAYNE COUNTY, OHIO, AREA IN 1979.

WHILE THE CURRENT WHEREABOUTS OF THE BOX ARE UNKNOWN, IT IS BELIEVED THE BOX MAY HAVE BEEN DISPOSED OF IN THE OHIO, INDIANA, OR MICHIGAN AREA.

ANY AGENCY WITH RELEVANT INFORMATION IS REQUESTED TO CONTACT SPECIAL AGENT ROBERT HILLAND OF THE FBI, NYO . . .

That was a longshot, too — and so was this new dig. But I was filled with single-focused determination. *We had to find this box.*

We whisked away the current owners of Unit 2019 to a hotel, promised a new garage floor when we were done, and got to work. Various tents and canopies were set up outside the garage, and the entire area was blocked off by bright yellow police tape to keep gawkers — and reporters — at bay.

I coordinated the Ground Penetrating Radar Team to come up from headquarters, and Speer coordinated a local Evidence

Response Team unit. The GPR Team dragged radar equipment across the garage floor to search for anomalies underneath.

"We found three," said Special Agent Jane Fisher, head of the Radar Team, pointing to "X" marks on the ground made with orange chalk.

"The largest anomaly is right here," she said, pointing to an X near the rear wall. "It's 36 inches from the surface and runs about four and a half feet long by two feet wide."

The other two anomalies were much smaller, she said, at depths of 28 inches and 14 inches. The GPR could tell us the depth and size of an anomaly, she explained, but not if the anomaly was a body or simply construction debris.

That was Duke's specialty.

Standing by was a dog handler and her cadaver dog, Duke, a black Doberman with soulful eyes. A police badge hung from Duke's collar; he and his nose were ready to go to work sniffing out dead bodies.

Before we set him loose, the country crew drilled a dozen holes near the anomalies to allow the trapped scent below to percolate.

"And if your dog alerts on something, how do you know?" Potts asked.

"He's trained to lie down on top of it."

After the holes were drilled, the team vacated the garage and closed the door so that the subfloor could release any secrets it might hold. Thirty minutes later, the handler and Duke returned.

"Find it!" she commanded, with an excited voice.

Duke dropped his nose to the ground and circled the concrete floor, tail wagging. After several passes over the largest "X" he stopped over it, took several deep, fast breaths, and laid down on it.

X marked the spot.

Potts, Cavan, and I donned masks as county workers sliced through the concrete with heavy masonry saws and thick waves of dust filled the air.

Wayne County's new command post arrived on the scene — a large RV with the sheriff office's seal prominently painted on the side. Reporters began to gather and ask questions, filming what they could from behind the yellow tape. A helicopter circled overhead. But the FBI had an unspoken rule: say nothing to the press. Not yet, anyway.

Once the concrete was cut up, everyone pitched in and carried or wheeled large, heavy slabs of it to a nearby backhoe. It was backbreaking work in sweltering summer heat.

After the concrete was removed, the digging began. We planned to dig at least three feet deep, all the while loading the dirt onto wheelbarrows and carting it out to the makeshift tents, where it would be sifted through giant screens to search for evidence.

This was going to take a while.

I stood at the edge of the garage and scanned the broken-up floor, wondering what lay beneath.

Wondering if she was there.

By early evening, we halted our work and arranged to continue the next morning.

At a local hotel, I washed off the dirt and concrete grime of the day and called home from the landline. The kids were also fresh from their baths, bubbling with excitement to talk to Daddy.

"Everything okay, Alex?" I said, when she wrangled the phone back from them.

"Sure," she said.

I could hear the loneliness and frustration in her voice. She had a new era to contend with beyond my late nights at the office: my absence for days and weeks out of town.

My cell phone rang — it was John Edward.

"Listen, I have to take this . . ."

"Go ahead."

Click.

"Hey, John."

"Hey, Bob. So . . . I'm seeing a big hole in the ground and dirt all around you."

"Yeah. We're digging."

"Okay. That explains it. Just . . . be careful."

"What do you mean. Am I going to fall into the hole?"

Pause.

"No. Not exactly. But I feel a tension at the office for you. Like you're getting into trouble. Watch that you don't push too hard."

"Maybe I'm digging my own grave. Ha!"

"Just . . . be careful. They're telling me to tell you."

I didn't take his warning too seriously. I was working my ass off, operating in good faith, and potentially on the brink of a big break in the case. How could I possibly get in trouble? As far as I could see, work was the only thing I was doing right.

After we hung up, I flipped on the TV and grabbed a cold beer from the mini bar. In the background, the local news came on.

"I'm at the scene of 2019 Grace Lane," said a female reporter, standing in front of the command post RV, "where FBI and police investigators have concluded their work for the day. Take a look at this earlier footage."

I turned to watch as the station cut away to an aerial shot of the garage from the helicopter, then closer shots of FBI agents pushing wheelbarrows of dirt.

"Investigators spent hours tearing up a concrete floor and sifting through the earth below a garage floor at the Grace Lane townhouse complex here in Medina. Officials were extremely tight-lipped concerning the investigation and provided no official release as to what they were looking for. But sources have suggested that the FBI is pursuing leads related to the disappearance of Chicago Teamster *Jimmy Hoffa.*"

I choked on my beer, nearly spitting it out.

Oh, shit.

Patricia's Backyard

As day two of the Grace Lane dig began, I went to investigate a mysterious message left on our tip line the day before.

"I know where Janice is buried," the woman said on the answering machine. "You're looking in the wrong place!"

Patricia Donnolly lived at the far end of town in a cramped, dirty, disorganized apartment. But until recently she'd lived two miles from Grace Lane, she told me, Potts, and Speer, as we sat around her kitchen table.

In a haunting way, Patricia reminded me of Janice Hartman's friend, Kelly Perdoni. She looked worn, sad, and much older than her actual age. But she came across as an emotionally stunted teenager, stuck and stagnating in a traumatic past.

Like many of the women linked to the Smith case, she was a victim of the evil that men do.

Patricia grew up sexually, physically, and emotionally abused by her three brothers, she told us. They took turns raping her as a teen, and when she was ten years old, they held up her pet rabbit by the ears and slit its throat in front of her as they laughed. She was not the only one they hurt, she claimed. They would pick up girls at the local truck stop, bring them back to the house, and rape and torture them in the basement for days.

"I heard girls crying, screaming for help," she said, sadly.

Two of Patricia's brothers were currently in prison for murder. Patricia's eldest brother, Kevin, was friends with Smith decades earlier.

She left us the message, she told us, because she believed "Janice is buried in the backyard of my old house."

Patricia told us about a day in the late

1970s, when she was sitting on the back porch at sunset.

"I saw Smith and two of my brothers carrying something in a rolled-up carpet or a blanket. They walked into the yard where a deep, rectangular hole — like a grave — had already been dug. They put this rolled up carpet in the ground and covered it with dirt.

They didn't see me at first. I was scared to death and tried to tiptoe away but Kevin heard me and dropped his shovel. I ran as fast as I could but he caught me. He pulled me by my hair and slammed my head in the ground. I couldn't breathe. I was crying for help."

She began to cry as she told us the story, and the pet Chihuahua by her feet began yelping. Patricia put the dog on her lap and held onto it like a security blanket.

"Kevin told me that if I opened my mouth, they would kill me and dig another hole for me. A few weeks later I saw a long concrete block over the hole. But there was also a second one. I went out to take a closer look. I don't know what they put under that one."

"And you're sure you saw John Smith out there with your brothers," I asked.

"Yes, sir."

I pulled out a photo lineup of several men, taken in the '70s.

"Do you recognize any of the men in these pictures?"

Without hesitation she pointed to Smith.

"That's John Smith, right there."

"Do you know for sure if there was a person in that rolled up carpet or blanket you saw?"

She shook her head.

"No. But the way they carried it and how it sagged in the middle, there was definitely something inside it."

"Patricia, did you know John Smith's wife, Janice?"

"Only that she disappeared. And I heard the rumors that he killed her. Everybody around here knows those rumors."

I handed Patricia a piece of paper and pen. She drew a map of the backyard configuration of her old house — the porch, the house, an oak tree with a swing, a row of high evergreens and bushes.

"They stopped by the bushes here, next to the tall evergreens," she said, tracing a path on the paper. "This was where they buried it and put that long concrete block over it. The second block was closer to the oak tree, over here," she pointed.

"Patricia," I asked, "when I go out there

and dig up these spots . . . what am I going to find?"

Her eyes welled with tears. She hugged her dog closer.

"I don't know. I don't *want* to know."

Less than two miles from Grace Lane, a long gravel driveway led to a nondescript ranch house on Guilford Road, the home where Patricia Donnolly used to live.

The dated structure appeared newly renovated with a new roof, new windows, a new garage door.

I pulled into the driveway with Speer riding shotgun.

"Bob, I admire your persistence," said Speer, "but we can't go around digging up every garage and yard until we find something. Heck, we're not even done over at Grace Lane yet."

"Who said anything about digging?" I said, getting out of the car. "We're just here to check things out."

After several doorbell rings and loud knocks at the door went unanswered, I pulled out Patricia's map and started walking toward the backyard.

"Whoa, whoa. What are you doing?"

"Working," I said.

Speer ran after me.

"We can't go around traipsing through people's backyards without consent."

"Roy, I've never *traipsed* anywhere in my entire life."

In the backyard, I climbed the stairs leading to a rear deck and a set of sliding doors, where I knocked again, loudly. Still no answer.

I turned and faced the yard, map in hand.

The property was expansive, with dozens of acres leading to a distant hill. I spotted the oak tree, the tall evergreens, and the nearby bushes as indicated by Patricia's map. But something was missing: No concrete slabs.

In their place, according to her map, I saw rows of firewood neatly stacked six feet high.

"Where the hell are those concrete benches?"

The glass doors slid open. A petite young woman stepped out with an infant on her hip and a cordless phone in her hand. She looked frightened.

"Can I help you?"

I pulled out my FBI credentials.

"I'm sorry to startle you," I said. "My name is Special Agent Bob Hilland from the FBI."

She placed her hand on her chest and sighed with relief.

"Oh, thank God. I thought you were Jehovah's Witnesses!"

"Nope," I laughed. "We're not here to save any souls. Well — not exactly."

Her name was Margaret Boone. She and her husband, Jack, bought the house two years earlier, she said. I explained that we were working on a case that led us to her home.

"We received a call from a woman who said she used to live here. She told us there used to be a couple of long concrete blocks in your backyard over by those trees."

"Yes," said Margaret, "they used to be where all that firewood is stacked. My husband dragged them away with his tractor . . . to there."

She pointed to the open field. Beyond the evergreens lay two long concrete slabs.

The dragging of the concrete slabs was one of many changes the couple had to make when they got the house, she explained, describing it as "an absolute wreck."

"To begin with, the smell in here was unbelievable. It smelled like cat urine, crap, and I swear to God I still think something must have died in here. We found dead cats in the walls. It was horrible."

Speer and I exchanged a look.

"And then there was the basement."

"What was in the basement?" Speer asked.

Margaret motioned for us to follow her inside, where she led us downstairs to the basement. She pointed to a fireplace built into the wall.

"For starters, I don't what they were burning down here but there were burn marks on the ceiling and on the wall. It looked like a crematorium. My husband had to rip everything out. The smell of smoke was so strong he power-washed the entire basement for a week and then scrubbed everything down with muriatic acid."

She was afraid to go into the basement, she admitted.

"It was like a dungeon. There was writing all over the walls. I think the people who lived here before must have been sick in the head."

"What was written on the walls?" I asked.

"Profanity. Lewd drawings, sexual stuff, and some crazy stuff like, 'Please help me.' We thought the previous family must've had a special needs kid or some out of control teenagers."

Margaret showed us the wall where the writing had been.

"It looked like girl handwriting. Pretty and flowery. Some of the things were written by different people though."

"How could you tell?" I asked.

"The handwriting was so different, there had to be more than one."

We went back upstairs and outside to the porch. I checked the map again.

"Why did your husband move the concrete slabs — to make room for the firewood?" I asked.

Margaret took a deep breath.

"You guys might think I'm crazy but when we first moved in here, I thought this house was haunted, possessed, you name it. Between the stuff on the walls, the dead cats, the smells, and that damn dungeon of a basement. I wanted to sell the place and get out of here.

"Jack told me it was all in my head and I was imagining things. Then one night we were in the living room watching television, and Jack suddenly jumped up and walked over to the sliding glass doors. He looked out and said, 'What the hell is this?' That's the first time we saw her."

"Her?" I asked. "Who?"

"That lady. I think her name was Patricia. It's got to be the same lady you're talking about. She used to live here with three older brothers."

"What was she doing back here?"

Margaret pointed toward the firewood.

"She was kneeling next to the long concrete blocks, crying and praying. Jack went out to talk to her but she kept crying."

"Did she say anything?"

"Not a whole lot the first few times."

"The first *few* times?" Speer repeated.

Margaret nodded. "She kept coming back. We thought she was crazy. She would be back here crying and praying for hours until we noticed her and my husband chased her off. It was very sad. I thought she was delusional or perhaps schizophrenic. I don't know what."

They dragged the concrete blocks away in hopes it would stop Patricia's visits, but "a couple of days later she came back and was kneeling on the dead grass where the blocks used to be. This time she was hysterical. We went out to talk to her. She kept saying was, 'Please leave them alone! Please let them rest!' She kept repeating it over and over. That really freaked me out. Jack told her that if she ever came back again, we'd call the sheriff's department. That was the last time we saw her."

I stepped off the porch and walked over to the oak tree. Loosening my tie and unbuttoning my collar, I lowered myself onto the swing and looked up to the sky, closing my eyes.

What fresh hell was this?

Now we had this new House of Horrors to deal with. But I had no idea how much we could trust this Patricia woman, who seemed mentally unstable. And I had no idea if I could convince the big bosses to approve another complicated dig with helicopters hovering.

I remembered what John Edward said.

Don't push too hard.

Speer and Margaret looked on in silence.

After a minute, I sprang from the swing and walked to the stack of firewood. I placed my hand on top of the pile, assessing the weight and number of logs.

"We need to move these," I said, unwavering, "and see if someone's buried underneath."

Grace Lane, Day Three

Back at the Grace Lane dig it was a fucking circus.

The garage looked like an indoor swimming pool. On the hour, the dog trainer would run out in animated excitement, saying Duke was "hitting" on something.

So, we kept on digging. And digging. And digging.

Tensions were high. The July temperatures and humidity were stifling.

Sheriffs from various Ohio divisions argued

about anything and everything, it was like watching a big dick contest on *The Dukes of Hazzard.*

The piles of dirt next to the screening stations kept getting higher.

By the time we excavated to a depth of five feet, we were all weary and cloaked in dirt and God knows what else.

Cavan motioned to me to join him on the ledge of the abyss. He pointed to a rotted piece of plywood with a garbage bag stuck to one end.

"There's our big anomaly," he said.

"Are you kidding me?" I asked, in disbelief.

"Nope. It's the same size and depth as the anomaly we picked up with the GPR."

"But the cadaver dog hit on that exact spot!"

"Don't know what to tell you."

Potts and Speer entered the garage and joined the briefing.

"What about the two other spots?" I asked.

Cavan pointed to them.

"Construction debris and garbage. We even brought in a second dog to make sure we weren't missing anything. The second dog didn't alert on anything. The handler said we could keep digging until we struck oil or started seeing Chinese people. But that there's no body in there."

My cell phone rang. It was Buckbee from the New York office. The guy had a knack for timing. He followed his call with a text: *911.*

"Oh, shit. This can't be good."

Cavan, Speer, Potts, and I filed into the command post, and I dialed Buckbee at the office.

"Exactly what in the hell are you doing out there, Bob?"

Buckbee's angry voice boomed throughout the RV.

"I've got the assistant director crawling up my ass because SAC Cleveland is not happy with us pissing all over his division."

"I don't understand, sir."

"Cleveland is fielding calls that we're looking for Jimmy-fucking-Hoffa! And on top of that you've got two local sheriffs fighting each other over this mess in the press and dragging us into the middle of their bullshit! If I were SAC Cleveland, I'd throw your ass out of there in a New York minute.

"So, unless you can tell me right now that you've got a body, you are closing down that fucking circus, thanking Cleveland for their help, kissing as much ass as you can, and getting the hell out of there! I don't want to hear another damn thing about this bullshit

case that has absolutely nothing to do with us! I should never have let you open it.

"Do I make myself clear?!"

Boone House Dig

Early the next morning a group of eight agents and detectives assembled in the backyard of the Boone house on Guilford Road.

We arrived in unmarked cars with shovels, and dressed in blue jeans, flannel shirts, and boots. We looked like a team of lumberjacks.

"Are you sure you want to do this?" Speer asked. "We should get approval."

"Roy," I said, putting my hand on his shoulder, "there's an old saying: 'Sometimes it's better to ask forgiveness than permission."

"Yeah," he said. "And there's an even older saying: *Pride goeth before the fall.* Proverbs 16:18."

"I'll keep that in mind, Roy."

But I didn't really. I was like a young bull that no one could stop from charging.

We didn't find anything at Grace Lane, and I was getting flak from work; I was desperate, now, to find something at the House of Horrors.

There was no way in hell I was getting approval for another official excavation at the Boone house, so I'd convinced a bunch of agents to dig with me on the down-low.

After we moved all the firewood, which took hours, we split into two teams. Each team focused on the area where one of the slabs of concrete used to rest.

By midafternoon, our two holes were three feet deep. I stood in one pit, dripping with sweat.

"If the FBI thing doesn't work out for you, Bob," said Potts, "you've got a future as a grave digger."

I laughed and dug my spade into the hole . . . and heard an unmistakable thud as the blade hit something.

"What was that?" Potts asked.

I scraped away some soil. Underneath, the tip of a blue tarp poked out. A jolt of adrenaline rushed through me.

"Someone hand me one of those small hand shovels!" I called out.

An agent brought one over as the rest gathered around.

I dropped to my knees and kept scraping as more blue emerged. We were all holding our collective breath.

I laid the trowel aside and with one hand, lifted a piece of the tarp. With the other hand, I reached in. After a minute of probing, I slowly pulled out a thin, grayish-white bone.

I handed it to Potts for closer inspection.

"Could be a bone from a hand," said Potts.

A body!

Speer grew anxious. "We should lock this down and get a medical examiner here," he said. "But I should call my supervisor first, before we do anything else."

"Hold on a sec, Roy," I said. "Before we spin this thing up, let's figure out what we've got. Does anyone have a flashlight?"

That request led to a loud sound of Velcro tearing. Three flashlights were thrown to me.

I dropped to the ground, lifted the tarp again, and shone a beam of light under.

With my head twisted sideways on the ground and cheek to the earth, I plunged my hand into the crevice.

"I think I have a tooth."

Seconds later I pulled out a long narrow jawbone. I climbed to my feet and sat on the edge of the hole, inspecting it.

I sighed and handed the jawbone to Speer.

"No need to call anyone, Roy."

My exhilaration a minute earlier plummeted to anger and frustration.

"We just found Lassie."

14

Smith and Smith

"Did you find her?" Michael asked.

Smith's brother jumped to his feet when we walked into his living room the next day. He was waiting on edge, eager to hear news.

Potts, Speers, and I came to give it. And unfortunately for Michael, I was in a confrontational mood.

"What do you think?" I asked.

Michael looked perplexed.

"I saw it on the news that you guys finished what you were doing at the garage and packed up and left. And now you're here, so I figured . . ."

Michael stopped talking as he watched me take a seat on the couch. Potts and Speers followed my lead. Michael sat down with us, searching our faces.

"What's going on?"

I was angry, frustrated, and humiliated in front of my colleagues — that's what was going on. And I was filled with doubt. I wanted to know: Had Michael fabricated parts of his story? Was he withholding important information? All that digging and manpower, and all we ended up with were giant holes of nothing.

I felt like after the hotel interrogation, part of me wanted to give up. But I knew such thoughts were fleeting. The more obstacles I faced, the more resolute I got.

I had to press Michael for more.

"You know, Mike, I appreciate everything you've done to help us with this case. It hasn't been easy and I'm doing everything I can to move the ball. But every time we have an opening, it closes. We run into a wall."

"Bob, I don't understand what you're talking about."

"Well, Mike, the story about the box is a good one. I want to believe it. Really, I do. But a lot of it doesn't add up. Nobody noticing a horrible smell in that garage for five years, the rainbow-colored hair, Janice's body not decomposing, Grace Lane, and you not knowing where that box went. I'm digging up half the state of Ohio looking for a box that might not even exist. I might as well be looking for bigfoot."

Michael stood up. He didn't have the high-pitched whine like his mother and brother, thank goodness. He could yell.

"That's bullshit!" he shouted. "Everything I told you was 100 percent true! If you don't want to believe me, I don't care. I found Janice in that box like I told you. You can go to hell."

I stood up next to Michael, towering over him.

"Listen. I just spent three days turning someone's garage into a damn swimming pool based on what you told me. If I didn't believe you, do you think I would have stuck my neck out like that? But if the roles were reversed, what would you think?"

"I told you the truth!" he pleaded. "I've had nightmares about it for years. Bad dreams of Janice chasing me down a field and beating me with her legs . . ."

Michael threw his arms up in the air.

"I don't know where the box is. Like I said before, it could be anywhere from here to Indiana."

"Hell, Michael. That really narrows it down."

I wasn't only frustrated with Michael. I was also questioning John Edward. Was I a gullible fool to believe in him and this psychic crap? I never went out to specifically prove the information he gave me. I used it as a compass to give me direction or confirm I was on the right track.

But moments like this, when I felt completely off track, I questioned everything, including John.

And yet.

He was so confident when he relayed information, and never wavered. He never told me what I wanted to hear. If I asked him a question and he didn't know the answer, he told me so. I reminded myself of the first day he and I met. How could he have known those details about Fran, Janice, Smith, Michael, and my family?

If he was correct with his information then, I had to believe him now, too. I had to keep my faith in him.

Michael ran his fingers through his hair. He too, was on the verge of giving up.

"I can't do this anymore," he said. "I can't take it. Between you and my brother, I don't know who's worse."

Hold the phone. What?

"What do you mean 'between you and my brother'?"

Michael ran his hands through his hair again.

"Well, you won't believe anything I say. And John won't leave me alone. It's too much, I tell you."

"Michael. What do you mean he won't leave you alone?"

"You know. He's calling me every night, wanting to know everything. 'What's the FBI doing now? Who are they talking to? Where are they digging?' I don't need this shit from him or you!"

I looked at him, flabbergasted.

"He's calling you every night? When were you planning on telling us this, Mike?"

He looked at me, Potts, and Speers with genuine confusion.

"What do you mean?' I assumed you guys already knew. I figured you were listening to my phone calls . . ."

I sat down on the couch with a sigh and pointed to the spot next to me.

"Sit down, Mike," I said, calmly.

He sat, keeping his eyes locked on me.

"Don't ever assume anything. How many times has your brother called?"

Michael shrugged — that was a family trait he did inherit.

"I don't know. He called a few times after the initial interview you guys did. He's called every night since you began digging a few days ago."

Holy hell.

"Has he called you tonight?"

"No," Michael said, as the phone began to ring in the kitchen. "That's probably him now."

I checked my watch and leaned close to Michael, speaking fast.

"Okay, Mike, here's what we're going to do. Answer the phone and cut him off right away. Tell him you can't talk . . ."

Riiiing.

"Lower your voice like there's someone else in the room and you don't want to be overheard. Tell him to call on Wednesday nights at seven o'clock, that's when Tawnya and Andy will be out of the house and you can talk freely . . ."

Riiiiiiiinnnnng!

"Tell him you need to talk to him and he has to call back. Then hang up, don't let him talk."

Michael nodded and ran to the kitchen phone. The three of us were close behind.

"Hello?"

"Hey, Mike, what's going on?"

It was Smith. Michael lowered his voice as instructed.

"Hey, John. I can't talk right now. But we need to talk. Can you call me on Wednesday around seven? Tawnya will be at church and Andy has piano. I need to talk to you without anyone around. I've got to go."

Michael hung up.

His hands were shaking. He went to the sink, filled a glass with water, and downed it. He slammed the empty glass on the table and covered his face with his hands.

I put a hand on his shoulder.

"Don't worry, Mike. We're in this together."

We had to lure John Smith in gradually. Lull him first, make him comfortable, that was the plan.

The first call the following Wednesday we kept simple and innocuous — the goal was to get Michael at ease speaking to Smith while being recorded. For the second call a week later, I instructed Michael to bring up "the box" so we could hear his brother's reaction.

When he did, Smith immediately cut him off.

"Don't worry about that box," said Smith quickly. "It was a stupid practical joke someone dropped off. They put a goat in that box."

Michael was taken off guard and too terrified to answer.

By the end of July, we had prepped Michael for call number three with a detailed script we rehearsed together. I placed a list of bullet points on the table in front of him before the call. If Smith brought up the BS goat story again, he'd be ready.

Michael was panicky. His wife, Tawnya,

paced back and forth. Their teen son, Andy, was at a friend's house.

"Are you sure you know where John is while he's making these calls?" Michael asked, terrified.

"Don't worry," I assured him. "We have agents watching him in California. Every week, he makes the call from work."

"But those other calls were nothing. This one is different," Michael said.

"I know, Mike. And it takes a lot of courage and strength to do what you're doing. But this is your opportunity now to prove to us the box really exists — with Janice in it."

"What if he comes here? What about my family?"

"I *promise* I won't let him near you," I said. "I won't let him hurt you or your family."

Michael took a deep breath.

Speers checked his watch. "It's time."

"You ready?" I asked Michael.

He nodded.

I put my hand on his arm to make sure I had his attention.

"You've got this. I believe in you."

The phone rang:

Speers activated the recording device and nodded. Michael took a deep breath, paused, and slowly lifted the receiver.

"Hello?"

"Hello," said Smith.

Michael let out an exaggerated sigh: "Can you talk, John?"

"Yeah."

"I've got some deep shit here."

"What?'

"Do you know that motherfucking FBI agent, that Bob Hilland son of a bitch?"

"Yeah."

"He brought me a grand jury subpoena and I've got to go testify in New York."

"Holy shit!" Smith replied. The fear in his voice was obvious.

"No kidding holy shit!" said Michael. "They're getting serious here, John. I mean what the fuck am I supposed to do? I'm not going to jail for you."

"No. I wouldn't expect you to."

Speers and I gave Michael an encouraging nod to keep going.

"I'll tell you what I'm going to do," Michael said. "I'm going to New York to testify and I'm going to tell them the truth. That I saw you build the box in the garage and that it stayed in there for years until Grandad and I opened it and that Jan was inside and . . ."

Smith immediately shot him down.

"No! That wasn't Jan in the box! It was a goat, a practical joke someone dropped off."

He fired back.

"John, that was Jan in the box! That was no joke and no goat! Grandad and I found the box in the garage, we opened it, and Jan was inside. For God's sake, you cut her fucking legs off! For years I've had nightmares of Janice chasing me down and beating me with her legs. I mean, come on!"

"Alright, alright," said Smith, trying to calm Michael down. "So, you're going to New York to testify. When?"

I scribbled on a piece of paper and handed it to Michael.

"Let me see," Michael said, reading the note as if he was reading the subpoena. "What the hell does this thing say. Looks like the fifth of September. That's three weeks from today."

"When did all of this happen?" Smith asked.

"Pardon?" Michael stalled.

"When did you get this subpoena?"

I heard a shift in Smith's tone. *He suspects.*

"Last Friday. Bob Hilland showed up at my front door and handed it to me," Michael explained. "I mean, what a way to start a fucking weekend."

Smith didn't respond. Michael looked over at us, nervously. I gave him the *keep going* gesture and pointed to the bullet points.

"Like I said, they're getting serious here," Michael said, reading from the bullet points.

"Hilland's digging up the whole fucking county. They're talking with people from way back. This whole thing is about to come apart. I can't do this anymore. I'm not going to lie and I'm not going to jail for you."

"You got to do what's right, Mike," Smith said, softly.

Smith's gentler tone unleashed something in Michael. Years of holding the dark secret poured out of him. The truth had been cathartic.

"For all I know they might put me in jail when this thing is over," Michael said to his brother. "But the only thing I'm guilty of is calling you to come get her. If they want to put that on me, then I guess I'll be going to jail with you."

"Alright, then," Smith replied, matter of fact.

"Okay. We're talking three weeks from today, John. At least you know."

"Alright, Mike. Thanks."

"Take care," Michael said, as we heard the click of Smith's phone.

Michael hung up and stared at the phone. He slowly turned to me; his face somber.

"Now do you believe me?"

In the New York office the next day, I played the recording for DeStano.

"You had Smith going," said DeStano. "You can hear it in his voice. He sounded shocked by what Michael was saying at first. But then it's like he suspected he was being recorded. That's when he started with that goat-in-the-box bullshit."

"I think you're right."

"Of course, I'm right," DeStano said. He pointed to the cassette player. "Your boy Michael did good. You've chummed the waters; let's see what the shark does."

I nodded with anticipation. I was back on track.

But as Speers liked to say, pride goeth before the fall. On cue, my desk phone rang. DeStano handed the receiver to me as he got up and returned to his desk.

"Bob. It's Roy."

He sounded worried.

"What's wrong, Roy?"

"We've got a big problem, Bob. Smith is gone."

"Gone? What are you talking about?"

"He took off last night and didn't show up for work this morning. The San Diego office got a call from Smith's wife, Diane. They sent her to the Escondido Police Department to file a missing person's report."

"You have *got* to be kidding me!"

"I wish I was, partner."

It took me a minute to digest what he was saying, and another to go into panic myself. *Michael! I promised him!* I sprang into action.

"Roy, we need to get to Michael and his family ASAP. Put them in a hotel right away."

"Already on it," said Speers. "Potts is with them now. They're packing bags, and we'll put them up in a secure location with protection until we locate Smith."

I breathed a small sigh of relief.

"I'll get hold of Raelene in California," I said, "maybe she can pull flight manifests and get more details on his disappearance. Anything else I should know?"

"I hate to be the bearer of bad news, brother, but . . ." Speers paused.

"What is it?"

"This thing has spun up to the front office. If it hasn't happened already, I'm guessing SAC Cleveland will be calling your office."

Trouble at the office, John Edward had warned. His guides are never wrong.

"Thanks Roy. I better go do damage control. I'll call you back."

I hung up and sat back in my chair, covering my face with both hands.

"Somebody give me a fucking break!" I yelled.

"What now?" DeStano asked.

I rubbed my forehead. "Smith is missing. He didn't show for work today. His wife's at the police department right now filing a missing person's report."

DeStano shrugged. "Maybe he decided to do the right thing and kill himself?"

I gave him a look: *Not likely.*

"Maybe he's headed to Ohio to kill Michael," I said.

In the blink of an eye, I was sitting in Dennis Buckbee's office with my supervisor, Stanley Nye. We'd been summoned, and now we were sinking into his leather couch.

Buckbee paced, hands on his hips, fuming.

"For the life of me, Hilland. I can't fucking understand you!" he yelled. "Between all that bullshit with the sheriffs in Ohio, the Jimmy Hoffa reports, and now this? You've made one hell of a reputation for yourself. The ADIC knows your name now, and not in a good way. He's taking calls from SACs in Cleveland and San Diego about this damn case that nobody gives two shits about. And when he asked me why the FBI New York office is working this, I stood there with my dick in my hand looking like a total fucking idiot!"

"Sir, if I could . . ."

"Don't speak!" Buckbee ordered. "Not one fucking word!"

His face was so red he looked like a mercury thermometer about to explode.

"You should be proud of yourself, Bobby. You're the first agent in the history of the fucking FBI to start a case with two missing people and now you have three!"

I stared at the floor.

"Effective immediately you're off this case, you're off the Cold Case Squad, and you're reassigned to C-10," he yelled. "And may God help you if I find out that you're still fucking around with this case. We're done with it!"

I couldn't bear it anymore. On top of the strain of the last few months, Buckbee's threats were the last straw.

I stood up and moved toward him. Stanley shot up and got between us.

"That's a bunch of bullshit!" I yelled at Buckbee. "I've been breaking my fucking ass around this fucking place. I've cleared more cases than anybody else on this whole squad, and all I get is shit for it."

I shook my head.

"I'm sorry about the bullshit in Ohio and the calls to the ADIC. But sometimes shit happens! So do what you got to do. Transfer me! Fire me! I don't give a damn!"

I turned and stormed out of Buckbee's office.

15

LADY IN THE BOX

Two decades later, when I was teaching a course on leadership at Quantico, I'd go around the room on the first day of class and ask each student what brought them to the Academy.

"Why are you here?" I asked. "Why do you want a career with the FBI?"

I'd get a variety of answers, but they were all a variation of the same theme: They wanted to make a difference. They wanted to stand up for people who couldn't stand up on their own. They wanted to be part of something bigger than themselves.

I praised their honorable motives, then warned them about the commitment involved with such an endeavor.

"Making a difference. It's not something you just say," I told them, "You have to *live it.*"

In 1999 I was living it, perhaps too zealously.

Soon after Buckbee kicked me off both the

Smith case and the squad, Alex and I went to see the film *Stir of Echoes.* I sat in the movie theater awestruck. The main character, played by Kevin Bacon, was a hardline skeptic of anything supernatural — like me the day I walked into John Edward's office — until his wife takes him to a party and a friend hypnotizes him.

My first shock when the film began was how much the wife, played by *Law & Order* actress Kathryn Erbe, resembled Janice Hartman. It was eerie. The next shocker was how much the Kevin Bacon character reminded me of myself. After he is hypnotized, it somehow ignites his psychic powers, and he becomes obsessed trying to find a missing girl from the neighborhood. He whacks through the walls of his house, drills under the floors, and digs up his backyard.

He has a crazed energy about him, intent on tearing everything apart until he finds this girl — which he finally does, secreted in the basement wall.

That's how I felt about finding Janice and Fran, that same desperate energy. Like I was thrust into a world I couldn't control and needed to tear everything down until I found them.

I followed that film with another new release in the theaters — *The Sixth Sense*

— about the little boy who "sees dead people." What are the odds? A psychic-medium doubleheader. Like the kid in that film, the Kevin Bacon character in *Stir of Echoes* also saw ghosts.

Thankfully, I wasn't experiencing that kind of energy.

Yet.

Back at the office, I was now officially assigned to the Organized Crime Squad. I was on squad C-10 assigned to the Bonanno and DeCavalcante families.

I cleaned out my desk and packed the Smith files into banker's boxes, careful not to let anyone except DeStano see me flipping through them. I was forbidden to do even that.

"This is bullshit," DeStano said, as he helped stack the boxes against the wall.

More bullshit arrived with a phone call.

"Agent Hilland my name is Mike McCabe. I'm an attorney from the San Diego area, and I'm sitting in my office with my client John Smith and his wife Diane."

I nearly dropped the phone.

"Did you say John Smith is there with you?"

"Indeed," said McCabe.

I couldn't help my outburst.

"Well, where the hell has he been!"

"I was going to ask you the same question," McCabe replied.

"Excuse me?"

The lawyer went on to say that Smith claimed to have been abducted in the Laforza parking lot by "several men wearing dark suits and dark glasses" — aka FBI agents — forced into a black van with dark windows, blindfolded, and whisked away.

"When the blindfold was removed, my client was tied to a chair in a hotel room and interrogated for three days without food and water."

I sat back in my chair and laughed. I mean, I *roared.*

"What may I ask do you find so funny?" he asked.

"I find you and your client funny," I said. "Look, I don't know who you are but if you're an attorney I assume you're an educated man and probably went to law school, right? Ask yourself some questions. Ask Smith to describe the agents who kidnapped him. What they looked like. How they spoke. Ask him to describe the vehicle he was in. How long was he in this van? Ask him to describe this hotel room. It's all nonsense. The FBI does not kidnap people! Why did he give Diane his wallet with his identification, as well as the keys to their house, before he mysteriously disappeared? And what were the circumstances that led to his sudden resurrection?"

McCabe was silent.

"The Escondido Police Department has an active investigation concerning Mr. Smith's disappearance. Diane filed the report herself. I suggest you take Smith to the police department so they can ask him these questions. In fact, I can put you on hold and conference them in . . ."

The attorney quickly cut me off.

"That won't be necessary," he said. "But please consider this call formal notification of my representation of Mr. Smith. Should you need to contact him in the future you may do so through me."

"Understood," I said. "And Mr. McCabe. I don't appreciate you initiating this dialogue by accusing the FBI of kidnapping a serial killer."

"A serial killer?"

McCabe gulped just as I was hanging up.

On Long Island, I sat across from John Edward as he closed his eyes and keyed into my energy.

I was used to the process by now — the scent of sage, the quiet, the focus, the way

John listened and looked at what his guides showed him. As before, I did my best not to give him any information.

Along with several other noted psychic mediums, John was currently taking part in a group of studies helmed by University of Arizona professor and psychologist Dr. Gary E. Schwartz, who wanted to explore the possibility of an afterlife from a scientific standpoint. The study would later be part of a series on HBO called *Life After Life.* The idea that what John did could somehow be captured scientifically intrigued me, it spoke to the hard fact–finder in me.

But at this moment, John was getting a sense of me on this side of the realm.

"There's *a lot* of shifting energy around you right now," he began.

"Yeah. No kidding," I said. "It shifted me right off the squad and off the case."

John furrowed his brow.

"What do you mean?" he asked. "You're not working on the case anymore?"

"I didn't say that, exactly." I smiled.

I had that crazed Kevin Bacon energy, remember? I was committed. I had to *live* it. There was no way I was letting go of Smith.

I was also a rule breaker adept at finding ways around obstacles, so I came up with a plan. I made sure the new agent in charge of Smith was a friend of mine, getting ready to retire. He didn't want any more work on his plate, especially this "hopeless" case. So, I convinced him to let me keep working it behind the scenes and we'd put his name on the paperwork. It would mean a lot of overtime on my part and working secretly — not a plan Alex was happy with.

"Officially, I've been reassigned to another squad," I told John. "And I'm not supposed to have anything to do with Smith anymore, but . . ."

"But," John cut in, "I see you taking your files with you. Either you literally did this, or it's their way of showing me that the case will follow you."

"I took them."

John shook his head and shivered.

"Wow."

"What?"

"There are a lot of dark energies working against us here."

"Dark? What do you mean?"

"It's like every time you make progress, even if it's small, something will happen to set you back or create problems. There are positive and negative energies on both sides of the veil. The ones in the physical world can cause physical harm. The nonphysical ones can cause blockages and obstacles."

I sat on the edge of my chair. I'd fought plenty of foes in my day, but never "dark energies."

"How do we fix this?"

"It's not that simple," said John. "All we can do is protect ourselves by being grounded and surrounding ourselves with positive thoughts, energy, and prayer. As for the dark energy, our best strategy is to be aware of its presence."

"That's it? I don't understand."

"It's hard to wrap your head around it," he explained. "But make no mistake, good and evil exist here and on the Other Side. And the forces on the Other Side can absolutely influence what happens here."

It was that Good versus Evil battle he talked about in our first meeting.

John listened to what his guides advised.

"They want you to be patient," he began. "Things will happen when they're supposed to. No matter how hard you might try, you can't make anything happen on your timeline. They will happen when they're supposed to."

"I know, I know."

Patience was a virtue; it just didn't happen to be one of mine. It was one of the two big lessons I would learn while working with John Edward. The second big one was yet to reveal itself.

John paused.

"Who's the G or J name like Jerry?" he asked.

"Gerry Downes?" I said. "He's an FBI agent working the Smith case with me."

John shook his head. "No. It's not him. Do you know another Gerry with a G?"

I shook my head.

"I keep hearing a soft 'G' or 'J' followed by two syllables. I'm pretty sure it's 'Gerry.' He has a son who crossed over. The son was a cop. I see a badge and uniform. He was shot. I feel the impact and burn. Gerry might be a cop too."

John Edward paused, a look of intense pain flashed across his face.

"Oh, man. This guy Gerry is heartbroken. When his son died, so did he."

I racked my brain but had no idea who John was talking about.

"You will," he said. "It has to do with this case."

John paused again and tilted his head.

"The answer you're looking for is in the garage."

"The garage? We already dug up the garage at Grace Lane and got zilch."

"No, no," John shook his head. He was looking off into the distance the way he does. "Not *that* garage. The dealership.

The answer is there. A fingerprint."

"John, once again, I have no idea what you're talking about."

"This one is for one of your *other* cases," he said, and pointed to my notebook. "Write it down."

One of my other cases? This was a first. He'd never given me information for a case that wasn't Smith before. An overlapping was taking place, and I was surprised. John wasn't.

"Anyone who has a connection with you can come through, not just the people you expect or want. Remember that movie *Ghost*? The scene where Whoopi Goldberg is surrounded by a bunch of spirits trying to get her attention? It can be like that. You don't know who will show up or who will get through."

Ghost. I made a mental note to put yet another film about psychics on my to-do list.

Now that I was on the Organized Crime Squad, I wondered if John's message was mob related. Those guys bumped each other off in garages all the time.

John looked confused.

"I don't understand what I'm seeing now," he said. "This doesn't make sense to me. Did you give Janice a birthday present? No, wait, that's impossible. You never knew her."

Once again, John tried to decipher the information he was receiving.

"When was Janice's birthday?"

"March 2, 1951."

John nodded with certainty. "They're saying thank you for the birthday present."

Again, I was at a loss.

"One, her birthday isn't for another six months. Two, I have no idea what to get her. And three, she's dead."

John paid no attention to my attempt at sarcasm.

"They're showing me a birthday present for Janice," he insisted.

"Well . . . can you see where she is?"

John squinted.

"She's buried. But it's strange. She's showing me a cemetery, but it's like she's buried in plain view with hundreds of other graves around her, but her tombstone is blank. She's pointing at her tombstone but there's nothing written on it. She's saying, 'Thank you for the birthday present.' "

"What does that mean?" I asked.

"I don't know." John shrugged. "I'm just telling you what she's showing me."

"Will I find her?"

John was silent for a moment.

"Yes."

"When?"

"Soon."

"Soon in real time or soon in Other Side time?"

"Be patient."

There was something neither of us knew yet, and John's guides were only giving us a glimpse on their timeline. It was this: On a beautiful spring day in 1980, road workers toiling on an empty stretch of highway in Indiana stumbled upon a box near a ravine — a four-and-a-half-foot-long, handmade, plywood box.

They opened it. Inside the box, they found the remains of a body with the legs cut off.

John's "Lady in the Box" was found in 1980 by road maintenance workers in Indiana. (COURTESY OF THE FBI)

I left John's office feeling a sliver of hope again.

Even though I'd been thrown off the case, the Other Side assured me that not only was I still on it but that I'd find Janice. That is, unless the Dark Energies got in my way. Before I left his office, John showed me how to surround myself with white protective light and gave me prayers to keep me "grounded."

As I drove home, I wondered who the "Gerry" was that John talked about, how he was involved with the case, and if I would meet him — *when* I would meet him. Through all the ups and downs of the year, I was still struggling to fully believe all this was happening, still fighting the logical, hard-nosed skeptic within.

I thought about the other piece of information John gave me.

The dealership. The answer is there. A fingerprint.

I ran through the organized crime cases the squad was working on in my head and couldn't match it with anything. I twisted and turned my Rubik's Cube mind, trying to line up the colors. As anyone who's tried it knows, the infuriating thing about a Rubik's Cube is, you make one wrong turn and the whole thing goes to shit.

As I drove, I twisted and turned . . . then I got it.

One of the oldest, coldest cases on the Cold Case Squad that I'd reopened was the 1958 murder of police officer Charles Bernoskie, 41, in Rahway, New Jersey.

Bernoskie was on patrol one night, back in the day when officers drove around and got out of their cars, shaking the doors of local businesses to make sure they were locked up. This night he was checking on a car dealership and stumbled into a burglary in progress. One of the guys started shooting and Bernoskie returned fire, but they got away.

Tragically, Bernoskie — a father of five with a sixth on the way — died.

No one had put much time or effort on the case for years, but it was one of the ones that pulled at my heart. I'd pored through volumes of police reports from the fifties and sixties, trying to identify potential suspects.

The car dealership was still there, forty years later, and I'd gone to look around. I interviewed all the old detectives from forty years earlier, men in their sixties and seventies now, still broken up and emotional about the murder, as if it was fresh.

I felt it, too.

It can be a very intimate act, to bring a case alive decades after all the headlines and hoopla are over. It's just you, alone, trying to bring it back to life. I wonder if sometimes that's how John Edward felt as he connected with energies from generations ago.

At times, I'd read files like Bernoskie's and think to myself: *I wasn't even born when this happened.*

I felt a responsibility to right wrongs committed so long ago, crimes left in the past and forgotten.

I thought again about what John said: "The answer is in the dealership garage. A fingerprint."

The Rubik's Cube locked into place.

He was right! There was a fingerprint!

A partial fingerprint had been recovered at the time, back in 1958, on a bottle of antifreeze. The fingerprint system, AFIS (Automated Fingerprint Identification System) ran it repeatedly, but it was never identified. Plus, so many hands had touched the items in the garage that at one point, they gave up on it.

Never mind that I was no longer on the Cold Case Squad, I needed to make calls about this.

I wondered if John was right.

I also wondered if, moving forward, his guides planned to assist me with future cases.

Four months later, in January 2000, we entered the new millennium.

The Y2K bug didn't bring down worldwide infrastructure and crash our computers as the alarmists warned, so that was good. I sat crammed into my claustrophobic cubicle in a sea of endless cubicles in my new office, rifling through my Smith files.

I glanced over my shoulder to make sure no one was watching and picked up a folder marked TELETYPE RESPONSES/LEADS. It contained teletypes spanning June 1999 to January 2000 that I'd sent out to law enforcement agencies across the country with the details Michael had given us about the plywood box.

Reponses? Nil. Leads? Nil.

I slammed the folder shut, grabbed my coat, and ventured out into the cold winter night to join a group of agents at our watering hole, Walker's.

Yes, patience was a virtue. But there was nothing like a shot or two of bourbon to ease the waiting time.

Making my way down Greenwich Street, I suddenly stopped. Did I forget something at the office? I had a nagging feeling. I turned around.

Back in the maze of empty cubicles, I zigzagged to my desk. Now I remembered! I had a roll of surveillance film I meant to send to the photo lab. I began to write out the necessary paperwork and noticed the red voicemail light blinking on my phone.

Beeeeeeeep.

Bob, it's Brian. I think we found her . . . Janice, I mean. Give me a call when you get this!

I got Potts on the phone in a New York minute.

"Bob, you're not going to believe this," said Potts, excited. "I'd mailed a bunch of letters to sheriff's departments and medical examiners in Ohio, Indiana, and Michigan — letters with the details of the box Michael gave us. Today I got a call from a sergeant from Newton County, Ohio, Gerry Burman. He said, 'I think I've got your girl.' I got chills when he said it, Bob."

I gripped the phone.

"Brian, did you say his name was *Gerry?*"

"Yes. Gerry Burman. G-E-R-R-Y . . ."

I remembered John's words four months earlier:

Gerry with a G. A badge and uniform. Might be a cop. He has to do with this case. His son was shot. Heartbroken.

"What did he say?" I asked. I was holding my breath.

"He said that in 1980 a road crew was fixing potholes along a county road outside of Hammond, Indiana. As they were patching a hole, they noticed a plywood box on the side of the road, down by a ravine. A couple of the workers went down and moved the box closer to the road. When they opened it, a skull rolled out."

"Brian. Is this for real?"

"Everything Mike told us about what he saw in the box was there. The legs were cut off right below the knees, the clothes were all rolled up and tucked inside, everything he described was in the box."

"What did they do with it?"

"They couldn't identify her back then. They ran articles in the newspapers but came up empty. They called her the 'Lady in the Box.' "

I gripped the phone tighter.

Potts continued. "They assumed she must have been a prostitute from Chicago. The Indiana State Police still have the box and all its contents in evidence. I'm going over tomorrow to review it all."

"What about the body?"

"She's been buried as a Jane Doe in a pauper's grave for 18 years. Doesn't even have a tombstone. Just a marker apparently."

Again, John's words echoed in my head.

Tombstone is blank. Hundreds of graves around her.

"Brian, do me a favor?"

"Sure," Potts replied.

"Michael said he saw a pewter crucifix in the box around Janice's neck. If it's in evidence, can you sign it out and send it to me? There's someone I need to take it to."

In midtown Manhattan, I dashed past a long line of people waiting to be let into the television studio where John Edward was taping

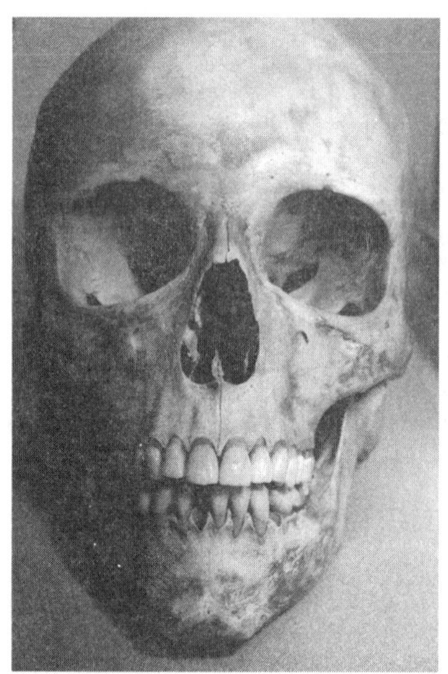

In 2000—on Janice's birthday—we exhumed an unmarked grave in Indiana and recovered her skull and bones.

(COURTESY OF THE FBI)

his new program, *Crossing Over with John Edward.* Hundreds were waiting to be part of the studio audience, hoping to get a reading from John.

I slipped into the studio's side door, made a beeline to John's dressing room, and knocked. One of John's assistants answered. I could see John in a makeup chair behind her. As soon as he saw me, he waved me in, removing the paper collar from his shirt.

"Hey! Everything okay?" he asked, worried.

"Yes. I'm sorry to show up like this when you're about to tape, but there's something I need to show you."

We went into an adjacent conference room with a long table.

"I want you to hold an item for me," I said.

I had the crucifix balled up in my hand facing down. John opened his palm under it.

"Do I have to?" he asked.

"No, John. You don't."

He took a breath and nodded. I dropped the crucifix in the palm of his hand.

A smile spread across his face.

"You found her!"

I nodded, smiling too.

John looked at me, waiting for more.

"What else do you have in your pocket?" he asked. "They're showing me you have something else to show me."

I reached into my pocket and pulled out an old, yellowing, newspaper clipping. I handed it to John. I could barely contain myself.

He unfolded it. It was a newspaper article dated 1980 with a photo of the plywood box found on the side of the road. The story's headline read LADY IN THE BOX.

John grinned.

"How cool."

On a cold Indiana morning, the FBI Evidence Response Team assembled their equipment and prepared to exhume the unmarked grave of Janice Hartman.

A front-end loader moved to a roped off area of the cemetery. The operator lowered the machine's outriggers and began to break ground.

A few feet away, I sipped a cup of coffee and was laser-focused on every minute move. Potts was there, too, scanning paperwork.

"Hey Bob, want to see something weird?" he asked.

"Always."

Potts held up his clipboard.

"Look at this date. March 2."

"So?"

"Do you know what today is?"

"Yeah, it's about 30 degrees too cold to be out here," I said, shivering.

"No," said Potts, his voice cracking a little. "Today is Janice's birthday."

I grabbed Potts's clipboard with my free hand and looked at the date again. I checked my watch to make sure.

Again, John Edward was in my head.

Thank you for the birthday present.

The FBI agents lifted a white plastic box from Janice's unmarked, nameless pauper's grave and placed it on the tarp spread across the cold ground in front of me.

I stared at it, hardly believing my own eyes, and whispered:

"Happy birthday, Janice."

16

PREMONITIONS, THE POLICE OFFICER, THE PRESIDENT

On the morning of October 1, 2000, John David Smith III was handcuffed in the parking lot of Laforza Automobiles and arrested for the murder of Janice Hartman.

Within an hour of the arrest, I was buzzed through a heavy door at the sheriff's office in Escondido, California. A narrow corridor led to Smith's holding cell, which was the size of a walk-in closet — enough for a sink, a toilet, a bed.

Smith sat on the worn mattress, looking lost.

When he looked up and saw me through the steel bars, his colorless face turned crimson. Anger? Defeat? Fear? Maybe all, maybe none.

It was the first time we'd seen each other since the hotel room interrogation a year and a half earlier. My last words to him then were, "Make no mistake. The next time you see my face, you'll be behind bars."

And here we were.

I crouched down to his eye level.

I wasn't gloating, I wasn't happy. Rather, I felt the weight of the moment on both of us. As John Edward said from the beginning, Smith and I shared a strange, unique, good-versus-evil connection. I was genuinely invested in it.

"Hello, John."

He acknowledged me with a simple nod.

"Are you okay?" I asked.

He shrugged. "I guess so."

"Do you need anything?"

"No."

I grasped the bars.

"I know you've asked for your attorney. I'm not here to ask you any questions like before. I just wanted to stop by to make sure you were alright."

He stared at the floor.

Once again, I remembered John Edward's advice before the hotel interrogation. It was the sword that pierced Smith's emotional armor.

Mention the grandmother.

"There is one thing I need you to know," I said. "Your mother Grace was with your grandmother at the hospital when she passed away."

Smith looked up, suddenly attentive.

"The last thing your grandmother said to her before she died was, 'I'm not looking for forgiveness or mercy, but that justice finally be done.'"

Smith froze.

I took my hands off the bars and left.

Justice had been done, and I was confident Smith would be incarcerated for a long time — hopefully the rest of his life.

But that didn't mean I was through with him.

My vow in Dansman's office the day I first saw photos of Fran and Janice was to find *both* women, no matter how long it took.

This was far from over.

We'd found justice for Janice, and now it was Fran's turn.

Back in New York, I met up with John Edward in a midtown Manhattan hotel after he'd finished a group reading event.

We were an odd pair when you saw us together. Our facial features and attention to neatness were oddly similar. But our height, clothing, and demeanor — not so much. I'd just gotten off work, so I was wearing my usual FBI uniform — suit, tie, badge, and gun. John was in his usual Long Island, guy-next-door, psychic-medium ensemble

— jeans, button-down shirt, wire-rimmed glasses, and hair gel.

At the hotel bar, I ordered a vodka on the rocks; John ordered a hot fudge sundae.

We were like Arnold Schwarzenegger and Danny DeVito in *Twins.*

Interestingly, our FBI-psychic relationship was evolving. The information John had given me the year before on the Charles Bernoskie case — a fingerprint in the garage of a car dealership — led to an arrest in Officer Bernoskie's mysterious 1958 murder in Rahway, New Jersey.

Ten days after I stood at Janice's Jane Doe grave in Ohio, convicted murderer Robert Zarinsky stood in a New Jersey courtroom, indicted for the murder of officer Bernoskie.

Age-old cases and Other Side–lives were converging.

As John would say: "How cool."

But now, I had Fran on my mind. And as usual, I was impatient.

"Did you see *What Lies Beneath* with Harrison Ford and Michelle Pfeiffer?" I asked John. "I saw it last night."

In the film, Pfeiffer's character is haunted by the spirit of a murdered woman who is trying to show her where her body is hidden. There's a vivid scene in which the dead woman pulls Pfeiffer into a lake to show her exactly where her body lies.

"I *just* saw it," said John.

"Well, why can't your guides tell us exactly where Fran is, like in the movie? Why doesn't Fran just tell us?"

It was a question I would ask John a million times. And a question he would try to answer so I would understand it, over and over.

"Look. I get it. I want that, too," John said. "After the movie I wanted to say to Fran, 'Why can't you tell me *I'm buried by the big tree* or whatever. You clearly know where you are. Why don't you just tell us? Why can't we know?' "

"Well?" I asked. "Why can't we?"

"In my world, it's no different than a parent not telling a child what to do because they have lessons to learn. It's not about getting answers or about success or failure. It's about the journey you need to take."

John's ice cream was melting. I waved to the bartender for another vodka.

"What journey do I need to take?"

He paused.

"We don't know yet."

The jury on the Other Side was also undecided on if I'd find Fran at all, it seemed.

While discussing the Smith case with his

friend, medium Shelley Peck, they had what he described as a "psychic stand-off."

Shelley gave John his very first medium reading when he was sixteen, and they'd been close friends ever since. John's mother, Perinda, passed away when he was a teen and Shelley (along with John's grandmother and an array of Italian aunts on mom's side) became one in a handful of strong, female forces in his life. She had a mentor-like approach with a Jewish mom vibe. She reminded John of a blonde Liz Taylor.

Not only did Shelley predict John would marry his wife, Sandra, before they'd even met, but "Shelley introduced me to my spirit guides," he explained. The guides were a motley crew that included an Asian monk, a goofy teenager, and a native Indian. They were "the Boys," as John sometimes called them, who helped me find Janice.

"For whatever reason, my guides trust you," he told me once.

John and Shelley compared incoming information from their respective guides from time to time to combine their two perspectives.

"Our guides are good at giving us a three-dimensional look at something," he said.

So, John asked Shelley to check in with her

guides on the whereabouts and timeline of my search for Fran.

On this question, John and Shelley — and their spirit guides — disagreed wholeheartedly.

John felt I would find Fran because his guides showed him a very specific detail during our first reading together — breast implants with serial numbers on them.

"I worked in healthcare and never knew implants had numbers on them," he said. "I mean, I knew about dental records, but breast implants? No idea. It was a very weird, random piece of information for them to give me. That's why I think you'll find her," he told me. "Because when you do, you'll be able to identify her from the serial numbers on the implants."

"You told Shelley about the implants?" I asked.

"Yeah. She doesn't see you finding her."

"But what about the . . ."

"She said, 'I don't care what you say. *She will not be found.*' "

I sighed and slapped cash on the bar for the bill. I had the other inevitable question to ask him, but I wanted to be careful how to word it. I didn't want to annoy John's guides. I didn't want to be impatient. I had to be subtle.

"So . . . *when* will I find Fran?"

John shook his head.

"I don't know. We could be, like, 97 years old when it happens. I don't know."

Patience.

But Shelley's conviction that I'd never find Fran made me want to search even harder.

I don't know if John was rubbing off on me or if I'd seen one too many films about psychics, but as I moved into the "Fran" phase of the Smith case, something odd — maybe supernatural — began happening to me.

John believed everybody has psychic ability, but because it's not encouraged or nurtured in our society, we learn to shut it down at a young age.

But now, I was starting to feel the doors of perception cracking open. My senses were acute. Like that Kevin Bacon character, something had been ignited in me.

That December in 2000, I heard Janice Hartman's voice for the first time.

I'd gone to Wooster, Ohio, to do prep work for Smith's trial, which was scheduled for the summer of 2001. While there, Potts handed me an old Christmas tape Janice's family had given him. I got in my car and drove, slipping the cassette into the tape deck. It was snowing, and the street was dotted with colorful, blinking Christmas lights.

Janice's voice boomed to life, a happy teenager laughing with friends at a holiday party. She sounded so young and full of hope, I choked up. I could *feel* her presence, as if she were sitting right next to me.

In that moment she came alive to me, more than ever. And her message was loud and clear — the way I imagined John received messages when his guides walloped him.

She said: *Don't give up. Keep going.*

An hour later, Potts and I met with Janice's brother, Gary, at the family jewelry shop nearby. It was late, and all the stores on Main Street were shuttered for the night. Only me and Potts and a cold wind blustered through.

We were there to show Gary photos of the rolled-up clothes found in the plywood box twenty years earlier, to verify if they belonged to Janice. We sat across from him at a desk and I pulled out a stack of 8 x 10s from an envelope.

One by one, Gary studied each photo and searched his memory.

When he recognized an item of Janice's clothing, he got excited for a moment, then his happiness would swiftly shift to sadness and grief.

"I remember those!" he said, of a pair of

bell-bottoms with a multicolored butterfly patch on the rear pocket. "Janny loved those jeans. She wore them all the time. I remember the butterfly."

We were halfway through the pile when I reached for the next photo and something caught my eye. From my position, I was seeing the picture upside-down. I leaned forward and studied it more closely.

I couldn't believe my own eyes; it was like I was seeing a ghost.

I quickly gathered the photos and stood up.

"I'm sorry, Gary . . . we're going to have to finish this another time."

Both Gary and Potts looked up at me, confused, as I bolted out of the shop. Outside, Potts followed me across the ice-covered sidewalk and into his car.

"What the hell is going on?" he asked, starting the engine.

I pulled the photos out of the envelope and flipped through the stack until I found it. Potts looked on, not understanding. With shivering hands, I held the photo up to Potts. It was a picture of a bright, lime green nightgown with discoloration and stains on the bottom.

"What do you see when you look at this?" I asked him.

Potts scanned the photo.

"An ugly green nightgown with stains on it," he said.

I turned the picture upside-down.

"Now what do you see?"

Potts' eyes widened and his mouth opened in shock. "Oh my God! That can't be!"

"Go!"

He shifted his car into gear and we sped off into the darkness.

Ten minutes later, we were in the musty basement of the sheriff's office, unlocking the door of the evidence room.

We made our way through a maze of boxes, files, and Rubbermaid totes marked with case numbers. The closer we got to Janice's boxes, the stronger the scent of death became.

With flashlights and rubber gloves, we hunted through box after box of Janice's belongings, on a mission to find a particular item. The stench was unbearable. Finally, I saw a flash of green.

"I've got it!"

Potts trained his flashlight on my hands as I reached deep into a box and pulled out the sheer nightgown we'd seen in the photo.

Carefully, I unfolded it and held it open.

An unusually large, multicolored stain covered its bottom. I slowly turned the garment upside down. The abstract stain took shape and form, revealing the secrets of the box. The visual was unmistakable; Janice Hartman's face was etched on the gown's fabric.

She was looking right at us. It was her own Shroud of Turin.

"I'll be dammed," Potts said, in a shocked whisper.

"Unbelievable," I said.

Bright rainbow colors surrounded the top of the image, where Janice's hair once rested.

"What do you suppose caused all those colors around her head?" Potts asked.

I lowered the nightgown and searched through the box some more, pulling out a pair of checkered, rainbow-colored pants.

"These pants. They must have gotten wet and the colors bled, dyeing Janice's hair. The green gown covered the front of her face and absorbed her image."

Potts nodded in agreement. We looked at the imprint of Janice's face with silent respect.

"Rainbow-colored hair," said Potts.

"Michael was telling the truth from the beginning," I said.

In July 2001, John David Smith III was found guilty of murder and sentenced to 15 years to life in prison.

For weeks, the small town of Wadsworth, Ohio, was abuzz with the dramatic trial. Women knocked at my hotel room door with homemade apple pies. It was like a scene out of *To Kill a Mockingbird.*

When Michael took the stand, Smith stared at his brother from behind the defense table like he was trying to suck the soul out of his body. The courtroom erupted in a collective gasp when the plywood box, essentially Janice's coffin, was carried down the gallery and propped up in front of the jury.

When it was all over and I was back home, I'd barely taken a breath before I got an urgent call from John Edward one morning.

"Bob. Do you know anyone in the Secret Service?" He sounded panicked.

"Yeah."

"I need you to get a message to them."

"What? Why?"

"I had a dream last night that the president is going to be assassinated!"

George W. Bush had been inaugurated earlier that year for his first term as president. That John had a dream about him being killed was alarming enough. Even more shocking was that John wanted us to tell the Secret Service about it.

He was private and always adamant about keeping our relationship a secret. And he didn't like talking to law enforcement (except me).

So this was dire. This was a big deal.

"Look. I need you to reach out to somebody," he urged. "If I don't do something and it happens, I'll feel responsible."

I called up a Secret Service buddy stationed in South Carolina who recruited two agents from the New York field office. A few days later, they showed up at John's studio. The female agent was apparently a big fan of John Edward's, a true believer. The other agent was a crusty, old curmudgeon of a fellow who treated the meeting as a joke.

They arrived bearing items from Air Force One — an ashtray, a paperweight, and other small objects that the president had touched, for John to hold.

In the dressing room, John explained his concern. He described the scene his guides had shown him:

"The president is walking through a doorway, to a podium . . . he's going to address the media, give a press conference . . . he's surrounded by people who have authority to be there, they're wearing badges, press credentials? But there is a bad actor in the group, a shooter. He has official credentials like the rest of them. I saw him raise a gun and point it at the president and shoot."

The way John described the scene reminded me of the time Ronald Reagan got shot.

The female agent listened intently, but the other agent — the old curmudgeon — was rolling his eyes, smirking.

That is, until John abruptly stopped.

He tilted his head, like he was listening to something. By now, I knew what that meant.

John turned to the female Secret Service agent.

"Um. May I be personal with you?"

Uh-oh.

"Yeah," she said.

As soon as she gave him the okay, a rush of details began rushing out of John like the Hoover Dam busting. John began listing personal information about the woman and she nodded as he hit everything on target. Meanwhile, the other agent was still rolling his eyes.

That's when John turned to *him.*

"Did your father pass recently?"

The color drained from the man's face.

"He passed away last week," said the man.

John nodded.

"Your father's coming through."

Once again, like a machine gun spitting out bullets, John gave the man personal information that blew him away. The look on that man's face reminded me of mine, the first day I met John. I have to admit, I was really proud of him.

Before the agents left that day, they asked John if he'd be willing to meet them in Washington, DC, and board Air Force One to see if he could glean any more information on the plane.

John agreed, but there ended up being no need for the trip. A few days after our meeting, I got a call from the female agent.

"Bob, I want to thank you and John and let you know we found a breach in security," she said. "We figured out what John was referring to concerning the issuance of controlled access passes. That's all I can tell you, but I wanted to let you know. We really appreciate you coming to us. Who knows what might have happened?"

John knows, I thought. I hung up the phone, grateful that the crisis had been averted.

Or so I thought.

For the next several weeks following our Secret Service meeting, John was on edge — almost depressed. He'd been in a major funk all summer, since June and the death of his friend Shelley Peck, but this was something more.

"Are you okay?" I asked. "You don't seem yourself."

"I don't know what it is . . ." he said, trailing off, distracted.

John was an exceptional communicator, but whatever was going on with him, he struggled to pinpoint it. Something dark was hovering, but he didn't know what it was or why.

As for myself, I tried to keep positive. Smith was in prison, the president was safe, and I was going full steam ahead with my search for Fran with encouragement from Janice on the Other Side.

Early on a bright, crisp, September morning, I kissed a half-asleep Caitie, now four, on the cheek and left for work. The trick was to make sure she *knew* I'd given her the kiss without waking her fully. If the sound of the front door woke her up without the kiss, she'd bound out of bed, run out the door in her pajamas, and chase after my car down the street.

Connor, now six, heard the front door closing on this day — his bedroom was at the front of the house. He and I had a morning ritual.

As I passed the outside of his bedroom on the way to my car, I knocked five times on his window — *knock, knock, knock, knock,*

knock. Half asleep and still in bed, he'd lift his little fist and knock on the wall twice — *knock, knock!*

It was our secret code and signal, like Batman and Robin. He wanted to be a caped crusader like his dad and fight crime.

Our special little exchange started my day with a smile.

I was still in great spirits as I approached the Holland Tunnel and sixteen lanes of traffic tried to squeeze into two like a zipper fit. Traffic inched along.

I looked up at the clear sky. The sun was dazzling.

I didn't think. It didn't occur to me before that the George Bush assassination attempt John saw in his dream might have meant something more, something bigger. Not an attack on our president, but an attack on our country.

As I marveled at the stunningly beautiful sky, I saw a plane streak across it.

One of the Twin Towers exploded.

17

Axis of Evil

John couldn't shake the "doom and gloom" feeling overwhelming him.

That's what he and Shelley Peck used to call the dark cloud of emotion that enveloped them before a tragic "big event" happened in the world. They both felt it before the space shuttle *Challenger* exploded in 1986, before the Oklahoma City bombing in 1995, and before the Columbine High School massacre in 1999.

But in the days leading up to September 11, John attributed his doom and gloom to grief as he struggled with the death of his dear friend, Shelley. But the grief kept getting louder, like a ticking clock.

Weeks earlier, he'd been *inside* the World Trade Center.

Sandra was working for the Empire State Ballroom Classic competition at the World Trade Center Marriott, and, during one number, he ducked out to take a call from a friend.

"I walked out of the ballroom, through a set of glass doors, and into the lobby of the Trade Center," he told me later. After an upbeat conversation with his pal, "I hung up and the lobby started to spiral," he said. "I broke out into a cold sweat and got nauseous. I was standing still, but the building was moving around me. I felt a swirl of dark, negative, angry energy."

"Dark, angry energy?" I asked.

"Yeah. Dark and bad. My immediate thought was there's going to be a mass shooting. Whatever was going to happen, it involved massive death."

John raced back to the ballroom to find Sandra, who excitedly told him she'd been asked to sign a multiyear contract to host the competition at the Marriott the following year and beyond.

"I asked her how long the contract was for at that hotel. Seven years, she said. I told her, 'They need to move it. They need to work with a different Marriott, *anywhere but here.*' She looked at me like I was nuts, then got pulled away to talk to some producers. But I muttered under my breath: *It won't be happening here next year.* I just didn't know why, or what that meant."

A few weeks later, on September 9, John and Sandra were going out to dinner to celebrate a friend's birthday, and Sandra suggested Windows on the World, the famous restaurant on the top of the World Trade Center.

"I flipped out," said John, "And told her there was no way I was going back into that building. I didn't want to go *anywhere* in downtown Manhattan."

He also didn't want to go out of town. John was flying out the next day, September 10, to Los Angeles be a guest on *Larry King Live.* But for some reason, "I did not want to get on a plane."

On the night of September 10, John's live taping in LA with Larry King went differently than usual. This was his fourth time on the show, which they usually packed with callers and readings. This time, however, his appearance was more of a discussion about the process of grieving.

"I had a feeling afterward that this show in particular was going to help a lot of people deal with death and dying," he said.

In the early hours of September 11, John was jolted awake by a call from the hotel front desk asking if he was okay.

"They told me a 911 call originated from my room minutes before," John said.

He had no idea how unless he did it in his sleep.

John went back to bed but was woken up again with a call from his *Crossing Over* producer, Paul Shavelson, in New York. Paul was on the Triborough Bridge uptown, staring at the smoldering Twin Towers right around the time I was looking at them while in the toll line for the Holland Tunnel.

* * *

I had to be daydreaming.

Or having an out-of-body experience, I told myself, as I watched a gigantic mushroom cloud blow up around the top of the North Tower of the World Trade Center.

I looked around to see if any other drivers were seeing what I was seeing. A woman on my right was checking lipstick in her rear-view mirror. A man to my left was reading the newspaper.

But the guy behind me was standing outside his car, pointing to the tower, and yelling into his cell phone.

Holy shit, this is real.

My FBI radio blasted: *All agent personnel report to the corner of Church and Vesey, across the street from the South Tower!*

As the cars merged into the tunnel, the first phone call I made, surprisingly, was to my father.

"Dad, it's Bobby."

"What's up?"

"A plane just flew into the World Trade Center, the Twin Towers."

"What?"

"A jet just flew into the tower."

"Where are you?"

"Going into the tunnel. They're calling all of us to the towers."

My radio crackled.

"I've got to go!"

I hung up and took the incoming call.

"Bobby, something just blew up! There was an explosion!" It was my supervisor on the Organized Crime Squad. "Where are you?""

"A plane hit the South Tower!" I told her.

"What do you think it is?"

"I don't know. I'm almost out of the tunnel."

I hung up and dialed Alex. No service. All the cell phones in Manhattan were dead.

The New York side of the Holland Tunnel was pandemonium — sirens, yelling, people running.

Our office was three blocks from the Twin Towers. I double-parked and met a group of agents on the street. As we threw on raid jackets, we heard and felt the next explosion, deep in our bones. It was so loud, the percussion reverberated through my body.

"What the hell was that?" I asked.

"A second plane hit the towers!"

No!

We began running, five of us wearing FBI jackets. As we ran toward the towers, a sea of people was running against us, the other way.

The streets were pure chaos, it looked like a scene out of an apocalyptic sci-fi movie.

In the middle of Church Street, a bunch of people stood motionless, petrified, staring down. I looked, confused by what I saw. It was a giant crater, as if a meteor had crashed into the street.

"It's an engine from one of the planes!" someone yelled, over the din.

Our small group of agents reached the corner of Church and Vesey, where we were told to report, but we had no orders what to do next.

We looked at each other and knew; we were going in.

Along with the rest of the city — and the world — we had no inkling those towers could ever, would ever, come down. They had the invincible aura of the *Titanic* — unsinkable — before it went down. I looked up at the smoke and flames engulfing floors 77–85 and worried: *How the hell are they going to put that fire out?*

Inside, I ran to one of the many elevator banks and, like the crater in the street, didn't understand what I saw. All the doors had been blown open by a fuel fireball shooting down the shaft and, on the bank, everything had evaporated.

The radio crackled again: *Agent personnel respond to the corner of Church and Vesey!*

We ran back outside, and the bedlam was worse than minutes before. A new, unfamiliar, ear-piercing sound greeted us — a combination of thuds and car alarms.

"What the hell is that sound?" asked one agent.

We looked up. People were jumping from the tower over a thousand feet above us and hitting the street and parked cars below, setting off car alarms. Some were lifeless as they fell. I watched as one man attempted to skydive to an adjacent building and miss. One couple, a man and woman, held hands as they plummeted.

Once they hit the ground, they disappeared.

Across from the South Tower, next to St. Peter's church, we took over an empty building and set up a command post. The first two floors of the building were concrete and windowless, and its entrance had two sets of heavy, clear doors, like a shopping mall, that acted like an airlock.

An assistant special agent in charge, Ken Waxman, and a high-ranking NYPD guy arrived to give orders. They directed us to establish land line communications and coordinate with various agency resources.

"Bobby, get 26 Federal Plaza on the phone!"

On the landline, I reached one of the highest-ranking special agents in charge, Rob Corvair. He was very military, no time for small talk, and was Waxman's superior.

"Bobby, where are you?"

I gave him details about the command post. By now, we had at least forty NYPD and FBI agents with us in the open cubicle area, plus a handful of civilians who'd run in for cover, including a journalist. I handed the phone to Waxman.

"Corvair, this is not an accident," Waxman said, voice shaking, face ashen. "This is a *fucking attack.*"

Before our eyes, Waxman began to fall apart. He was shaking uncontrollably.

"The Pentagon's been hit!" someone yelled.

He looked at me confused.

"What did they say?"

"I think they said the Pentagon was hit."

Waxman's shoulders slumped with complete resignation. He put the phone down and walked away. I stood there, not sure what to do. None of us knew what to do. But I could hear Corvair, still on the line, still thinking he had Waxman there.

I grabbed the phone.

"The military jets just took off from McGuire Air Force Base in Jersey and will be in lower Manhattan in 12 minutes," he was saying. He sounded like a leader in a war zone.

I cleared my throat.

"Who the fuck is this?" asked Corvair.

"Sir, it's Bob Hilland again."

"Where the fuck is Waxman?"

"He . . . got called away."

"You get his ass on the phone right now!"

"Yes, Sir."

But by now, Waxman was at the far side of the room in full shellshock, like a zombie.

"Everyone, get under your desks!" another agent yelled.

We all dove to the ground, the phone still in my hand.

Three blocks away, Corvair could see what was happening. He was watching the Trade Center from his window high up at Federal Plaza.

"Oh my, God. Bobby, GET EVERYBODY OUT RIGHT NOW!"

The phone went dead.

The lights went out.

When metal twists, it sounds like crying.

That's what we heard first. Then, we heard a deafening boom-boom-boom. It got faster and faster and louder and louder. Crouched under our desks in the dark with no communication, we had no idea what was happening. *Another plane? A bomb?*

Manhattan sat on bedrock and the island was shaking. Something was about to hit us, I thought.

This is it; this is the end. God, please let it be quick. Please take care of my wife and kids and family.

I was strangely at peace, facing death. It was a moment of complete acceptance and surrender. Maybe it was because of what I'd experienced with John Edward. I didn't think about dying the same way I used to.

Suddenly, the crying metal and thunderous booming stopped. In its place was an eerie quiet. It was the loudest quiet I'd ever heard in my life.

We still had no idea what went on outside our airlocked doors, until . . .

"Oh my God!" someone yelled. "The South Tower fell!"

* * *

Another agent and I crawled our way to the two sets of doors at the front of the building. The room was so dark, I couldn't see my hand in front of my face. Within a minute, emergency floodlights came on. They were dim but enough so we could see.

After opening the interior set of doors, we reached the outer doors and were again puzzled by what we saw. The clear glass doors were black, we couldn't see through them. It was 10 A.M. and dark as midnight out there.

Maybe we're trapped under debris, I thought.

We pushed against the double doors, releasing the air lock, and they flew open. An incoming tsunami of dust, ash, and shards of god-knows-what sucked in and smothered us. We couldn't see anything, but now we could hear. Screaming.

We wrestled the door shut. Without flashlights, how could we get to people and help them?

A strobe light flashed in the room. One of the civilians who'd run into the command post was a TV reporter with a video camera.

"Hey!" I yelled. "We need that camera!"

He clutched it.

"But this is a $60,000 camera!"

We took the camera with the light from

him. Several agents and I positioned it by the front doors and turned on the strobe, shooting the beam out into the blackness. Every few minutes, we cracked the door open and yelled, "Come to the light! Come to the light!"

Yeah, it sounded like a corny near-death experience in a B-movie. But every few minutes, a bloody hand would slap across the glass and we'd open the door, grab the person, and pull them inside.

After fifteen minutes, the debris began clearing from the air and the sun pierced through, making it possible to see again.

We ventured out. The streets looked like the morning after a heavy snowstorm. The entire Financial District was blanketed with a coat of white, chalky powder.

When I returned home around dinnertime, I was greeted by the same little guy who sent me off that morning. Connor heard my car pull in the driveway and ran out to the porch.

"Daddy, daddy! Did you see it?"

He had two toy planes in his hands and whooshed them through the air, simulating the crashes into the Twin Towers.

"Two airplanes came zooming in and knocked the buildings down, Daddy!"

I grabbed him and hugged him tight.

Inside, Alex was in the living room with her sister and mother, as if they'd been holding vigil for me. All day, she had no idea if I was dead or alive. I stood in front of them caked in ash, looking like a ghost.

Alex jumped up and hugged me, crying.

I was a mess, in so many ways. And I was never so glad to be home.

John's guides tried to get his attention, that's for sure. But could they have done it in a way that would have prevented the attack? Like they had a month earlier for the George Bush assassination attempt?

"No," he said, when I reached him later by phone. "Because I wouldn't have been able to stop it," he said.

"Who did this?" I asked. "Do you know who is responsible?"

He didn't even pause.

"Osama bin Laden."

For the next year, like thousands of others, I lived and worked at Ground Zero. I put my search for Fran on hold.

The USS *Intrepid,* docked on the West Side Highway, became our new command post as agents rotated assignments: two weeks climbing through the pit at Ground

Zero . . . two weeks at the morgue, helping to catalogue recovered evidence that might contain DNA . . . two weeks chasing down leads and interviewing family members of missing people . . . two weeks at the Fresh Kills landfill on Staten Island where rubble from Ground Zero was dumped and sorted.

Posters of thousands of missing faces were all over the city — on lampposts, covering the walls of Grand Central Station, on trees in Central Park. Civilians lined the streets of the West Side Highway near Ground Zero and cheered for us. Wearing hazmat suits, we'd climb through the piles, looking for body parts that might identify those who'd perished.

As I sorted through the rubble and picked up lost objects from someone's desk, I felt nothing. I couldn't let myself. A job needed to be done and there was no time for feelings. I had to compartmentalize. There was too much to do.

The FBI coordinated with the New York City Medical Examiner's Office to collect DNA samples of people reported missing. After weeks of climbing through the piles, putting on a clean suit and knocking on someone's door to get a toothbrush or hairbrush would be a welcome respite, I thought.

I was sent to an address in New Jersey

belonging to a missing man in his thirties. A young mother answered the door, holding a baby. A toddler clung to her leg.

She glanced at my credentials and then, joyously, looked past me and over my shoulder, to my car in her driveway. She must have thought I had her husband with me. She thought I had found him and was bringing him home.

For a fraction of a second, she had hope.

Once I realized that, I couldn't get words out. As I asked for her husband's toothbrush, the look of despair on her face was more than I could bear.

When I got back into my car, I leaned my forehead against the steering wheel and called the command post.

"Put me back in the morgue," I said. "Put me in landfill. Put me in the pit. But please, don't send me to any more families."

We never found that woman's husband or the father to those two children.

I was working long, endless days, six days a week. Every morning, I began saying a specific prayer — the Prayer of Saint Michael the Archangel:

Saint Michael the Archangel, defend us in battle. Be our protection against the wickedness and snares of the devil; May God rebuke him, we humbly pray; And do thou, O Prince of the Heavenly Host, by the power of God, thrust into hell Satan and all evil spirits who wander through the world for the ruin of souls. Amen.

In the span of a few weeks, about 1.6 million tons of rubble came to the Fresh Kills landfill for sorting. More than 1,600 personal effects were retrieved and 4,257 human remains were found. We were able to identify 300 people.

"Be careful about the air," John told me, those first few weeks.

"We've got paper masks," I said. "But the air is like wet concrete and metal. It leaves a copper penny taste in my mouth and nose and back of my throat. No matter how much water I drink or how many times I blow my nose, I can't get rid of it."

John coughed. His guides were showing him.

"There's something bad with it," he warned me.

A few weeks later, air-testing stations appeared all over Ground Zero — little metal boxes that gave off a humming sound. Soon after that, we were issued better masks — rubber, with a filter. Not long after that, we had to get fitted for the top-of-the-line kind that let nothing through.

"You were right about the air," I told John, during our next chat.

He was quiet.

"John?"

"You're going to find a tattoo."

"A what?"

"You're going to find a piece of a person, a young female, and it will have a unique tattoo on it. This is significant because the tattoo will identify her," said John.

He paused. Then . . .

"When this young woman got the tattoo, her mother was angry at her for doing it. They argued. But when you find it, her mother will be grateful for that tattoo. It will help the family say good-bye and grieve her death."

"What kind of tattoo?"

John paused.

"I don't know. They're not showing me. But it's unique, one-of-a-kind. That's how they will know it's her."

A few days later, I was with a group sifting the ruins with a rake when we found a piece of torn, burned flesh. It was from a hip or a shoulder, and it had a tattoo on it; a rare flower with a bumblebee flying above the petals.

We photographed it, bagged it, documented it, and sent it to cold storage.

The young woman with the tattoo was one of the 300 people we were able to identify.

Even though I did my best all year to stuff my feelings in a place I couldn't feel them, a question loomed large. It had to do with the battle between Good and Evil that John mentioned at our first meeting, and several times since.

What made one person choose to hate and another person choose to love?

What made one person act heroically and another descend to villainy?

In the wake of 9/11, I witnessed the best and worst in people, and it wasn't always where I expected.

I was surprised to receive cards from Wayne County, Ohio, where we'd just finished the Smith trial. The judge, his court officer, the prosecutor's office, the victim/witness office, the Hampton Inn hotel staff, and even Smith's attorney sent notes of encouragement.

"We're thinking about you," they wrote, "and praying for everyone in New York."

I will never forget the bravery of those members of the Fire Department, the Port Authority, and the NYPD who, without hesitation, ran into the burning towers to help people, not knowing if they'd survive themselves.

On their faces they wore expressions of intensity and focus and shared an unspoken understanding: this is the right thing to do, no matter what happens.

FBI agents from all over the country showed up at Ground Zero: "We're here to help," they said, "we're all in this together."

I also saw the opposite. People looting and stealing from the underground mall, among the fresh graves of thousands of victims we were looking for. Witnessing this, I had a difficult time holding back one emotion: *Anger.*

President George Bush gave his now-famous speech at his first State of the Union address, four months after the World Trade Center attack. He talked about the "axis of evil" and outlined his "War on Terror" that would define US foreign policy for the next two decades.

But in the weeks after 9/11, I learned that sometimes Evil didn't reside in a foreign land or a place of biblical punishment. It can live and thrive in your own backyard.

And I decided that in life's existential battle, each person had to pick a side. And if we didn't, it would be chosen for us.

"We all have free will," John said. "The

general rule for me is, who is putting humanity first? Who is using their free will to forgive and who is using it for vengeance?"

I was far from perfect and had plenty of my own internal demons to fight as I tried to slay other external ones, out in the world.

But I tried to choose humanity, pushing aside the anger I felt. I would discover later that you can't hide from emotions. The rage would catch up with me in time, and it's something John would help me with. Another lesson I would learn.

By August 2002, my time in the pits of hell was over.

John, too, had been doing intense work all year. His readings were dominated by friends and families who'd lost loved ones at the Trade Center, starting with hero firefighter Michael Kiefer, who came through to John three weeks after the attack. (The following year John would name his son "Justin Michael," partly after Kiefer).

Kiefer's company was last seen in the lobby of the Marriott just before the towers fell, the spot where John had his spinning, spiraling, dark energy incident weeks before the attack.

"I know I'll be working with September 11 families for the rest of my life," John told me.

It had been a year of tragedy, of loves lost and appreciated, of grief and closure, and about trying to make families whole again.

John did it one way; I did it another.

One of the more bittersweet aspects of John's work, he told me once, is that he can pass along incredibly intimate information to people who are mourning for loved ones. And often, it helps them tremendously. But even so, it's never quite *enough.*

"Because what people truly want," he said, "is to have their loved one alive again, standing next to them. So, I try to let them know that they are with them in spirit. And even though the body is gone, the energy and love never dies."

After a year of death and destruction, that was a good reminder to have — and give.

On a bright fall morning, as crisp and dazzling as the September before, Sergeant Brian Potts of the Wayne County Sheriff's Office pulled into a driveway with a very special package.

"Janice wanted you to have this," he told Dee Hartman, her sister, when she met him on the front porch.

Potts handed her a purple velvet jewelry bag, newly released from the evidence room at the sheriff's office.

She opened the bag and pulled out an item

she hadn't seen in nearly 30 years — the birthday watch with the silver, herringbone band and green face encrusted with diamonds and emeralds. The one she helped pick out for Janice.

Dee stared at it, covering her mouth to hide her astonishment.

"I knew she would love it," Dee whispered.

She burst into tears and hugged Potts.

"I don't know how to thank you."

18

FATHERS

A year after the September 11 attacks, I could still smell the charred, metallic Ground Zero air wherever I went. It would stay locked in my senses, smoldering, for decades — maybe forever.

But at least after my work was done and I'd left the pit, I could let go of some of the emotion.

That September, I began training for a new position — special agent polygraph examiner. It was a four-month program, five days a week, in the Deep South at Fort Jackson Army Base in Columbia, South Carolina — the largest US Army installation for basic combat in the country.

Conducting polygraphs was considered a tough job, requiring keen interview skills. The FBI routinely went to countries all over the world to suss out truth tellers and identify liars whose evils could harm the fate of many.

When they had an opening, the polygraph team reached out to me and asked if I'd join them. I had a knack for getting information out of people, they said.

I liked the process of polygraph testing, it appealed to my meticulous nature. Based on the "fight, flight, freeze" concept, there was a clear-cut black-and-whiteness to its biology that I took to. It worked with our nervous system, recording respiration, heart rate, blood volume, and changes to galvanic skin response (GSR) — aka sweating. When it came down to it, we were all animals. Our bodies didn't lie.

That's what I was learning about on the morning of September 11, 2002, when the program director came into the classroom and gave a brief speech to acknowledge the one-year anniversary of the attack.

We were a class of about thirty, from various agencies — FBI, Secret Service, Department of Defense, CIA, and the Drug Enforcement Agency.

"All of you here strive to keep the country safe," said the director. "What we do is important."

"Sir," someone spoke up, pointing to me. "There are a couple of guys here who were at Ground Zero when the towers fell."

The director looked over at me, shocked.

"Agent Hilland, would you like to say a few words?"

A tidal wave of emotion whacked me hard, taking me by surprise. All year I'd been so used to damming up the feelings. I looked down and shook my head, trying to stay composed. I glanced at another agent in the room from New York. He was feeling it, too.

The director asked us to form a circle and hold hands. He recited a prayer. I tried not to make eye contact with anyone, I couldn't. When we were done, the class took a break and I found an empty room. There, I cried about what had happened and what I'd seen. For the first time.

The end of that era and the start of a new position also meant I could get back to my quest — finding Fran and putting Smith away forever. I had every intention of continuing to work the Smith case on the sly, as planned.

Before arriving in South Carolina, I had returned to Ohio to cultivate a new source — Smith's cellmate at the maximum-security Trumbull Correctional Institute. Convicted murderer James Rivers was doing time for hacking up his son-in-law with an axe. Put those two butchers in a cell together and you had to wonder: which one is more nervous to go to sleep at night?

Rivers was a heavyset guy with a heart problem and had monthly appointments with a cardiologist outside the prison. After one of those visits, I had the police bring him to me at the state police barracks instead of back to his cell.

He was sequestered in a back room with chains on his arms and ankles, angry as hell, wondering what was happening, when I walked in.

"Mr. Rivers, I'm Bob Hilland from the FBI."

"Well, well, well," he said, with a sneer. "So, *you're* the famous Bob Hilland I've been hearing all about."

I asked the police to remove his chains and motioned for him to join me at a table.

My goal was to find out if Smith had divulged anything about Fran — what he'd done to her, where he'd put her. Was there a plywood box between here and Timbuktu with Fran's well-preserved body in it?

Anytime you talk to someone in jail, nine out of the ten things they're going to tell you will be lies. They want to get out, so they'll tell you anything. And as well as a murderer, Rivers was a known con man, too. He proceeded to blow smoke up my ass for hours, with bizarre stories about Smith that my own internal human bullshit detector rejected.

After three hours of his BS, I ordered pizza. Eating was a good way to break down barriers. Sharing such a primal act creates a unique bond; the conversation gets more real.

"Let me tell you something," Rivers said, eyeing me as he shoved a slice in his mouth. "If Smith ever gets out of jail, you've got a problem."

"What do you mean?" I asked. "He'll kill more women?"

"Oh, he'll do that for sure," said Rivers, spitting out bits of pepperoni. "But you, Bob Hilland, *you* have a problem."

"What's my problem?"

He chewed another mouthful and swallowed.

"Smith's afraid of you. He's afraid if he ever gets out, you'd kill him. He also says, 'There can't be that many women with the last name "Hilland" in the New York area.' So, if you have a daughter or a wife and Smith gets out of jail, you have a problem. Any female with your last name is going to disappear."

His words jolted me. If I was angry and focused before, now it was multiplied by a thousand. Not only did I need to prevent

Smith from ever killing again, I had to keep him away from my family. I needed to keep my wife and children safe.

Along with as my search for Fran, something else continued in a way I didn't expect — my collaboration with John Edward. I'd gone to him about the Smith case and considered the New Jersey police officer tip, the George Bush warning, and the 9/11 tattoo premonition as collateral bonuses, if you will. Since Smith was now behind bars, I wasn't sure if — or how — our sleuthing partnership would evolve.

Apparently, the Other Side was certain. They had plans.

"My guides trust you," John repeated, when I went to him about a case later that year. "You and I have a unique karmic tie. We were probably connected in another lifetime."

"Another *lifetime?*"

"Yeah. Maybe we were like Sherlock Holmes and Watson in previous lives."

"Really?"

"Definitely."

Talking to dead people was one thing. Past lives and reincarnation were too much for this Lutheran to absorb. I mean, how far out of one's compartmentalized comfort zone could one man — especially a structured, just-the-facts guy — mentally, emotionally, and psychologically go?

Back in New York after training was over, I was officially assigned to the Polygraph Unit in Manhattan. Which, of course, didn't mean I stayed in that lane.

The new case I took to John Edward was an unsolved double murder mystery in Florida. It came to me courtesy of then-journalist and *20/20* co-anchor John Miller, whom I'd gotten to know when he covered the Smith case.

Miller was friends with siblings Sheila and Bill Tendy, Jr., two former prosecutors who were now in private law practices in the New York area. Everybody knew about their father, William Tendy, Sr., the US Attorney for the Southern District of New York, who'd passed away in 1986.

The Tendys were dear friends with the family of one of the murder victims, Chris Benedetto. So close, in fact, that they considered him a cousin. Chris's parents died when he was 19, only six months apart from each other. The Tendy family embraced him and his siblings as their own.

On a chilly winter evening near the end of 2002, I trekked uptown to meet Sheila at the famous Upper East Side eatery

Elaine's, where she told me the tragic story.

Chris and his wife, Janette Piro, were living a simple, happy life by the beach on Florida's oceanfront peninsula, Singer Island. In their early forties, they'd retired early after Chris received a million-dollar settlement after falling off scaffolding at work and fracturing his spine.

"Chris was dynamic," Sheila described, "handsome, strapping, he loved to cook. He was a very endearing guy and would do anything for you. The ladies loved him."

But he was crazy in love with Janette, who was "just as dynamic and pretty. They were inseparable."

In November 1998, the couple went missing. After nearly two weeks of frantic searching by friends, family, and police, two of Benedetto's brothers, both police officers, found Janette dead in a freezer in the couple's garage. Police who'd searched the house before had missed the bait freezer, which was tucked under a workbench.

Janette's body was there, but Chris was nowhere to be found. There was no forced entry into the house, no sign of struggle. Missing from Janette's wedding finger — her beautiful, custom-made, $58,000 diamond ring.

It didn't take long before the Tendys and

local police had a suspect — Janette's New Jersey–based brother-in-law, Michael Koblan — "Big Mike," he was called. The day the couple went missing, Mike and Chris had gone fishing together to sort out a money conflict they were having. As witnessed by a neighbor by the boat dock, only Mike returned in Chris's boat — alone. As family compared notes, there was talk of Mike being a gambler and having connections and shady business with the New Jersey mob.

Even with this information, the investigation dragged on. "We didn't find the investigative skills of the police to be so crackerjack," says Sheila.

So, she and her brother Bill began investigating themselves. Through law enforcement connections, they learned of an inmate in New York's Otisville prison who might have information. Kenny Marino, in jail for several bank robberies, was a mob associate — one of those guys who knew unsavory types and had the dirt on everyone. He'd been a reliable informant for other law enforcement officials over the years.

The Tendys urged the FBI in Florida to get involved. Agents there pulled Marino out of prison, flew him to Florida, and interviewed him.

Mike Koblan owed money to a high-ranking

mob guy, Marino claimed, and they threatened to kill him if he didn't pay them back. He borrowed a few hundred thousand from Chris to get the mob off his back, promising to pay it back. But when months turn into years, and Mike still hadn't paid the money he owed Chris, his brother-in-law confronted him.

"Pay me back," Chris told him, "Or I'm going to the FBI to tell them about you and your friends from New Jersey — including a certain mob associate."

Chris and Mike arranged to go fishing to discuss the matter.

"Koblan flew out from New Jersey to Florida using an alias," said Marino, "went out on the boat, shot Chris in the back of the head, then tied the anchor to his body and threw him overboard."

When he arrived at Janette's door after the murder, of course she let him in — he was her brother-in-law.

"He strangled her," said Marino, "took the ring off her finger, and stuffed her in the freezer."

Once he got back on the East Coast, Mike took the ring to a jeweler in Manhattan's Lower East Side — a friend of his, and the same jeweler who'd custom-made the ring. He had the jeweler break down the diamond into smaller pieces so he could sell them for cash.

The information was so damning, Sheila and the rest of the family thought for sure it would lead to Mike's arrest. But it didn't.

Four years after Janette's body was found, the case was still "unsolved."

Why? Because the FBI in Florida conducted a polygraph exam on informant Marino and he failed it, so they dismissed him as a liar and put him back on the plane to Otisville. They didn't even pursue the information on the jeweler.

"Agent Hilland, my father raised my brother and I to seek and do justice," said Sheila. "Please, can you help us?"

I wasn't on the Cold Case Squad anymore, and even if I was this case was out of my jurisdiction, it belonged to Florida. *And* it was sacrilegious to mess with another agent's open case or talk to one of their sources, especially if they've been dismissed. This case was untouchable for me.

And yet. After my months of polygraph training, I knew that while the body never lied sometimes other things got in the way of a conclusive test result. Like life, polygraphs were not always black and white, as I had thought, and as I was discovering. I hadn't seen Marino's polygraph exam but, for many reasons, there was a chance his information was good. Enough of a chance to pursue that jeweler.

I devised a cover story so I wouldn't get jammed up.

First, I went to Otisville and talked to Kenny Marino myself, getting him to repeat the full story in detail. I didn't polygraph him; I couldn't break the rules that far. But even though I knew prisoners lie like hell to get out of jail, I felt the information he provided should be followed up on. It was too specific and detailed to not be true. It had the ring of truth.

The next day I called up the Florida FBI office and spoke with the agent in charge of the Benedetto case.

"Hey, I'm up here in New York on a case and I happen to be in Otisville conducting an unrelated investigation and I interviewed this source, guy's name is Kenny Marino. He told me about this case you were working on, something about a jeweler and a diamond and two victims down there."

As soon as I mentioned Marino, the agent went off.

"That lying piece of shit!" he yelled. "We flew him down here and he lied. Don't believe a word he's saying to you!"

"I hear ya . . . but hey, this jeweler is right

here in Manhattan. If you want, I can go over and talk to him no problem . . ."

"Bob, I appreciate the call but no thanks. It's a waste of time."

In other words, leave my case alone. Door closed.

The next week, I passed by John Edward's studio when he was on break from taping and asked if his guides had any thoughts about a jeweler I intended to flip.

John immediately got a visual.

"This jeweler is a little guy," he said. "He's a cagey little rat. Oh, man, he's going to shit himself when he sees you. He's not the kind of guy who would do well in jail. Tell him that. You should tell him that. It will have an effect."

A few days later, I returned to John's studio — this time with Sheila Tendy. She brought items belonging to Chris and Janette and settled on the leather couch for a reading. I told John she was linked to a murder I was looking at, but that was it. He didn't know Sheila and the murder had anything to do with the jeweler I'd asked about.

After a few pleasantries, John went right into it, doing that thing he does.

"You're married. You have two children. Their names start with the letters . . ."

John began listing names, letters, people. Sheila nodded and nodded.

"They're telling me your son has psychic ability, did you know that?"

They talked a bit about it.

"All children are born with the ability, but because we live in a world that doesn't allow it to develop, it wanes over time. If you're able to cultivate that in him, you should."

Sheila agreed and nodded some more.

John paused.

"Um. May I be personal with you?" John asked.

Uh-oh.

"Yes," she said.

"You have two children, but they're telling me you had three pregnancies . . ."

My heart skipped a beat. Sheila's eyes looked sad, but she nodded.

John mentioned Sheila's brother Bill, and that they were both involved in law.

"But you have other law enforcement in the family, too," he said. "Someone who's passed, above you. Wow, his energy is taking up the whole room! Your *father.*"

Sheila smiled.

"That sounds like him."

For the next hour, Sheila's famous father — who'd passed sixteen years earlier — dominated the reading with the excitement of a father reuniting with his cherished daughter. He also had some scolding to do.

"Your father's saying that in your mother's bedroom, there's a bookshelf filled with junk," said John. "And in the middle of all that junk, there's a vinyl record of your mother singing from a radio program from, like, the 1950s."

Sheila's eyes widened.

"This is incredible," she said.

She explained that her mother was a professional opera singer before getting married and having seven kids. The existence of the record, on that shelf filled with junk, was something no one would know about.

"Your father is saying you need to protect that record," said John. "It shouldn't be sitting in a pile of junk in the bedroom on the bookshelf."

"He's right!" Sheila said, with a laugh. "He's so right."

After father and daughter finished a happy, tearful catching up, the revered federal prosecutor got to work on the case.

"Your father is saying someone to your side is with him there. Like a brother to you. I'm getting a C or K sound . . . a Cuh. Not an S sound like Cynthia . . . a Chris or a Christine."

Sheila nodded. "Chris."

His body hadn't been found. But even though everyone knew he was dead, hearing it from John made it real.

"He's with your father and with his parents," said John. "They are all together, it's important you know that. He died from an impact to the head?"

"We think so."

"I'm asking more about it," said John. "They're showing me a casino and slot machines. Someone involved was a gambler."

"Yes."

Sheila and I exchanged a glance. *Koblan.*

"They're showing me Chris's watch. It's in the cove. The cove he always went to. If you look, you'll find his watch there."

After John gave more details, I pulled out a file folder from my briefcase.

"Sheila, I'm going to show John photos from Janette's crime scene. Maybe you want to leave the room for this part?"

She shook her head. "I'll be okay."

But when I opened the folder, I could see the pain on Sheila's face when she saw them. She'd seen photos like this many times in her work, but it was different when the victim was someone you know. *Family.*

John looked at the photos intently.

"Someone's wearing this woman's ring," he said. "This woman . . . she has a J-name, like Jenny or Janet . . . her ring is on another woman's finger. They're showing me someone wearing her ring."

I looked at Sheila and we both thought the same thing.

Marino is telling the truth. We had to get to that jeweler.

The cagey little rat of a jeweler, as John saw him, was key to this case — damn whatever the FBI in Florida said.

Marino had given us the name of the jewelry store. I staked it out for a few days, and five minutes before closing one day, I walked in with an NYPD detective and flipped the OPEN sign to CLOSED.

Until he saw our badges, I think the guy thought we were about to rob him.

"Am I in trouble?" he asked, looking up at me, afraid.

He was just as John described him, a weaselly little rat.

"Should you be?" I answered.

I put a photo of Janette's diamond ring in front of him and watched the color drain from his face.

"You are either one of two things," I said. "Either you're one of those guys tied to the mob who fences stolen diamonds taken from the bodies of dead women for a piece of the profit," I said, "or you're a family jewelry shop owner trying to get by and make a living. Now, I don't know what Koblan told you . . ."

"He said he needed to sell the ring to raise cash to help search for Chris and Janette," the jewelry guy squeaked.

"You and I both know that's bullshit," I said.

"Problem is, now he's involved you in something you don't want to be a part of. Here's the deal: I know you made the ring. I know you sold it to Chris Benedetto. And I know Koblan brought it back to you, and you cut it up into little pieces. So, you have a decision to make . . ."

Now I used John Edward's line, with extra emphasis.

". . . because to be honest, *you're so not the type of guy who's going to do well in prison.*"

The little guy looked up at me — way up — and shriveled even more. I could see him flip before my eyes. A minute later, he confessed everything.

A few days after that, I wired him up, and he made a call to Mike Koblan. The script was similar to what I'd given Smith's brother years before.

"The fucking FBI is up my ass, Mike, and I'm scared to death about this thing," he said to Koblan. They talked about the murder. I was recording it all.

The next day, I called the FBI office in Florida and talked to the Benedetto agent.

"Hey, I got something you're gonna be interested in."

I put the recording to the phone and pushed PLAY.

"Holy shit!" the agent said. Funny, but he didn't care anymore that I'd gone out of my lane.

In June 2003, Michael Koblan was charged in a five-count federal indictment with the murders of Chris Benedetto and Janette Piro. At his trial, he was found guilty of all five counts and sentenced to two life terms in prison.

"I feel like my father was present throughout the entire case," Sheila said. "Everywhere we turned, and I don't say that lightly, somebody connected to my father popped out of the woodwork to offer assistance."

Sheila Tendy's father came through loud and clear from the Other Side to help his daughter find justice. It was the family business, after all, to put criminals away. He had taught her well. It was also very touching to watch her reconnect with a father who'd been so loving and inspirational to her.

During all this, I couldn't help but notice an interesting parallel happening for John Edward and me with our own fathers.

We didn't know this in the beginning, but one of the energetic pulls that brought John and me together was how similar our fathers were, and our respective need for their validations.

Our dads were not like Sheila's. They didn't tell us they loved us or that they were proud of us. It was a lack John and I recognized in each other subconsciously, and one we help each other heal from.

By helping me solve crimes, John by proxy was getting validation from his police officer father. On my end, I had tried to be a "super cop" to get my father's attention. I excelled in sports for the same reason. I threw myself into the FBI and tried to catch serial killers for the same reason — to get my father's attention.

That year, around the time Sheila's incredible father showed up, something shifted for John and me and our fathers. The timing was eerie.

In early 2002, the infamous, dial-a-psychic lady with the fake Jamaican accent, "Miss Cleo," was accused of fraud by the Federal Trade Commission. John got a rare email from his father, John Sr.

It's people like this that make what you do look bad, his father wrote.

"I can't believe it," John said, when he told me about it. "That was a compliment coming from him. And the only validation he's ever given me about my work. I'm going to have to *frame* this," he laughed.

John had heard secondhand from his aunts that his father was proud of his success with *Crossing Over,* but he never heard it directly from his father.

That September, two weeks after the 9/11 anniversary, John became a father for the first time when his son, Justin, was born. Like me, he vowed to be a different kind of father than his own.

Six weeks after that, right around the time I was meeting Sheila at Elaine's, John's father passed away from diabetes and throat cancer. The two had been out of touch, and news of his death was a shock to John, who didn't know he was ill. Even though he has psychic abilities, John still was a human learning his own earthly lessons. His father-son pattern was one of them.

They hadn't mended their differences before he died, but instead of being upset by that, John was optimistic.

"Now that he's on the Other Side, we can probably start having a relationship for the first time," he told me.

"What do you mean?" I asked. Like our

conversation about past lives and reincarnation, this was a new, foreign concept for me to grasp.

"My guides have shown me that when a person crosses over, the first thing they do is reflect on the life they led here and the choices they made. They try to understand their decisions and see how their actions affected others. And they see what they still need to learn while on the Other Side."

"We learn on the Other Side?"

"Our learning doesn't stop just because our bodies do. In fact, we can probably learn faster on the Other Side because we're no longer dragged down by earthly obstacles. If you think of it like school, life on earth is like kindergarten, and we're distracted by toys. When we get to the Other Side, we're in college."

"But how can you and your father have a better relationship now?"

"Not only does learning continue," John explained, "but so does the exchange of energies between two people. We can communicate with our loved ones after they've passed. If the relationship was troubled, you can continue to work on it. Especially because the person on the Other Side has grown wiser and cleaned their energy of negative patterns. I already feel a different 'vibration' between my father and me because I can drop my guard against the established relationship dynamic and allow myself to heal on a different level."

I wished the same was true for my father and me. All I ever wanted was for him to believe in me.

One of my favorite inspirational speeches is "Cutting Down the Nets" by legendary basketball coach Jim Valvano. I first heard it in 1990, when I was a recruit at the police academy. In the speech, Valvano says the greatest gift his father gave him was having faith in him.

"He believed in me. Even when I wasn't the best son, father, husband, coach, friend. When I didn't live up to my own expectations. My father always said, 'You're going to make it. I know you will. And when you do, I will be there with you. My bags are packed.' "

It spoke to my heart. Like John, I'd heard from others that my father talked about me as if he was proud, but he never told me himself. And every young man needs his father's affirmation.

But was my father capable?

I took a cue from John and tried to change the vibration between my father and me while we were both still alive, on *this* side. Maybe we still had time.

In June 2003, I dropped my father and mother off at a Marriott Hotel on Long Island for a one-on-one reading with John Edward.

Somehow, I felt like the key to breaking down the walls between my father and me was related to breaking down rigid beliefs, and the black-and-white thinking I'd learned from him. It had something to do with learning, stretching, and widening our comfort zones, as I was trying to do with my work with John. It was about realizing there was a universe of gray residing between the black and white.

And maybe I wanted them to meet John and understand my world and what I was doing and trust it and me. I wanted them to pack their bags for me.

I made the appointment in secret through John's assistant, without him knowing. I didn't tell my parents where I was taking them until we arrived at the hotel, and then I explained.

My father was resistant; my mother was curious. I sent them down the hallway and I waited in the lobby bar. When they walked into John's suite, he had no idea who they were.

An hour later when they returned, both my parents were wide-eyed, astonished, and emotional. They had a look of profound shock on their faces.

On the two-hour drive back to Jersey, my mother replayed every moment of the reading — the details of their parents coming through, the specifics John couldn't have known about them and their lives and their past but did.

"You and John could be brothers, you look so much alike," my mother said.

For much of the drive, my father was speechless. He kept shaking his head, saying, "How did he know that? How did he *know* that?"

He reminded me of my first meeting with John, when my belief system felt like a snow globe that had been shaken up.

Looking at my father in the passenger seat, I wondered if he was experiencing what John would call an "energy shift" and if the vibration between us would change.

Or maybe, like John and his dad, we'd have to wait until one of us was on the Other Side to finally mend our father-son relationship.

19

THE HONEYMOONERS

In early 2005 I moved the family to upstate New York and joined the FBI office in Albany.

Alex had fallen in love with the state's capitol and yearned for a change. And, fed up with my overly long workdays, she wanted me to arrange a job closer to home to cut down on commute time. The kids were getting older, too — Connor and Caitie were turning ten and eight — and I wanted to be more involved in their lives.

So north we went, settling in a beautiful home on the west bank of the Hudson River.

Alex and the kids loved it, but only months into it I found the move professionally stifling. After seven years at the FBI's flagship office in Manhattan, embroiled in cases of big money, murder, and the mafia, I struggled to downsize my ambition to fit the bureau's smallest office where the investigations paled in comparison to those in New York.

Maybe it was my ego that needed downsizing? For too long I'd linked my identity and self-worth to my professional success, to saving people. As John Edward might say, there was a lesson for me to learn in this.

It wasn't long, though, before I was crossing seas and oceans again, figuratively anyway. And John knew about it before I did.

In the summer of 2005, John and I were having dinner at a steakhouse in Albany — he was holding an event nearby — when he suddenly looked up at me from across the table in surprise.

"Hey!" he says, "you and Alex are going on a cruise?"

"What?"

"Yeah. Like, next week."

I dug into my ribeye and laughed.

"I have no idea what you're talking about."

After six years with John, you'd think I'd know better.

"They're showing me a cruise ship," he insisted. "I'm telling you; you're going on a ship."

He stopped midsentence, fork in air.

"Oh, wait. You'll be working a case *involving* a cruise ship. That's what it is."

I continued to argue with him about it (I mean, why? *Why?*), telling him he was wrong.

Meanwhile, thousands of miles away in turquoise Mediterranean waters, a murder was taking place.

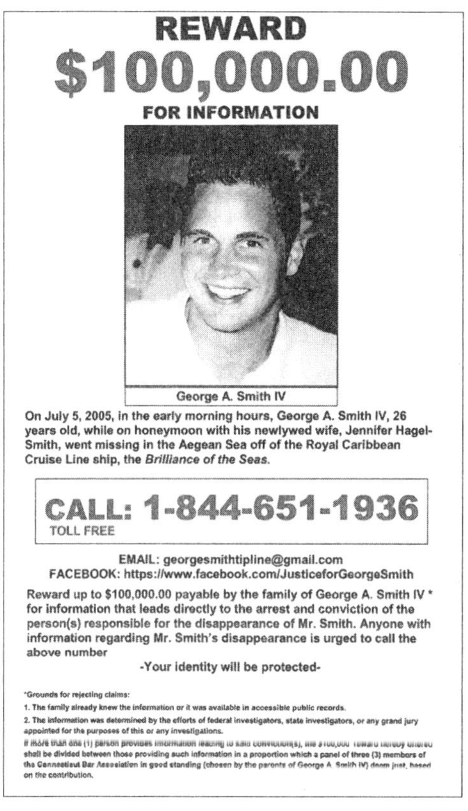

Poster seeking information about George Smith's disappearance aboard a cruise ship

On June 29, newlyweds George and Jennifer Smith, both Connecticut natives, boarded Royal Caribbean's *Brilliance of the Seas* cruise ship in Barcelona, Spain, and set sail on a two-week honeymoon.

George was a handsome former football star who came from an affluent family.

Jennifer was a beautiful honey-blond schoolteacher. In their twenties, they were just beginning their perfect life together.

Less than a week later, George went missing on the *Brilliance of the Seas*. Blood was splattered on one of the ship's lifeboats. Did he fall or was he pushed? It was a mystery.

The case hadn't hit the news yet when John and I were wolfing down our steaks, but it did a few days later. I still hadn't seen the headlines when I got a call from an FBI supervisor in New Haven, Connecticut.

"Bobby, I need your help with a difficult case. Did you see the cruise ship story in the news? We need you to come and talk to the wife."

Holy shit.

I called John right away.

"Hey, remember you said I was going on a cruise? I just got assigned a case on a cruise ship."

"The one in the news today?"

"Yeah. I'm going to polygraph the wife of the guy who's missing."

Pause.

"I'm not feeling it's her."

"Oh? Well, I don't really know details yet. But there must be a reason they're asking me to interview her . . ."

"All I'm telling you," John repeated, with

utmost confidence, "is that I'm not getting a feeling like she's involved. I'm getting the feeling she had nothing to do with it."

"Okay . . ."

He paused again.

"When you talk to her, there will be pieces of the night she won't remember. She won't remember a lot of things. People are interpreting that like she's deliberately hiding something. But the reason she doesn't remember is because she was drinking."

"Got it. I'll keep that in mind."

"One last thing," he said. "There's more to the story that they're not telling you."

"Who's 'they'?"

"The FBI."

"John, I work for the FBI."

"Yeah, I get that. But they're not telling you the whole story."

"Why wouldn't they tell me the whole story? I'm on their team."

"I'm just the messenger, Bob. All I can tell you is what they're showing me."

The next day I set up my polygraph equipment at the FBI office in New Haven, preparing to interview Jennifer Smith, fresh off a flight from Turkey.

A group of high-ranking agents gathered in the observation room next door, behind a two-way mirror. With so much media attention on the case, they were under a lot of pressure to solve it.

The information I knew so far was scant. The couple had an argument a few hours before George disappeared, that was it. The agent leading the case was a brash, young, new guy in the bureau. His lack of experience and my history working homicide was the reason I was asked to help — not only to polygraph Jennifer but to coach the agent along the way, too.

As I set up, he offered his opinion of the case.

"The wife hasn't told us everything," he said. "She's conveniently not remembering important parts of the night. There was some type of domestic on the ship between her and George. I think she may have hooked up with somebody on the ship. I don't believe her.

"This is a domestic gone wrong. She's denying it."

The agent left to take a seat in the observation room with the others and left me in a state of confusion. John Edward said she didn't do it; the agent in charge of the case said she did. Both were adamant.

Minutes later, I would find out for myself.

Jennifer Smith arrived — young, beautiful, and devastated.

I began the pretest by asking her to walk me through a timeline of events for July 4, the day her husband went missing. The ship had docked in Mykonos, Greece, she said, and the happy couple spent the day touring the island in the searing sun.

"We were drinking beers all day and smuggled a bottle of Absolut Vodka onto the ship," she said. It was taboo, but cruise guests were often guilty of this misdemeanor because alcohol was so expensive aboard the ship.

And the newlyweds wanted to drink. A lot.

Before dinner, they downed vodka and Red Bulls in their cabin, then continued with wine at the meal. During dessert, they ordered Irish coffees. Jennifer drank so much that she ran to the bathroom and threw up.

She went back to the room, changed clothes, and they went to the casino where they drank more. After the casino closed, they moved to the disco and drank more, still. It was estimated that George had at least 16–22 drinks in his system that night, mixed with prescription meds. Jennifer wasn't far behind.

"Do you remember having a fight with George at the casino?" I asked.

"I remember some guy trying to dance between me and George and George got upset and called me a 'whore.' That's the last thing I remember," she said, sadly.

There will be pieces of the night she won't remember, John said, *because she was drinking.*

According to crew members, security found Jennifer passed out in a chair in another section of the ship at 4:30 A.M. and took her back to her room in a wheelchair. George was not there. The ship sailed on from Greece to Turkey, and a few hours later, passengers on their way to breakfast saw a large amount of blood splattered on a lifeboat. George was still nowhere to be found.

"If George was murdered or thrown off the ship, what do you think should happen to the murderer?"

"I want them held responsible," she said, upset. "I want them to go to prison."

"Did you have relations with any other man on the ship?"

"No."

Jennifer talked about her husband, George, like a woman in love with a man who was still alive.

"George is a great guy," she said to me, through tears, "you would love him. You have to meet him."

"Do you think George is still with us now?"

She broke down.

"I love George. My life is destroyed. All our hopes and plans are gone. I can't live without him."

The first set of questions were "behavioral analysis questions." With the polygraph sensors now attached, I asked Jennifer more targeted questions to determine what happened on that ship.

"Are you withholding any information about what happened on that ship?"

"No."

"Are you withholding any information about George's disappearance?"

"No."

The results of the test corroborated what my gut and her demeanor told me from the first moments I met Jennifer. She had the cleanest test charts I'd ever seen, not a whiff of deception. This young woman was telling the truth.

I walked into the next room with the paper in my hand. The group behind the two-way mirror were expecting me to say she failed the test.

"Look," I said. "I'm not discounting what you think happened. But based on my interaction with her and the results of the polygraph, she had *nothing* to do with her husband's disappearance."

The case agent sighed. The others had a look of confusion on their faces.

"Dammit, there must be more to the story with the European kids from Brooklyn," muttered the case agent.

"What European kids?" I asked. "What are you talking about?"

"The night that George disappeared, he was last seen partying with some European kids from Brooklyn."

I could hear John Edward's warning ringing in my ears: *There's more to the story that they're not telling you.*

"Wait a minute," I said. "You led me to believe Jennifer was lying. Meanwhile, there's more to the story? Why didn't you tell me?"

"I didn't want to overload you with information," he said. "I wanted to resolve this issue with Jennifer first."

The last people to see George Smith alive was a group of young men, aged 16–20, on vacation with their parents. Three were of Eastern European background from Brooklyn — Ronald, Gary, and Jack — and the fourth was Jimmy, a kid from Florida they met on the cruise.

Questioned by Turkish officials as soon as

the boat docked on its next stop, the young men claimed they had drinks with George then helped him back to his room and put him to bed.

I rushed to a phone and called John.

At this point, I trusted him and his guides way more than I trusted my own colleagues. I told him what happened.

"And she tested clean, John, she had nothing to do with it. Just like you said. And then they told me this whole tangential thing about these Europeans . . ."

I could practically hear his intake of breath.

As soon as I said "European," John fired away. He described them like they were standing in front of his face. This one has severe acne. This one was a big guy with a tattoo. This one's a little guy with a Napoleonic complex.

"He's the alpha male," John said. "The smaller one. He's orchestrating the others and telling them what to do. A real condescending ass."

I frantically took notes. John took a breath.

"Did you see the tape?" he asked. "There's a tape."

"What tape?"

"You've got to find the videotape, Bob. *There's a videotape. Look at the video.*"

I could feel John's distress rising.

He described a violent struggle in one of the ship's cabins between George and the boys, with George too intoxicated to fend them off.

"Oh, my God, Bob," he blurted out, horrified. "I can see them holding him by his feet upside down off the balcony. Then they let him go."

Both of us were quiet for a moment.

"You'll have a chance to get a confession," he said. "But you'll only get one shot at it."

"What's the shot?"

"You're going to get one of these European kids by himself. The big guy with the tattoo. And if you play it right, he'll talk."

It would take a lot of interviews and CC footage over the next few weeks to piece together what happened that night, but it went something like this, according to law enforcement's theory of the case:

While the intoxicated newlyweds danced at the disco, the boys from Brooklyn watched. Trying to impress his buddies, the puny ringleader, Gary, got up and started grinding against Jennifer on the dancefloor, simulating sex acts.

When George realized what was going on, he grabbed Gary and wound up for a punch. His buddies rushed to the dance floor and intervened. Jennifer was crying. George was highly intoxicated, disoriented, and raging with anger and jealousy. The couple argued and she staggered away, ultimately finding a chair to pass out in.

Meanwhile, the European guys tried to calm George down. At their table, they offered stealthy shots of absinthe — once banned in the US because it's so strong — that they smuggled onto the ship.

George tossed back the shots, and soon bragged loudly about his fabulous wedding and the cash he had in his room. Fifteen thousand dollars as wedding presents, he said, but the Europeans misheard and thought he said $50,000. That error might have cost him his life.

They "helped" George back to his room with the intention to steal that $50,000. After dropping George on the bed, they quickly woke him up with a sense of urgency and told him "Jennifer is not here, we need to go look for her."

Two of the four boys ushered him out to the hallway and the other two began ransacking the room, looking for the cash.

But moments after leaving the room, George felt sick and returned, catching the two Europeans looking for the money. All hell broke loose and a fight ensued.

The boys beat the hell out of George, took

him out on the balcony, and dropped him into the dark night waters.

Basically, what the investigation strongly suggested is that it was a robbery gone terribly wrong.

I called a colleague, a supervisor in the White-Collar Crime Squad in Manhattan, and asked him to run the boys' names through the system to see if they were involved in any cases. This specific European group in Brooklyn were well-known to be involved in every conceivable type of fraud scheme. This is why I reached out for the White-Collar supervisor.

He called back fast.

"Bob, you're not going to believe this. We picked up Ronald about two months ago. He was working the phones making cold calls in a boiler room operation."

You're going to get one of these guys by himself, John said. *You'll have a chance to get a confession. One shot.*

I thought up a plan and immediately called John to strategize.

"One of the boys was picked up on a separate case," I told him.

"Bob, this is it," said John. "This is the opportunity I was talking about. He's the one-off."

John paused.

"He's the big, muscular guy, right?"

I checked the photo and description my colleague had emailed.

"Yup."

"Okay, listen. *This is the guy.* He's scared to death, but you gotta play it right. Create a ruse. Bring him in under one pretense and then talk to him about the cruise guy."

I told John about the boiler room operation that I could bring Ronald in to talk about.

"Perfect," said John. "He'll come in. And at some point, he's going to ask you for a cigarette. That's when you really gotta inflate the kid's ego. That's the moment that will put you on the yellow brick road. He's insecure. He's big, but he's like a child."

"Got it."

"And then you've got to play like you're going to use him for a bigger case."

"Right."

"He'll be angry at one of his friends, the little one. The ringleader. Use that anger. He'll bite on it."

"Okay."

"And his father. He's afraid of his father. He doesn't want him to find out about any of this. Bring up the father."

"I will."

Once again, I was scribbling notes as fast as I could.

"If he doesn't confess when you talk with him, you have to figure out where he'll go or who he'll call once he leaves your office."

"Will do."

"And Bob," he said, with an anxious tone. "The videotape. They're telling me it's important. Have you seen it yet?"

"Not yet."

That was my next call.

I got the case agent on the phone, the one who assumed Jennifer was guilty. The one who didn't tell me about the Eastern Europeans.

"Have you told me everything about this case?" I pressed.

Apparently not. There was one other thing. *A videotape.*

After George went missing from the boat and the blood was discovered on the lifeboat, the ship docked in Turkey and police interviewed the four boys. Other guests had seen them with George at the disco.

As Turkish authorities questioned the boys, one of the parents secretly videotaped the interview. The boys told their unconvincing story — that they helped George back to his cabin and left him to sleep it off. They were released.

They boarded the ship, with their parents' video camera in hand.

I imagine they felt pretty high after that. As if they'd gotten away with murder — which maybe they had. The boys strutted down the ship's deck like a wild pack of wolves and surrounded two teenage girls in a hot tub.

One was an innocent 17-year-old, I'll call her Jane. She was on the cruise with her best friend and the friend's parents.

Out came the absinthe. The boys coerced the girls to drink. After a few shots, Jane felt sick and wanted to go back to her room. The boys offered to escort her, but took her to one of their rooms instead, where three of them had sex with her and videotaped the incident.

When she regained consciousness in her own room, she ran to the ship's doctor in tears. The doctor alerted the captain, who realized these were the same boys questioned about missing George Smith.

The ship's security team searched the boys' rooms and seized the video camera.

Look at the video, John Edward told me.

At the New Haven office, I searched through the evidence file and found it — a DVD copy of the video from one of the parents' cameras, turned over by Caribbean security. I slipped the disc into my laptop and nearly went out of my mind.

Although the boys later claimed that the tape contained evidence of "consent," it was clear to me from what I saw that this girl was raped and abused in other ways.

I pressed REWIND.

An earlier scene showed the European boys eating a hearty breakfast in the dining room. They passed the camera around, seemingly joking and boasting about what they did to George Smith.

What they said was, "He went parasailing without the parachute," laughing hysterically.

The group high-fived one another and devoured their pancakes.

My next chat with the case agent was tense.

"The Turkish authorities saw this video?" I asked. "These guys are boasting about killing George Smith and assaulting a girl. It's all captured on this videotape!"

The agent shrugged.

"They don't want to deal with it," he said. "They saw it and said it looked like a drunk American girl having fun."

I was stunned.

"And what about the boys and George Smith?"

Turkish authorities were deferring prosecution to the United States concerning George.

The jurisdiction question was a tricky one. The FBI had authority to investigate crimes involving American citizens regardless of where the crime occurred, but prosecuting was another matter. If a crime happened in a foreign country's waters, that country typically had first right of refusal. If the crime happened on "international" waters, cases were typically prosecuted by the US Attorney's offices in New York, DC, or Miami.

In this case, the sexual incident happened in Mediterranean waters, and the suspected murder happened somewhere between Greece and Turkey.

I called John again, sick to my stomach.

"I saw the videotape," I told him. "We have to get these guys."

"Bring that kid in, the big one," John repeated. "Gain his trust. Then flip him against the others. But be careful. He's a big guy, but he's like a little boy. He's scared to go to jail."

"He should be."

"He's more scared than the others," said

John. "And it's going to be a problem for you."

"Why?"

"Because two guys held George Smith upside-down and threw him into the water. I can see it. And the big guy knows who."

Like John said, I needed to get this kid alone. I needed him to talk.

I coordinated with my friend in the White-Collar Crime Squad to arrange for Ronald to come into the Manhattan office under the pretense that we needed his help with the European fraud scheme.

When he arrived, I presented myself as the supervisor of the squad and began asking questions. Ronald was a big, muscular guy, like John said. About 6'2" and 250 pounds. We sat in a polygraph room across from each other at a small table, two hulking men balancing on creaky metal folding chairs.

Ronald was chatty, but nervous. I began the process of blowing smoke up his ass.

"Look, Ronald, I'm going to be upfront with you," I said. "You're a small fish in a big pond, right? We don't care about a young kid who's cold-calling people. But we do keep our eyes open for people who can help us in other cases. Big ones. And you seem like a street-smart kid."

"Yeah."

"Do you have any interest in working undercover?"

"What do you mean?"

"We have another very high-level case we're working on. I'm thinking, depending on your ability, we could educate you about it and plant you in the scheme. We want you to work for us, but I've got to know you can think on your feet."

Ronald's nervousness turned into excitement.

"I can do that."

"This is going to be one of the biggest cases the FBI has ever worked on," I continued, "and I'd be putting my reputation on the line for you, which I'm happy to do. But if I'm going to do that and make you my guy, I've got to know what skeletons you have in your closet."

He was a kid from Brooklyn, already running with criminals. There was no way he was going to resist my next move; it was a beauty.

"You remember John Gotti, the boss of the Gambino crime family?"

Ronald's eyes widened.

"Sure, I do."

"How about Sammy 'The Bull' Gravano?"

"Yeah, of course!"

"Well, Sammy 'The Bull' killed 19 people, Ronald. But the government didn't charge him with any of those because he helped us dismantle the Gambino crime family."

I leaned forward on the table.

"The case I want you to work on is *bigger* than that. So, I don't care if you have baggage. I don't care if you've killed 19 people. But before we go any further, I need to know your skeletons."

And then it happened.

"Can I have a cigarette?" he asked.

I could hear John's voice in my head: *He's going to ask for a cigarette. That's the moment.*

I wasn't a smoker, and it wasn't allowed in the FBI offices. But I always kept a pack handy for subjects who did. Sometimes, I joined them. Like eating together, it built rapport. I specially made sure to bring some today, because of what John said.

I slid a pack of Marlboros across the table. He put a cigarette in his mouth and I lit it for him. Ronald took a thoughtful, clumsy drag.

"Well," he says, "there's this one thing . . ."

He began talking about the cruise ship. I played dumb.

"What cruise ship? You mean the one they're talking about on TV?" I asked.

"Yeah."

"You were on that ship?"

"Yeah. Me and some friends, we met that guy."

He went on to give me the same white-washed story they gave the Turkish police. The boys bumped into George, partied with him, helped him back to his room, and tucked him in.

"What happened after that?" I asked.

"Nothing."

"Ronald, you're not telling me anything," I said. "That's not a skeleton. Are you telling me you killed this guy? Because if you did, I don't care. This cruise ship case is meaningless to me. I'm worried about my big fraud case. I don't give a shit about some kid being thrown off a cruise ship."

Ronald was quiet, trying to figure out what to do.

"So do us both a favor," I said. "Don't bullshit me and say you're not involved. Let's get it out in the open so we can start working on this other case together."

He fidgeted. He was about to explode. Almost.

Instead, he shook his head.

I stood up.

"Okay. Sit here while I go make a phone call. I don't even know if the FBI is looking at this cruise ship thing. I'll go see what I can find out and will be back in fifteen minutes. But before I walk out of the room, I'll ask you one more time. Is there anything else you want to tell me? I'm trusting you to be honest."

"No. That's it."

In the next room, my laptop was ready and waiting with the incriminating DVD keyed up. I left the room, checked my laptop, then returned to Ronald.

"I just spoke with the agent in New Haven who's on the cruise ship case. He's sending me some kind of video. I'm waiting for the file to download. The case agent mentioned a young girl being assaulted on the ship. Do you know anything about that?"

He paled. I could see beads of sweat form on his upper lip and across his forehead.

"No, I don't know what you're talking about."

He squirmed.

"I mean . . . I remember partying with some girls, but I don't know anything about a rape."

I nodded and left the room, letting him sit longer. He looked like he was about to pass out.

I returned to Ronald, frowning like I was angry, and placed the laptop on the table.

"Hey, Ronald. I told you I didn't care what

you've done. I want you to help me crack open the biggest case in FBI history, that's what I care about. But you aren't being truthful with me about the cruise ship."

He squirmed some more.

"Let me refresh your memory," I said.

I pressed PLAY: On the screen Ronald's pants were down, his tattoo was filling the frame as he attempted to have sex with the girl. It was obvious on the video that he didn't want to participate because he couldn't "perform." The whole time he tried, Gary was yelling at him.

I pressed FORWARD: On the screen, Ronald was high fiving his buddies, joking about George parasailing over the balcony to his death.

This time, finally, it was Ronald who looked like he was going to vomit.

It was time for John's next maneuver: *He'll be angry at one of his friends, the little one. The ringleader. Use that anger. He'll bite on it.*

I sat down next to him.

"Ronald, you know what I don't understand? You're a tall, well-built, good-looking guy with everything going for him. But you let this little, 5'4" piece of shit Gary tell you what to do and he put you in this bad situation."

He was getting more and more upset.

"Let's get this out of the way," I said, calmly. "I don't care if you threw this guy off the ship. You were pressured into it; anyone can see that. You were drinking and Gary put you up to it. You were defending yourself. We can explain this away, but you must be honest with me."

I segued to another John tactic: *He's afraid of his father. He doesn't want him to find out.*

I'd done some digging. Ronald's father was born and grew up in Eastern Europe but came to America to work hard and make a better life for his family. He was elderly and not in good health.

"Look," I said. "Let's not put your father through this. You could be the hero here, but I need your help. Don't sit here and tell me nothing."

It was like he had a good angel on one shoulder, and an evil one on the other. He went back and forth, not knowing what to do.

By 11 P.M. we'd been in that room for four hours. I'd trotted out every trick in the playbook but none had worked. It was like that moment with John Smith in the hotel room when he was on the verge, about to leap, then pulled back.

When Ronald left the FBI office, a surveillance team followed him on foot.

He scurried two blocks to the City Hall subway station, screaming into his phone the entire way.

"You motherfucker! You put me in this situation! I was just interrogated by the FBI you piece of shit! I'm going to kick your ass!"

We knew he was talking to Gary.

If he doesn't do the right thing, John had said, *figure out where he'll go, who his first call will be.*

The agents followed Ronald into the subway and onto the train.

He was sobbing so much, they told me later, he missed his subway stop and had to backtrack. When he finally got off and made his way home on the streets of Brooklyn, "he looked destroyed," the agents told me.

"He looked like a broken man."

I called John the next morning and gave him the full report.

"Man, Bob. I don't know what to tell you. I can see it. You had him right there. But he slipped away, like sand through your fingers."

"What can I do now?"

"You need to figure out who he's closest to, who is most important to him, and go to that person."

We both thought it and said it at the same time: *The father.*

The following day, I knocked on the door of Ronald's family's apartment in Brooklyn. Ronald wasn't home, but his father and older brother were. The father was one of those old-country, old-school Europeans who was genuine, respectful, but wary of authority.

I explained who I was and why I was there. His son hadn't told anyone about our meeting the day before.

"Sir, I'm going to be honest with you," I said, sitting on the living room couch. "Your son was put in a really bad situation by that Gary and some others."

The father slammed his hand on the table.

"I never like this family!" he said, in heavily accented, broken English "They trouble! I told my son stay away from them!"

"Your son knows what happened on the ship," I said. "He was a part of it. And I need his help."

The father stood up — he was big and tall, like his son.

"You no need worry about Ronnie. He needs to worry about me! You come back in two hours. We will fix. Ronnie will tell you everything."

I left their apartment convinced I'd broken

the case wide open. The old man would kick his son's ass if he didn't do the right thing.

When I returned a few hours later, Ronald was there — eyes red and swollen, like he'd been crying. The father and older brother were on the phone, speaking a foreign language.

The older brother handed the phone to me.

"It's our attorney."

My one shot came and went. Sand through my fingers, as John said.

Ronald did not cooperate, and neither did anyone else. And even though we had strong circumstantial evidence including the video, testimony from passengers, security footage, access card information . . . the case fell apart.

I didn't want to give up, though. John and I both felt a righteous indignation to seek justice for the victims, so I kept pushing.

I went so far — over the line, I'm sure — as to meet up with Ronald's fiancée and her mother. I showed them the videotape. The fiancée turned away in repulsion and called off the wedding. But still, Ronald would not cooperate.

The problem was this: no one saw the crimes except the criminals — and John

Edward. He saw it all, and I believe the evidence showed that he had been spot-on the whole way.

To this day, two decades later, no one has ever been charged for the murder of George Smith or the rape of that teenaged girl.

I wasn't sure if people atoned for their sins on the Other Side, but the harsh reality of this world, and a truth I have trouble accepting, is that a person can get away with murder and never be punished.

John reminded me of something his colleague, psychic Char Margolis, said to him once:

"It takes multiple coats of light paint to cover the dark, but it only takes one coat of dark to cover the light."

I hoped and prayed that John Smith would not get away with killing Fran.

20

Then I Saw Her Face

I felt disheartened after the cruise ship case that I couldn't get justice for George, Jennifer, and that teenage girl. For the longest time, I believed any case could be solved with the right amount of hard work, dedication, and persistence. But that wasn't always true. Timing and luck were also big factors.

Sometimes you make your own luck. Other times, unseen forces or energies beyond your control could make or break a case. Bits of evidence swirl together like the chemicals in an old-fashioned photo lab. They develop the case, then suddenly you see the answer all at once, like a picture in a frame.

I directed my energies back to Fran, trying to keep that in mind.

By the fall of 2005, I'd conducted at least a dozen physical searches to find her body. I'd used cadaver dogs, ground-penetrating radar, and old-fashioned shovels — focusing my search on Smith's former workplace, the

Carborundum Company Plant, in the Keasbey section of Woodbridge Township, New Jersey.

Smith's factory, Carborundum, circa 1950s — where we dug for Fran's body . . . and found her spirit (COURTESY OF THE FBI)

The factory had been closed for years, but that's where Smith was working when Fran disappeared.

At our first meeting in his office, John Edward's guides showed him an image during our reading.

"She's encapsulated in something. I keep seeing gray cylinders," he told me, years earlier. "Like those storm water pipes when they construct a new road or highway. And she's in something to keep her preserved, like fluid . . . or concrete."

Concrete. Smith's factory produced

masonry blocks of different sizes. The kilns were the size of a four-car garage, with heavy steel doors. Inside, the blocks of cement would bake for hours at 1,800 degrees Fahrenheit. At night, after the employees went home, the kilns stayed on at 400 degrees, never turning off.

Smith had 24-hour access to the plant, so there was decent reason to believe he might have done something with Fran's body there.

At first, I wondered if he'd tossed it into a burning-hot kiln. But after researching kiln mechanics, I ruled that out. The massive kilns required two people to operate, with each person using a separate key on opposite sides. Plus, alarms went off and firemen were present when the kilns were fired. So, he couldn't have done it alone.

Cylinders. The factory also had large stormwater drainpipes that ran into a creek and fed into the nearby Raritan River. As soon as I saw those pipes, I searched every inch of them, along with the surrounding area. I found nothing.

I'd crisscrossed the 40 square acres of Carborundum by foot so many times that the new owners of the land knew me well enough to invite me to their son's wedding.

I'd dug, searched, inspected, researched,

jackhammered, drilled, and trod on every blade of grass.

The only thing I hadn't done was take a psychic with me. Or two.

As the years went by John's guides began pulling back from showing him insights about Fran ("Nope. They won't budge," he said once), so he began introducing other psychics into the mix in case their guides could open a new door.

"I never want to disappoint you," John would say. "But I also want to make sure I can still be objective."

His friend Char Margolis was one psychic he would send me to. Her guides gave accurate information about Fran, but nothing new that would help me find her.

On an early Saturday morning, John met me in a parking lot on Crow's Mill Road, across the street from the abandoned industrial complex. He brought reinforcement — a friend of his, also a psychic, Jonathan Louis.

A former Long Island home builder, Jonathan completely shifted his career and life path as an adult after a chance meeting with John, who helped him onto his new path the way Lydia Clar had helped him when he was a skeptical teen.

After years studying metaphysics and

psychic phenomena, Jonathan embraced his "true calling" as a psychic and now described himself as a "psychic builder."

The two psychics parked their car and climbed into mine, ready to be my tag team for the day on yet another search of the factory.

"I'm going to drive around the property," I told them, "and you tell me if you feel yourselves being pulled in any direction. Okay?"

John closed his eyes to clear his mind and slow his breath as I began circling the grounds. Minutes later, he opened his eyes and pointed.

"This way, Bob, over here."

I drove straight ahead, passing a building so large it reminded me of an airplane hangar. Suddenly John sat forward.

"I want to go to the end and turn right. What's at the end of this building to the right, do you know? Something's around the corner . . ."

I drove to the end, then turned right. In front of us, a giant water tower loomed. At its base stood a white, cinderblock building, about 25 feet wide and 40 feet long.

"What the heck is that?" John asked.

"A pumphouse. It was used to pump water up to the tower."

"We need to go in there."

Jonathan nodded. "Definitely."

A second later, John got more animated. "She's in there!"

I'd barely come to a complete stop in front of the pumphouse when John jumped out of the car. Jonathan quickly followed. I parked and ran after them, reaching John as he entered the unlocked pumphouse.

It was a dark little place; I'd been in there many times before. One wall was lined with a row of lockers with old girly magazine pages still taped on. In the corner, an old diesel engine stood on a slab of concrete.

Half the pumphouse floor was covered by heavy, steel grates. Underneath those grates was a 10-foot pit that held the industrial pipes and valves acting as main arteries to the water tower.

John's eyes darted around the room like a kid hunting for Easter eggs. He was usually a stoic, especially during readings. Unless an energy from the Other Side was extra forceful, which seemed to be happening now.

"She's here!" he repeated, absolutely convinced. "I can feel her energy!"

My heart was racing.

"John, we've torn this place apart," I said. "There's nothing here."

John took a deep breath. "All I can tell you is her energy is here. I feel like she's here right in front of us, but for some reason we can't see her. Something's in the way."

He looked at the grates.

"Did you check below these grates?"

Jonathan and I lifted the filthy grates and stood them on their sides. I pulled a flashlight out. John stayed on floor level as Jonathan and I climbed down into the black pit.

We crawled along the floor and through the maze of industrial pipes — everything was covered in a thick layer of grease, dirt, and slime. We were covered in the stuff, groping around, as John egged us on.

"I feel her," he kept saying. "She's *here.*"

Jonathan saw my flashlight hit on something and he crawled to it.

"Oh my God, look at this!" he said.

Laying on one of the grimy, sludge-covered pipes — and to this day, I don't know how this was possible — was a white, pristine, 14-inch feather.

John and Jonathan both freaked out. The feather was so bright, it glowed against the darkness.

"How'd it get down here?" I asked, picking it up and handing it to John.

I didn't understand the significance and didn't know that a white feather was John's recurring sign from his mother on the Other Side.

("I immediately thought it was from my mom," John told me later. "I took it as a sign that I was using my ability in a positive way. Like working on my dad issues, which is something she always wanted me to do.")

Jonathan and I searched every nook and cranny in the pit for two hours until every inch was accounted for.

When we were done, the three of us sat on a jersey wall outside the pumphouse.

I was sitting in the middle of two psychics, but you didn't have to be psychic to see how deflated I was.

"Bob, all I can tell you is that if her body isn't here now, it *was,*" said John. "This place has great significance to what happened to her. I don't know that she was necessarily killed here or brought here after to do something with her body. But this place has a direct connection to her disappearance. I can feel it. I feel her energy. She's here with us now."

I was already a believer in John and what he did, but . . .

"You don't believe me?" John asked.

"What do you mean?"

"You don't believe Fran's really here?"

"I believe," I said.

"No, you don't."

I did, but . . . he was so certain her body was here, and he was wrong. How could he misinterpret the information to such an extent?

"Look, I told you I'm worried I'm developing a bias," he said, "that's why I brought Jonathan. I want to find Fran as much as you do and maybe that's interfering. But I'm telling you, her body was here at some point when she was killed . . . and she's here now."

I nodded, but I was still confused. I had two powerhouse psychics with me. Why couldn't they help? Why couldn't they find her? Why wasn't this working?

"Bob, it's okay to have doubts and question things. That's why you're good at what you do. I'm not asking you believe me. I am asking you to believe in yourself."

"What does that mean?"

"I told you she's here with us."

"Yeah."

"Ask her yourself. Ask Fran a question. Ask her to show you that she's here."

"How do I do that?"

"Ask her for a sign."

A sign. I looked around. Next to us stood a wooden pole about twenty feet high with a streetlamp attached.

It was in the middle of the day and I felt goofy doing it, but no one else was there except us. Or so I thought. I made an impassioned plea out loud:

"Fran, I don't know if you can hear me," I said. "But I'm trying. God knows I'm trying. I've gotten in trouble at work and at home. I've made messes of things. I'll keep looking for you. But you've got to help me. You've got to show me a sign. If you're here, please let me know. If you're here and you can hear my voice, turn that streetlight on . . ."

The light burst to life, blazing like a torch. Bright, even against the sunniest of skies. I raised my hand to shield my eyes.

John smiled. "I told you she was here."

I looked at John and Jonathan like they were magicians.

"Is this for real?" I asked.

"Ask her," John directed.

"What?"

"Ask her for another sign."

"Fran . . . if that's really you," I said out loud, "and I'm not losing my mind . . . shut the light off."

BOOM, the light went dark.

I couldn't process what I'd just seen. My hands were shaking.

"What does it mean?" I asked John.

"I think she's telling you not to give up."

Back home, I didn't tell Alex what happened. I worried she'd roll her eyes and belittle an experience that had a deep, profound effect on me. Besides, she'd embargoed talk of the Smith case and John Edward years before. I was cut off from sharing these moments with her.

"You keep looking for people who aren't there," she said recently, "and you're going to lose the people right in front of you."

But Fran *was* there, right in front of me. She'd given me a sign. I wasn't psychic, but I saw that light flare with my own eyes after I asked Fran to do it.

It was an important moment for me, a turning point in my spiritual evolution, as John might say. I spoke to an energy on the Other Side and got confirmation from her that she'd heard and understood me. What was going on?

"A natural shift happens to people when they're around 'the work,'" John explained. "They begin to open up to the energies around them. Plus, you're an Aquarian, Bob," he added, "that makes you even more open than others to the unseen world."

Astrology, that was another modality I had yet to embrace. But all in good time.

For now, I was still spinning about my first direct back-and-forth interaction with the Other Side. It would be the first of many.

A few months later, just before Christmas, I went back to Carborundum to do another search. I was walking outside by the pump-house, along the stream that runs through the property. I poked around through the tall grass with a stick, probing the dirt. You never know what you might find doing that. You never know.

The sun was setting, so I headed back to my car.

As I passed the water tower, a wave of fragrance hit me as if someone had stuck a bottle of perfume under my nose and sprayed. An intense, all-encompassing scent I'd never smelled before overtook my entire olfactory system.

A few steps further, the scent disappeared. I looked around and couldn't see a soul in sight.

I wasn't sure what to make of it, until later that night.

I was in a hotel room in New Jersey and had just said good night to Alex and the kids on the phone, then got into bed and flicked on Monday Night Football.

I was half-sitting, half-lying in bed, lolling in that in-between place of not awake but not asleep. I started drifting and then . . . I shot straight up in bed and gasped.

What the fuck? Who touched my hair?

My heart jumped.

Then came the perfume. The same scent

that wrapped itself around me at the factory instantly filled the room, sapping all the oxygen out.

I got up and checked my suitcase. Maybe I spilled my aftershave? Nope.

I went to my door and walked out into the hallway. No one was there, and no perfume scent, either. I went back in my room and there it was, overpowering.

I tried to use reason, logic, and physics to explain to myself what was happening but it was no use. The context was indisputable.

Someone was trying to get my attention in a big way, and I had an idea who.

I remembered something Janice Miller, the Bridgeport prostitute, told me years ago when we talked in prison. Smith's garbage bags filled with clothes in the Milford house attic were infused with strong perfume.

I remembered what John said during our first meeting.

"I smell cigarette smoke and strong perfume, like when a person tries to cover up the odor with a lot of perfume . . ."

Fran.

On my drive back to Albany the next day, I called Fran's daughter, Deanna.

"I have a crazy question," I said. "Did your mom wear a lot of perfume?"

"Oh my god, yes," she said. "She was always trying to hide the fact that she smoked, so she'd use gums and mints, and especially a lot of perfume."

"Was there a particular brand she wore?"

"Only one," said Deanna, "Opium by Yves Saint Laurent. It was her favorite."

I pulled into the next shopping mall and spotted a Macy's. The store was packed with holiday shoppers, and Christmas carols were playing on a loop.

The lineup at the perfume counter looked endless. When I finally got the salesgirl's attention, I asked if she sold Opium.

"Of course," she said, and reached for a bottle.

"No wait!" I said, "please don't show it to me."

She looked at me like I was crazy.

"Please, bear with me. I have an odd request," I said.

I asked her to pick out two other strong perfumes that were similar to Opium and, with my back turned, to spray three paper "test" strips with each fragrance. Then, without telling me which was which, I wanted her to hold the strips up to my nose, one at a time, to see if I could pick out the Opium.

Dozens of tired and impatient customers

were vying for the salesgirl's attention, tinsel was everywhere, but she was game.

She sprayed the little papers, then I turned back around for the smell test.

The first two were strong and distinct, but not what I smelled in the hotel room or at Carborundum. She held up the third.

I took a whiff . . . and got goosebumps. It was the one.

"That's Opium," I said.

She nodded and handed me the bottle.

"Merry Christmas!"

I left the store with the scent of Opium on me and continued driving north. As soon as the traffic eased, I called John.

"Hey. I'm driving home," I told him.

"Okay. But what's with the perfume?" he asked.

I caught my breath.

"John, I can't believe you're asking me this," I stuttered. "Why are you bringing up perfume?"

"As soon as I heard your voice, I smelled a very strong perfume," he said. "No, wait. I'm not sure what this means, but they're showing me Fran putting on perfume."

I was so jarred by what John was saying, I had to pull off the highway.

Parked on a side road, I explained to him what happened with the perfume and the sense that someone was touching my hair.

"I thought I was going crazy or imagining things," I said. "I didn't sleep all night. I felt like I was being watched, like someone was in the room with me. I hid under the covers like a scared little girl and prayed."

John chuckled.

"It wasn't a dream," he said. "It was Fran. And she wasn't trying to scare you. She was letting you know she was with you."

Fran was with me, and she was getting closer. I could *smell* her now. I felt her *touching* me.

John wasn't surprised, or even concerned. He was more worried about the people around me who were alive.

I'd begun traveling with the FBI polygraph team to conduct examinations of judges, prosecutors, and investigators in foreign countries to help weed out corruption. Often, I'd find myself in situations where I didn't think I'd make it out alive.

On one assignment, I was sent with a team to Bogotá, Colombia, to investigate corrupt government officials. They'd been accepting bribes from drug lords and compromising cases.

I wasn't allowed to pack my gun, which worried John. The streets of Bogotá were so dangerous, people bought kidnapping insurance. Carrying a gun depended on what country we were in. Afghanistan, Iraq, and places like that, I could take my weapon. Countries like Colombia or Kazakhstan, nope.

"Be extra careful," John warned, uneasy. "Something unexpected is going to happen."

The "something unexpected" unfolded a few days later.

Before I even got on the plane, another flight carrying US drug enforcement agents and other US government officials crashed in the mountains just outside Bogotá. Several agents died in the crash, but there were also survivors who were missing. The US government were trying desperately to locate them.

At that time, the guerrilla narco-terrorist group FARC — who lived up in the mountains — was making money through drugs and kidnapping. They had the survivors and were holding them ransom for millions of dollars.

That was all happening as eight of us sequestered in a hotel conducting two polygraph exams per day, trying to determine which officials there were dirty and which were clean.

Today it's all electronic, but back then

the polygraph machines spit out paper like in the movies. After each exam, we'd show the paper to the program chief, who'd look it over and give the subject a thumbs up — he's clean — or a thumbs down — he's not.

On day two, my colleagues bought me a hard hat for protection. The first time I walked into our hotel elevator, my head crashed into the low-hanging Tiffany lamp sconce and it came crashing down. The hat was a gag gift — sort of.

"It'll also come in handy if any snipers are around," one agent said, "you're so tall, you're an easy target."

On our third day of work, a local stranger walked into the US Embassy a few miles away, claiming to know where the DEA agents were being held. He'd tell them for a price, he said.

The Federales in Bogotá brought the informant to us at the hotel to polygraph and see if he was telling the truth. Could we trust the Federales? Not always. Some of them are corrupt, too.

One of my colleagues, a Spanish-speaking agent, administered the test.

"Do you know where the American citizens are?"

"Are you setting up an ambush?"

The guy failed the test miserably. Not only

did it quickly become clear to us that this was a potential FARC member who might be setting up an ambush, but now he knew where to find eight FBI agents — we were easy targets, hard hat or not.

The Federales assured us they would take the "informant" to the local police and put him in a cell for a few days to keep us safe while we finished our job and got out of the country. But that's not what happened. Instead, they released him. And now all eight of us, with no guns, were compromised.

"Everybody! Go back to your rooms and pack your shit fast," the chief ordered, "we have to get out of here!"

We scrambled. As we waited at the front of the hotel for our US Embassy cars to pull up, several dark vans swooped in and a bunch of goons armed with machine guns jumped out and ran toward us.

We dove into our cars.

"Drive!" we all yelled.

We flew through the streets of Bogotá, weaving in and out of traffic, running red lights, as the dark vans chased us.

We're about to die, I thought. But unlike the time under the desk during 9/11, I didn't feel so at peace with it.

A minute later, we reached the gates of the US Embassy and zipped in. The Marines standing guard shut and locked the gates behind us.

It was a close call, one of many to come. And I often wonder, looking back, why I never worked out a sign with John if I was ever to cross over during one of my perilous assignments. John's mother had her white feather. What would be my sign? An FBI badge was too general. Would he get Big Bird?

Fran was getting closer, and the sign she was about to send was beyond question.

A month or so after the pumphouse visit with John and Jonathan, I went back to Carborundum to do another search of the area. I'm always checking, *Did I miss anything?* I'm always wondering, *Is there a new way to look at something?*

In the pumphouse, I jackhammered the slab of concrete that lay under the old diesel engine, thinking Fran could be "encapsulated" there. She wasn't.

When I was finished, I took photos with my digital camera. It was standard operating procedure for the FBI to take "entry" and "exit" photos each time we searched a property.

Again, as always, I left the industrial complex disappointed and frustrated that I didn't find anything.

Late that night, after I got home to Albany, I was getting into bed when John called. He didn't usually call so late.

"Hey John, is everything okay?"

"Yes. Bob, did you take photos at the pumphouse today?"

He had that fervent sound in his voice again.

"Yeah. I didn't find her. Again."

"Yeah. I know. But Bob . . . have you looked at the photos yet?"

"No."

"I need you to go look at them. They're showing me the number 18. I don't know what it means but they're telling me you need to look at the pictures."

"Okay, hold on . . ."

I took the phone with me downstairs to the living room where I'd left my camera bag. I got the camera out and switched on the digital display. Tucking the phone under my chin, I began flipping through the gallery of photos.

"Okay, I'm looking," I said to John. "Nothing stands out so far, everything looks normal. What am I looking for, by the way?"

"I don't know," said John. "They keep showing me the number 18."

When I got to the 18th "exit" photo, I nearly dropped the phone.

"Oh my God," I said.

"What's wrong?"

"Something's in the picture. It looks like . . . a face."

I flipped back and forward, checking photos 17 and 19. They were clear. But frame 18 looked like an entity had stepped in front of my lens as I snapped the picture. The shape of a head, a face. It was Fran, looking directly into the camera lens at me.

Like John at the pumphouse, I could feel her energy. It wasn't the same as Janice Hartman's, which I felt that day in the car when I listened to her voice on the cassette. Janice's vibration felt young and lively. Fran's felt more mature and confident. But I also felt Fran's sorrow.

After I hung up with John, I realized something.

I'd now seen both their faces. Janice looked at me from the shroud of her lime green gown. And now Fran was looking at me in the photo.

John would tell me later, as I continued to search for her, that Fran had in a very real sense become "the other woman" in my life. Not because she visited me at night wearing her favorite perfume and touching my hair, but because she would become the enigma I would obsessively pursue and not give up on. She, along with Smith, would become a main character in my own personal quest narrative. Like Ahab's white whale in Melville's *Moby-Dick*.

After I understood that Fran just wanted to assure me that she was with me, I wasn't afraid of her appearing anymore.

John's work and mine were not so different, I realized. We both based our conclusions on evidence and facts, but mine were in the physical world and his were in the energetic.

The feather, the lamplight, the perfume, the photo, the fingers in my hair.

Like an old Polaroid picture developing before my eyes, unseen forces and energies came together, and into view.

21

Goat Eyes and Whitey

For the next several years, John Edward became my go-to secret weapon as I traveled the country and the world with my polygraph equipment, rooting out liars and identifying truth tellers.

By now we'd honed our back-and-forth communication skills into an organic flow. Like two musicians who'd jammed together for years, we knew our parts; we knew what notes to hit.

John was the more "surgical" one, like a doctor using a scalpel. He worked with a clinical eye and kept enough of an emotional distance so that he could receive information from his guides clearly and protect himself in the process.

I was the sensitive, demonstrative one. I dove into my cases as if the victims were family. I got deeply involved and pushed hard, sometimes *too* hard.

Even though John's information about

Fran had slowed, he continued to get hits on my other cases. Sometimes his thoughts on a case made sense to me right away, like a piece of a puzzle clicking into place, like an AHA! moment. Other times they'd seem cryptic until later, when his words would become clear like writing in the sky.

He helped me undisputedly, whether it was with questioning strategies, insights, suggestions, assurances, validations — oftentimes just warnings, like with Bogotá. My gut instinct combined with John's "Be careful!" kept me alive in some situations.

In early 2006, I landed in a former Soviet Socialist Republic amid chaos in the streets.

An immensely popular politician, poised to unseat the sitting president in a landslide victory, had been assassinated months before an election. The political candidate, his driver, and his bodyguard were taken up the side of a mountain and executed, all shot in the back of the head.

After the murders, foreign government officials and local officials claimed to have solved the case and arrested two men. One was a champion athlete in his early twenties, a former Olympian for the country. Another was a businessman in his fifties. Officials claimed that after a failed business deal between the candidate and the businessman, the man hired the athlete to kill the politician.

The whole scenario stunk of an inside job and cover-up. The current president, in power for many years, was known to be corrupt. He'd even installed family members in top cabinet positions. The US government was convinced his regime had orchestrated the assassinations.

So were the people. After officials released their fake story, it caused a backlash, and mass rioting and looting erupted in the streets.

Because the US government was trying to establish and maintain relationships in this country, it was in our best interest to monitor any espionage, instability, and corruption. So, we offered to "help" the foreign government officials by "confirming" their findings.

I was to lead the team, which required me to sit through an agonizingly long meeting with the FBI's International Operations Division, in which they presented an elaborate PowerPoint presentation of the key players.

"This makes no sense," I said, once they were finished. "All our intel says this was a political hit. Do you think we're going to walk in there and get people to confess? The intel confirms that corruption exists in this country. Are we supposed to walk in like in the scene from *Casablanca* when Captain Renault says, 'I'm shocked! Shocked to find that gambling is going on here!' "

"Even if we got a confession," I continued, "which we won't, what difference would it make there? What's the point of this?"

I was angry. Why send us into dangerous, hostile territory, without guns, for no good purpose? It was reckless.

"Nothing good can come of this," I told them as I left the meeting. "It's a no-win situation."

John Edward begged to differ.

"You're going to get a confession," he told me, when I called him right after the heated meeting.

"What? I am?"

"Yes."

"How am I going to do that?"

He gave me a line he's given me dozens and dozens of times.

"Just do what you do."

"Okaaay. Are you getting anything else?"

He paused.

"Whatever this is, I feel like a wet blanket thrown over me. That's what the energy will be like for you there. Oppressive."

"Yeah, well, it is the former Soviet Union.

The FSB, formerly the KGB. I expect it to be bad."

"You'll be under a microscope," said John. "They'll be watching everything you do. Don't trust anyone, *not anyone.*"

He was more emphatic than usual.

"I mean it. Not *anyone,*" he said. "And don't push too hard. Do your job, but once you get the truth, get out."

"Okay."

"Whatever this is, it's exactly what everybody thinks it is. I don't understand the specifics, but whatever you are thinking . . . they're showing me you are right."

The former Soviet Union was like a Cold War spy novel; "Don't trust anyone," John warned.

I wasn't afraid of much.

But traveling unarmed to the other side of the world to interrogate foreigners allegedly involved in an assassination and not being able to communicate with headquarters back home was . . . frightening. FBI agents had power and authority in our country and many others, but where I was going, I was a nobody with nothing.

Landing in the former Soviet Union was like being plopped in the middle of a Cold War spy novel. The next week would be a blur of hammers and sickles, bugged hotel rooms, foreign government officials lurking in black turtlenecks, horse meat dinners, limitless vodka, and achingly beautiful women. All of these, especially the women, were perilous.

Arriving at our ornate hotel — majestic lobby, marble floors, glass elevator — I waited by the lobby elevators with two other FBI polygraph examiners who'd be working with me that week under my direction.

It took one minute before we were surrounded. A handful of women — we're talking Cindy Crawford circa 1992 supermodel types — appeared from nowhere.

I pulled the agents into the elevator and hit the "DOOR CLOSE" button.

"Go straight to your rooms," I told them. "Put the chain on your doors, and don't let anyone in."

The next day, we met with the US ambassador and the deputy chief of mission (DCM) in "the bubble" — a room in the basement of the US Embassy with soundproof metal walls.

"We rank counterintelligence threat on a scale of one to five, with five as the most severe threat," said the RSO. "This country rates an *eleven.* Everything you do here will be monitored and recorded. You'll be followed. All your rooms will be bugged. They'll know how many times you take a piss in the middle of the night."

Oppressive wet blanket feeling, said John. I already felt smothered.

In the days leading up to the polygraph tests, we worked with various local government officials and police. And other shady figures, who never identified themselves. Which made everything even more ominous.

The interrogations occurred in a US-controlled condominium on the outskirts of the city. It had that cold war feel to it — dated wallpaper, cramped rooms, flickering lightbulbs. On the morning of our first polygraph test, we set up the equipment in one of two bedrooms and had a US electronics technician sweep the place.

The first subject arrived, a bloated businessman in his fifties with a round face, goatee, and a bad hair-dye job.

I waited in the living room area with the leader of the foreign delegation, his staff, the police investigator, the mission RSO, and the local FBI legat while the other two agents and a translator went into the bedroom with the man to conduct the polygraph.

The leader of the foreign delegation wore a black suit and tie and had great presence. When he walked into the room, all the men stood up. He was introduced as the "General."

Foreign security officers positioned themselves outside the bedroom door and outside the condo, under the windows. They looked like Eastern European thugs — jeans, black turtlenecks, black leather jackets, and short military-style haircuts. I'm guessing some were former boxers or fighters because I saw a lot of broken noses and cauliflower ears.

"Are you withholding any information concerning the politician's death?" the agents asked the man.

No answer.

"Did anyone direct you to plan this death?"

No answer.

He said nothing, except to tell the agents he was sick with pancreatic cancer. Then he pointed to his ear and up to the ceiling — indicating the previously hidden microphones.

"My friends, this matter does not concern you," he warned. "The best thing you can do is get on your plane and go back to the United States."

After an hour of no cooperation, the agents called me into the room and briefed me on all that happened. My usual instinct would have been to sit down and drill into this man to get him to talk. But I remembered what John told me.

Don't push too hard.

I went back out into the living room, where everyone was waiting to hear the results.

Don't trust anyone.

"The test was inconclusive," I told them, and made up some excuses as to why.

The room was unsettlingly silent. I'm sure they knew I was feeding them a line, but they also knew it was better than me telling them the guy had failed the test. That would have meant we were onto them.

The next day, it was the athlete's turn. His attorney arrived first, chain-smoking and shaking with fear. A few minutes later, the athlete entered the condo with a black hood over his head, handcuffed to two SWAT-type guys, the Russian version. I was surprised; I'd never seen that before.

The two other agents and translator went into the bedroom with him and removed the hood. Again, I waited outside with the others.

"Are you withholding any information concerning the politician's death?" they asked.

"No."

"Was anyone else involved in planning the assassination?"

"No."

He failed the polygraph test and, like his predecessor, gave no information.

As I listened to the Russian group rant about vodka, women, sex, and cigars, one of the agents signaled me to come into the room.

"Bob, he's scared to death," said the agent.

I looked over at the athlete, slumped in a chair, and had a hunch.

You'll get an admission, John told me. *Just do what you do.*

I pulled a chair up close to him and sat down.

"Listen, we're here to help you," I told him. "People at the highest levels of the US government including the president and the director of the FBI sent me. We already know what happened here and who was behind it. There's nothing you can tell us that we don't already know. If you want our help, you must at least confirm for us what we already know."

He was petrified. He pointed to the bedroom door and whispered:

"Can they hear us?"

"No," I told him.

"Are you sure?"

"I'm sure they can't hear."

He had tears in his eyes.

"On the way here, in the car," he said, "the man handcuffed to my right arm — I don't know which one he is because of the hood — he told me: 'If you talk to the Americans we will torture and kill your wife and children.' "

I leaned in close.

"What is it they are worried you will tell us?"

He hesitated.

I leaned forward and said in a low voice: "I told you we already know what happened here. As a show of good faith, that you want our help, at least whisper in my ear the name of the person who set up the assassination."

He slid toward me until his mouth was an inch from my ear:

"The president's son."

I put my hand on his shoulder and nodded.

I knew what we had to do next.

Once you get the truth, John said, *get out.*

I went out into the living room where the Russian contingency was waiting, dying to hear the results. John said not to trust anyone — *not anyone* — he emphasized.

But I had to trust my colleague, so I told the rest of the group that the test results were incomplete and the agents needed more time. I waited about 10 minutes or so before I calmly asked the legat into the back room. I didn't want it to be obvious. I told him what happened.

"Oh my God," he said, running his fingers through his hair and pacing.

"In a few minutes, I'll tell my guys to pack up," I told him. "We're going back to the hotel and the three of us are going to sleep in the same room tonight because I don't want to wake up with a dead hooker in my bed tomorrow. We're getting on the first plane out tomorrow morning. We've completed our mission. We got the admission. We're out of here."

The local FBI representative looked astonished and pointed toward the living room.

"We have to tell them!"

I look at him, dumbfounded.

"If you tell them," I said, "you're going to get someone killed."

But he was already out the door.

A minute later, the FBI legat was telling the Russian group everything the athlete said — including the fact that one of the SWAT-type guys in the room threatened to torture and kill the young man's family.

My heart felt like it was going to explode. I wanted to vomit.

"There's nothing to worry about, my friend," one SWAT-like guy in a crummy leather jacket said to me. "Everything will be taken care of tonight."

A few hours later, I was in the backseat of the General's black Phaeton luxury Volkswagen sedan, with blacked-out windows. Beyond those windows, it was pitch-black outside. My two FBI colleagues were in cars behind me.

The sedan moved up a winding road on the side of a mountain.

The General sat in the front passenger seat and the interpreter sat with me in the back. He was freaking out.

"Bob, do you see where we are!"

"No, where?"

"This is the hill where the assassinations happened!"

I cursed myself. *Why didn't I listen to John?* Was there a way I could have gotten us out of that condo without ending up in the back seat of the General's car, going up this god-forsaken road?

I tried to get the General's attention, giving him every excuse I could think of to take us back to our hotel. I was sick, I said. I had essential medicine in my hotel room that I needed. We were exhausted from the day. We had a plane to catch.

"You'll be fine," said the General. "We're going to take good care of you."

The translator gave me a look, like: *We're about to die, and they'll never find our bodies.*

Obviously, thankfully, we did not die that night.

Instead, the General led the entourage of five cars to a mountaintop restaurant and presented us with the local delicacy — a boiled goat's head. As it turned out, the General was so insistent on getting us to the dinner because he wanted to ask for our help on a local, unrelated murder case. (We didn't do it.)

As the vodka flowed, the General stabbed a fork into one of the goat's eyes, twisted it, and held it up in front of the two-dozen guests at the table.

"Every part of the goat's head has symbolic

meaning," he announced. "We give the eyeballs to the elders and the leaders, so they will have vision to see the future!"

He handed the fork to me. The eyeball was dripping with sinew.

"I give this to my new brother, Agent Hilland, the leader of our table!"

After that night, I don't know what happened to that athlete or to the businessman sick with cancer. Did they live or die? No clue.

But I do know what happened to me and that goat's eye. I got out of the former Soviet Socialist Republic the next day, but not without paying a small price: I chewed and swallowed that eye.

It was gray and rubbery, like a hard-boiled egg cooked too long. When I bit into it, a vile, viscous fluid shot to the back of my throat.

And I do know what happened to the sitting president whose son orchestrated the murder of three men. He remained in power, and his corruption continued. Anything more than that, I'm not at liberty to say. Any other details and outcomes, I can never talk about.

When my plane touched down on American tarmac, my adrenaline was still pumping from my supposed near-death experience. I thought about that politician, shot in the head. About that athlete, who probably met a nefarious end. And about that panicked drive up the mountain, certain I was heading toward my execution.

I was grateful to be home. The goat's eye was getting away easy.

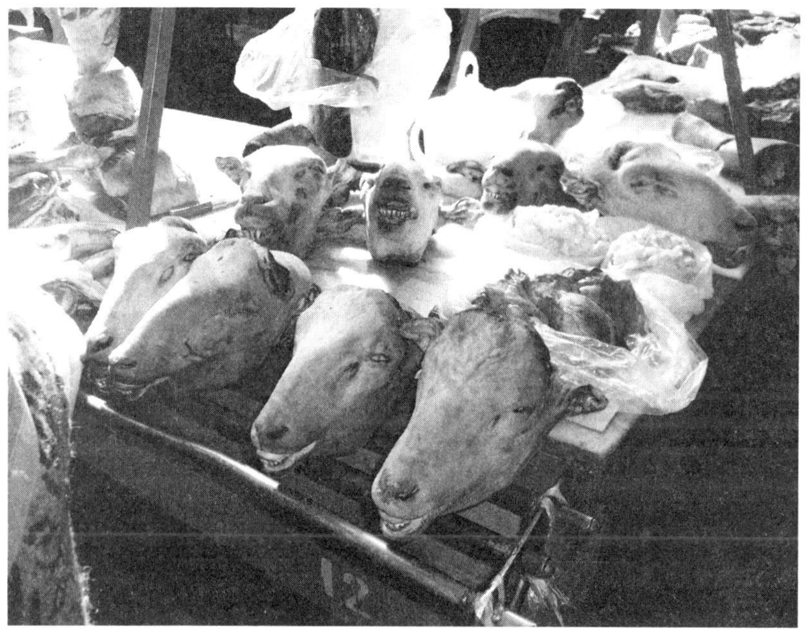

No shortage of goats' heads, a local delicacy, at the market

* * *

By 2006, organized crime boss James "Whitey" Bulger — also known as the "Irish Godfather" — had been on the FBI's Most Wanted Fugitive list for seven years, second only to Osama bin Laden.

Bulger was the longtime leader of Boston's Winter Hill Gang in the '70s and '80s and had been on the run as a fugitive from the FBI since 1995.

My boss in the Albany office, Bill Chase, was part of the original Bulger investigation team when he lived in Boston. He currently served as the special agent in charge of the Albany Division.

I admired him for many reasons, one of which was because he was as passionate about catching Whitey Bulger as I was about John Smith. Whitey was Bill's white whale.

I didn't know a lot about Bulger or the case. I was aware of what had transpired a year earlier, in 2005. Bulger's handler, FBI agent John Connolly, had been indicted on murder and conspiracy to commit murder charges. In the years before that, Connolly was indicted on charges involving racketeering, falsifying FBI reports, accepting bribes, and basically helping Bulger evade capture. It was a mammoth stain on the FBI's reputation.

When I strolled into Bill's office one morning in early 2006 to join him for a coffee, he was in front of the television cursing.

"We *just* missed catching Whitey!" he told me, ticked off and moving around the room like he wanted to hit something. He explained that FBI agents were tipped off that Bulger would be at a specific location in Piccadilly Circus in London, but the timing got messed up. The agents arrived 20 minutes after Bulger left the scene.

"We've done everything humanly possible to get him," Bill lamented, as I sat down with my coffee and put one on his desk for him.

"We've spent millions of dollars in source payments, we've done undercovers . . . and we can't get this fucking guy," he vented.

He sat down. "What we need," he said, "is a miracle."

Bill took a sip of coffee. The word "miracle" hung in the air.

"You know, I saw this guy on TV last week — a psychic," he said. "He was amazing. He can talk to dead people and predict things. Man, I wish there was a way we could contact this guy. Maybe he could help us. His name is John Edward."

I nearly spilled hot coffee in my lap.

"Um, Bill. I *know* John Edward."

"Fuck you."

"No, really."

"You know John Edward?"

"Yeah."

"You shittin' me?"

"Not shittin' you."

I told Bill the story of how I met John eight years earlier, a cynic determined to take him down. I told him about the reading John gave me that shook me to my core, and how he then helped me with the Smith case — and others.

"Please set up a meeting," Bill pleaded. "Tell him we'll pay."

"He doesn't want money," I said. "His two stipulations to me from the start have been that he won't take money and what he gives us is off the record. His name can't appear in any paperwork. I made those promises to him, and I've honored them."

Bill promised to do the same and implored me to call John, which I did as soon as I returned to my desk.

I should have known John would be wary.

Not only were he and his guides leery of me bringing "new energy" into our unique, well-honed relationship . . . but they were especially sensitive about *cop* energy. As I discovered recently when I called John about another case and neglected to inform him that two other law enforcement officers were on the phone with me. John's guides gave him nothing. Crickets. And I got a scolding about it later.

"My guides will work with you," he said, "but they don't want to work with anyone else. They were put off that you didn't ask if you could bring new people in."

"I understand," I said. "But listen. This case is a big deal. I want you to know that."

John paused for a moment — consulting with his guides, I'm sure.

"Okay."

* * *

A week later, Bill and his buddy from the Boston FBI office, Agent Dave Donahoe, met John and me for a clandestine meeting in a hotel room on Long Island. Donahoe was the lead on the Bulger case, and he'd known Bill for decades. He, too, had to be convinced to take this meeting.

"What are we seeing a damn psychic for?" he grumbled to Bill, on his drive over from Boston.

I told them to bring items that belonged to Whitey, if they had any, and to add "control" items — but not to let me know which was which.

"John has no idea what the case is," I assured them.

In John's hotel suite on Long Island, the living room was configured with a long coffee table, a couch on one side of the table, a small love seat on the other side, and a wingback chair alone at one end.

I made introductions, and then something odd happened after we all sat down. Dave and I sat next to each other on the couch, John sat across from us on the loveseat, and Bill took the wingback chair.

Bill and Dave laid out a dozen items on the coffee table including a passport, a watch, a book, a skull ring, and a hunter's knife. But as John scanned the items, I could tell he was bothered. He looked up at Bill.

"I need you to do me a favor," John said. "Can you switch places with Bob?"

We did as he asked without questions, and I relocated to the wingback chair. Then, it was time to begin. Or not.

John looked at me with an odd expression.

"Bob, can we talk in the other room for a minute?"

We excused ourselves and I followed him into the bedroom. He shut the door.

"Hey, is everything okay here?" he asked.

"What do you mean?"

"I mean, can we trust these guys?"

"Yeah. I mean, I think so."

"I keep getting the feeling like something's not right. They're showing me a bad cop or a bad agent."

Ah, I thought. *He must be picking up on John Connolly, Whitey's indicted handler who was now in prison.* That explained why he asked me to sit on my own, on the wingback chair. To "separate" my energy from the others.

But now with his question, I wondered about Bill and Dave. I didn't know Dave at all, and Bill I'd known about a year. He seemed to be a genuine guy who truly wanted to find Bulger. If they had ulterior motives, why would they meet with a world-famous psychic?

"Okay, let's go back in," John suddenly said.

We returned to the living room and sat down again. John scanned the items on the coffee table for a second time and picked up the passport.

"Whoever this is," he began, "he is a very powerful guy. He's alive. And he's very, very smart."

Again, John stopped and looked up at Bill. He put the passport down. Apparently, it still wasn't time for Whitey.

"May I be personal with you?" he asked Bill. I knew what that meant.

"Sure," said Bill.

"You lost your father recently?"

The energy in the room shifted. Bill looked like someone had shot an arrow through his heart.

"Yes," Bill said.

"He's here," said John. "Your dad is showing me you and your brother standing watch over his body. You wouldn't leave his side."

Bill nodded. He was trying not to cry. On the emotional Richter scale, he jumped from one to ten in seconds.

John continued.

"He's literally showing me you and your brother in the hospital, right after he crossed over, standing by him. Like you refused to leave him alone."

Bill kept nodding, tears streaming down his face now.

"We're a military and law enforcement family," he explained. "We don't leave the dead unattended until they are buried. My brother and I took shifts guarding him. We didn't leave his body."

John paused.

"Your father wants me to acknowledge that you have two boys, and your younger son is very sick."

That was a trigger that set all three of us non-psychics in the room off. Bill, the big boss, broke down in tears. I put my head in my hands. And Dave, the cynic, had his mouth open in shock.

"Your father wants you to know that he's watching over your son," John said. "And that when it's time for your son to cross over, he will take care of him."

Bill tried to respond, but he was too choked up to talk.

"I needed to pass this information along from Bill's father," John explained to us, "before we did anything else."

We all got it. Except for John, there wasn't a dry eye in the room.

It took Bill, me, and Dave a few minutes to compose ourselves.

Once we did, John picked up the passport from the table and began again. The information came like a torrential downpour.

"This guy has a 'J' name, like John or James. I think it's James or Jimmy. Whatever this is, he was in charge. A very powerful guy. I'm getting a John Gotti feeling, like a powerful gang or mob family. But whoever this is, he's not Italian."

We all nodded. John looked at Bill and Dave with the same expression of discomfort he had earlier.

"Look. I don't know you guys. And I don't mean any disrespect. I know Bob, and I trust Bob. And I know he wouldn't bring you to me if he didn't trust you. But I'm going to tell you right now, there's a dirty cop in your organization who has something to do with whatever this is. Someone who . . .”

John thought for a moment.

“. . . helped this James get away. He tipped him off. But this was not a one-time incident. There was a relationship between the FBI guy and this James for years.”

Bill and Dave both nodded vigorously.

“And there was money back and forth. This guy James was working the FBI guy.”

John put down the passport and picked up the watch.

“Who died by suicide recently? Like, a week or two ago?”

Bill looked surprised.

“Someone involved in this case, close to James, killed himself two weeks ago.”

John paused again.

“This guy James is a sociopath,” he stated, as fact.

“He has no empathy for anyone. And the crazy thing is . . . in the same way that some people thought of John Gotti as a hero and loved him even though he was a cold-blooded killer — this guy James is like that. People idolize him, even though he’s killed people. John Gotti used to throw block parties with fireworks and people loved him. But they were also afraid of him and his extreme power and control. This guy is the same. But I feel like you guys already know all this and I'm not telling you anything new, right?"

"Right," they both said.

"The dirty agent," John said. "You guys know who he is. He's a 'John' too. He's already in jail."

"Yes," they said.

"But . . ."

John looked directly at Bill.

"I need to ask you something."

"Go ahead," Bill said.

"I know you're all FBI agents, but I feel like Bob and Dave are the same and you're different, you're higher up. Three or four levels up."

"Yes. I'm a special agent in charge, so I am in charge of an office."

"But you answer to somebody above you, like a headquarters?"

"That's right."

Pause.

"I don't know if it's your boss," said John, "but there's a person above you. Whatever the next level is. One person at that level, maybe two, they don't want this guy James found."

I noticed John only called Bulger by his true name, "James" — never by "Whitey."

"Because when he's found," John continued,

"he'll have a book with all sorts of names and notes, going back years. So, when you catch him, he'll have this dossier . . ."

Bill and Dave sat up on the couch. The energy in the room doubled.

"So, we're going to catch him?" asked Dave, revved up.

"Yep. Absolutely," John said, matter-of-factly. "You're going to get him."

"When?" asked Bill. They were both on the edge of the couch.

"I'm bad with time," said John. "So, I can't say. But there's no doubt you're going to catch him."

They were electrified, hearing this. Suddenly full of piss and vinegar.

John went back to the dirty agent.

"One person who doesn't want James to be caught," he said, "I'm getting an 'N' or 'H' name."

John said a male name out loud.

Bill and Dave exchanged a look, like, *holy shit.* Dave scribbled a name down on a piece of paper and held it up to Bill. They nodded to each other. They knew exactly who John was talking about.

"He's somebody higher than you," John repeated to Bill. "Someone in Washington. He doesn't want James found because he's worried something will lead back to him."

John put the watch down and picked up another item. He shook his head and put the item back down again.

"I'm not getting anything from that," he said. *A control item,* I thought.

John picked up the book.

"This is crazy," he said. "You guys were close to catching him recently."

He looked at Dave.

"You missed him by *minutes*?"

"Yes."

John described what he saw. The setting was an outdoor café or restaurant, with tables and umbrellas.

"You had information that this guy James was going to be there, and you had agents all over the place. But you missed him by, like, 20 minutes. He showed up early or you guys got there late."

"Exactly," said Dave.

John looked like another scene was unfolding in front of him.

"Oh, this guy is unique. Very smart," said John. "I feel like for years, before he disappeared, you guys were looking at him and he knew it. He would walk up to the agents surveilling him and talk to them. He was bold. I see agents sitting in a car watching him and James walking over and talking to them. Like in *Beverly Hills Cop.*"

As John described each new detail, the agents' faces lit up. Especially with the quirkier stuff.

"This guy is very health conscious," John said. "He works out a lot. I see him exercising in the middle of the night."

Yep, they said.

The next image John's guides showed him was straight out of *Silence of the Lambs.*

"I see a pit," he said, looking off into the distance and frowning.

"This guy James would take people to a pit and torture them or kill them. It feels like a garage setting or a warehouse, with a concrete floor. Like an underground room. I see this guy taking people there and . . . killing them."

John looked at Bill and Dave.

"I hear your accents. I assume you're from Boston. But whatever this pit thing is, it's linked to Boston."

"Boston is right," said Dave. "But . . . where is he now? Where is James *now*?"

John thought for a moment. I imagined him posing this question to his guides.

"They're taking me south and west. He's on the other side of the country. Does he speak Spanish?"

They didn't know.

"I keep seeing Spanish, like he's by the

Mexican border and goes back and forth. Either South Texas or Arizona or California. Yes, *California.* He's with a woman, she has blonde hair. You know who she is."

"Yep," said Bill.

"She has a 'C' name, like Cathy. They live like a married couple and blend into their environment. James walks around like this nondescript guy out in plain daylight. No one would pick him out of a crowd. No one would ever suspect. They're this nice older couple."

Dave couldn't take it anymore.

"How will we find him" he asked John. "What should we do?"

John thought some more.

"Follow the medicine," John said. "He takes medicine for the blood or heart. Try to trace the medication. And find the woman he's with, the 'C' name. When you catch him, it will have something to do with either the medicine or the woman he's with."

By this point in the meeting, John had picked up most of the items Bill and Dave brought with them. One item stood out, though — glaringly untouched on the table; an old '70s hunter's knife with a fixed blade and a leather wrapped wooden handle.

"You didn't pick up the knife," Dave said. "Would you mind picking that one up?"

"Do I have to?" John said, a bit nervously. He'd obviously avoided it.

John slowly lifted the knife, held it in his hand for a few seconds, then dropped it on the table. I don't know what he saw, but I can tell you what I saw on his face: complete and utter repulsion.

"Please tell me he used that knife to kill or skin a deer," he said.

Bill and Dave were quiet. We all knew the answer.

Before they left the hotel room that day, John reminded Bill and Dave of the three main takeaways of the meeting: to focus on southern California, the medicine, and the woman.

"You're going to get a break with the female," he repeated, more and more sure of that.

Bill and Dave thanked John and left the meeting with renewed optimism about and focus on how to catch the elusive fugitive they'd been hunting for years.

John's validation of the case details — all accurate, they told me later — his insights, and his assurance that Bulger would be caught one day left them revitalized.

That John knew so many details about

Bulger was especially astounding to me, considering the conversation he and I had after Bill and Dave left.

"How do you think it went?" he asked me.

"John, do you have any idea who it is you were talking about?"

"No."

"Whitey Bulger!"

In classic John tradition, he asked: "Is he a baseball player?"

I had a good laugh. I laughed all the way downstairs to the hotel bar, where I met with Bill and Dave and we rehashed the entire meeting, word for word, over many beers.

In June 2011, five years after our hotel meeting, Whitey Bulger, 81, was arrested in Santa Monica, California. The FBI were tipped off by an acquaintance of Bulger's girlfriend, Catherine Greig.

Just as John said.

22

SOCCER IN THE JUNGLE

I lasted in the Albany office for about a year before eagerly accepting a temporary duty assignment based in Washington, DC, in the spring of 2006.

For the next 18 months, I commuted back and forth between Albany and FBI Headquarters, sleeping on an air mattress in a room I found on Craigslist during the week, then returning home for weekends.

I decorated my new office desk with two items — framed photos of my family, and a bronze figurine of winged and armored Saint Michael. The archangel stood atop a serpentine Satan, clutching a dagger in victory.

That was the endless theme: The fight between Good and Evil.

My new position was a promotion — supervisory special agent of the FBIHQ Polygraph Unit — and I dove into it, packing my suitcase once again.

One of my first assignments was to take a team to Guyana in South America and investigate a major weapons theft at the Guyanese Defense Force (GDF) military base.

Stockpiles of automatic guns, rocket-propelled grenades, and other explosives had been reported stolen by the GDF, and the intel funneled its way to US agencies, who worried the weapons were in the hands of terrorists intending to harm our country. The initial intel suggested that members of the GDF had conspired with powerful drug lords to steal and ultimately sell the weapons on the black market.

Our goal was to find out who took them and where they were, and get them back.

All I knew about Guyana was that it was mostly jungle — and it was the location of that Jonestown massacre in the '70s when hundreds of cult members drank cyanide-laced Kool-Aid and died. It was also the largest illegal drug depot in the world, I was told, where drugs from South America passed through to get to the ships in the north.

"Be careful," John warned, before my flight out. "Don't trust anyone. People on the inside did this. Trust your intuition."

It was like what he said before my Soviet trip, and the same words I would hear in the future, time and again, as I headed off to hostile, foreign lands. The clincher this time was a unique detail he added, something that made no sense at the time.

"They're showing me a soccer ball."

"What? A what?"

"A soccer ball, like in sports. Watch for the soccer ball. Trust the soccer ball."

"John, what does that mean?"

He paused.

"I have no idea."

The hot, broken roads of Guyana were populated with donkeys pulling carts and bugs the size of Buicks. Run-down shacks stood next to multimillion-dollar estates owned by drug warlords.

Like in Bogotá, kidnapping for ransom was rampant. Also, like Bogotá and the former Soviet Union, we were not permitted to take our guns into the country. Instead, we would have armed personal bodyguards with us day and night for protection.

Soon after landing, a military captain and major whisked my team and me off for a formal tea and photo-op at the office of a top general. He was the head of the GDF base where the stolen weapons had been kept.

The next stop was the scene of the crime — a mammoth hangar on base. We had to pass three armed checkpoints to get to the area where the weapons had been. You didn't need a polygraph test to know that there was no way anyone could get past those checkpoints without being military. This was an inside job, for sure.

Our three-story hotel was off a dirt road. It had no elevators, bad water, and rabid wild dogs running about. The hotel was U-shaped, with rooms on each floor opening to a walkway that overlooked a middle courtyard, where you could get food and drinks.

I thought of John. Not a soccer field or ball in sight.

What the hell did he mean?

Our personal bodyguards were young men ranging in age from 18 to 23, armed with machine guns. There were seven of us and fourteen of them, so that made me feel a bit better; two bodyguards per agent. They spoke English, but except for greetings or ordering food from the courtyard restaurant, the bodyguards were forbidden to speak to us.

"They are here for your security only," said the ranking military captain and major, who planted themselves in the courtyard to monitor us throughout the day, every day.

"You must communicate with us directly for anything important."

The bodyguards were clearly afraid of the officials, and I didn't trust them, either. Could we even trust the bodyguards?

Don't trust anyone, John said.

When another FBI agent arrived to stay for one night, I watched him pull a heavy rope out of his duffel bag and tie one end to the foot of his bed.

"What are you doing?" I asked, as he coiled the other end of the rope on the floor, across the room.

"Setting up an escape route through the window," he said, "just in case."

The next day, my team started running polygraph examinations in their respective rooms on soldiers brought to us by officials.

These polygraph examiners were the most experienced I knew, real heavy hitters. So, when they brought me their first batch of printouts and I scanned them, I was baffled. Something was wrong. The physiology recorded on the charts was erratic and indecipherable. The first round of tests was inconclusive across the board.

"Go back and talk to these guys," I told the examiners. "Find out what the hell is going on."

What we discovered was that military officials were torturing these soldiers to get information on their own before bringing them to us. One device they were particularly fond of was the "Guyanese water-ski" — tying a soldier's feet and hands, throwing him off a boat, and pulling him in the water until he lost consciousness.

From the walkway outside my room on the third floor, I spotted the major and captain lurking in the courtyard and signaled them to come up.

"We're here to help you," I told them, after they were in my room and I'd shut the door. "The men you brought to us were already interrogated. They were too stressed for us to test them. If you continue to send us men in this condition, we cannot help you and will have to return to the United States."

They assured me the problem would be corrected and the first batch of tests the next day looked more "normal." Which was good. But, as the day went on, we still weren't getting any useful information about the stolen weapons. The soldiers' charts were coming back clean; they didn't know anything.

I stood in the walkway outside my room, looking down at the courtyard. The major and captain were there eating. Some of the bodyguards were standing by.

But this one kid stood out, a bodyguard

for one of the other agents. He was surreptitiously looking up at me. In fact, since we arrived at the hotel, I noticed that every time I glanced in his direction, he was staring at me. Not in a malicious way. In a way that made me think he wanted to talk to me. *A lot.*

By day three, I knew I had to talk to this kid. But how? The captain and major were watching.

While the examiners were conducting tests in their rooms, I went out to the walkway again and looked down at the courtyard. The captain and the major were there. So was that kid, shouldering a machine gun bigger than he was. He was standing next to a table set up with coffee and tea.

He looked up at me, our eyes locked.

A minute later I had descended the hotel steps and stood at the coffee table, fiddling with the paper cups.

"Hey, how are you doing?" I asked nonchalantly. The kid was four feet away from me.

He smiled. The captain and major were ten feet away in the other direction.

I poured myself a coffee and glanced over at the kid again. I couldn't see it before, from my perch on the third floor. Maybe because it was blocked by the giant machine gun. But now I saw it clear as day. His shirt. It had the bold red, yellow, and green colors of the Guyana flag.

And smack dab in the center of his chest was an image of a black and white soccer ball.

Holy effing . . .

I casually stirred my coffee.

"Hey, do you play soccer?" I asked him.

"Yeah," he said, nervously.

"Are you good?"

"Yes," he smiled. "I'm good."

I kept stirring. The eyes of the captain and major were on us.

"Do you play a lot?"

"Hmm-hmm."

"How old are you?"

"Twenty-one."

I added sugar to my coffee and glanced at the kid's face. After fifteen years in law enforcement, I knew when someone was bursting to give information. This kid wanted to talk. And he had John Edward's soccer ball.

I turned my back to the officials and faced the kid.

"Don't look at me," I said quietly, "stare straight ahead like I'm not talking to you."

He obeyed.

"You look like you want to talk to me, right?"

He began turning his head toward me . . .

"Don't look at me," I said quickly. "Keep your eyes forward."

He stared straight ahead.

"I get the feeling there's something you want to tell me," I continued, "maybe I'm wrong, but . . ."

"I know where the weapons are," said the soccer kid.

Holy effing . . .

I took a sip of coffee.

"Okay, keep staring ahead so it doesn't look like I'm talking to you," I told him. "I'm going back up to my room and in 30 minutes, I'm going to order food. I want you to bring it up to me."

Thirty minutes later the soccer kid knocked on my door holding a tray of food, his machine gun slung across his shoulder. His hands were shaking so much, the dishes were knocking against each other, making a clinking sound.

I ushered him in and looked at my watch. I had three minutes to talk to the kid before anyone got suspicious.

"We don't have much time," I said, taking the tray from him. "What's going on?"

"I know where the weapons are."

"Where are they?"

"They're at the house of a drug lord."

"How do you know?"

"I have a source. But I can't tell you who the source is."

I checked my watch. Two minutes.

"Why not? What are you afraid of?"

The kid started crying.

"You clearly care a lot about this source," I said.

"He's my brother! I'm afraid he'll get hurt. I'm afraid they'll kill him!"

I checked my watch. One minute.

"I understand. When did you last speak to your brother?"

"Last night. He knows some of the people involved with the theft."

Probably an errand boy for the drug czar, I thought.

"When did your brother last see the weapons?"

"Last night."

Time was up.

I ushered him out, promising I'd protect him and his brother and think of a way for him to "give" me the drug lord's address without anyone knowing he spoke to me.

John said not to trust anyone, but he also said to trust my instincts. And my instincts told me this kid was telling the truth.

After he left, I waited a bit then went out

to the corridor again. The captain and major were still in the courtyard. I caught their attention and gestured for them to come up.

Once inside, I sat them down and lowered my voice.

"Listen," I told them. "I need to share some very sensitive information with you."

They leaned forward, like dogs salivating for a treat.

"We have intelligence coming in," I said, "I check in with Washington, DC, using a satellite phone. About two hours ago, I learned of three potential locations where the stolen weapons might be. I have three addresses."

"Give us the addresses," the captain demanded.

"I can't do that."

The next minute was very, very uncomfortable.

"This is very sensitive information," I continued. "If I give it to you and something goes wrong, it will reflect badly on all three of us. I need to pick three of your men to run down the intel on the addresses for me."

The captain hesitated.

"Okay," he said.

I walked out of my room with the officials at my side. The kids with machine guns were spread out everywhere.

"You, and you, and you!" I pointed at

three of them, including the kid with the soccer shirt.

"Come up here right now!" the major yelled, and they came running. My soccer kid looked terrified, worried I'd sold him out.

Once assembled, and with the blessings of the captain and major, I told the three bodyguards that I had a special, secret assignment for them. I handed each kid a piece of paper.

"I'm giving each of you an address. Your job is to go to the address and check what vehicles are parked in the driveway of the house. Don't talk to anybody. Be back here as soon as you can and report directly to me — not the captain or the major. Just to me. Do you understand?"

They nodded and scurried off.

For two of the bodyguards, I'd written down home addresses I found in a map in my hotel room. To my soccer kid, I gave a blank piece of paper and hoped he was smart enough to figure out what to do with it.

Within 90 minutes, they returned one by one.

The first kid was covered in sweat.

"I'm sorry, sir. I went to the house but the cars were not there."

I nodded.

The second kid showed up.

"Sir, I went to the house, but I didn't see any cars."

More nodding.

Then my soccer kid returned. He handed me the piece of paper and on it he'd written the address of the house and a note: THE WEAPONS ARE STILL THERE.

I folded up the piece of paper, stuck it in my pocket.

"Thank you, I'll let you know if I need anything else," I said, and dismissed him.

I shut the door.

"I know where the weapons are," I told the captain and major.

"Give us the address," the captain demanded.

"No."

"We insist you turn that piece of paper over to us," said the major.

"I'm sorry, but I can't do that," I told them. "I need to meet with your general, the one we met on the first day. I'll give him the information, and he can do whatever he wants with it. But I can't give it to you."

They looked royally pissed off.

"Look, if I give it to you and it goes bad, someone could get hurt or killed. So, if you want to put me in jail go ahead. But I'm not giving you the address."

"Agent Hilland, give us the information."

These guys looked like they were about to put a gun to my head. And we all knew I didn't have a gun. I didn't even have a rope to escape out the window.

It was time to put on a big show.

"This is FUCKING BULLSHIT!" I yelled, loud enough for all the guests in that hellhole hotel to hear me. "We're here to help you, and you jeopardize our lives and the lives of our sources? Take me to your commander or arrest me and throw me in jail," I shouted, practically spitting in their faces.

"But if you arrest me, it's going to be an international fucking incident. Take this piece of paper from me and there will be more US personnel here crawling up your ass by morning than you can imagine. And they'll be looking at things you don't want them to look at!"

As all this was going on, the other FBI agents were finishing up polygraph tests and arriving at my room to give me new charts. They got there in time to witness the standoff, and the officials backing down.

"Mr. Robert, we're sorry. Our apologies," the officials said. "Please calm down. Can we get you a drink?

"I don't need a drink!" I kept yelling. "I need to see your fucking general!"

A few hours later, my team and I — and the captain and major — were sitting with the general in an elevated, screened-in patio. We were on the military base somewhere, but it seemed more like the middle of a jungle. Exotic bugs and monster-sized mosquitos crawled up the mesh, trying to get to us.

Yellow fever, I thought. *Malaria. Did I just hear a jaguar?*

It was dark and ungodly hot and humid.

Back at the hotel, I memorized the address the soccer-kid gave me and ripped up the paper, flushing the bits down the toilet.

"Mr. Robert," said the general. "It is my understanding that you have information for me. Please, tell us the address where the weapons are."

The general and his staff were drinking cold cherry juice. They didn't seem hot at all, while I was sweating like I was en route to the electric chair. My heart was about to jump out of my chest.

"General, with all due respect, you're putting me in a very difficult situation," I said. "Even if I was back home in the United States, I would never divulge such specific information in front of so many people because it could be compromised."

"Mr. Robert," he said, "I trust these men with my life."

I didn't.

"I appreciate that, general. But I'm not going to publicly announce this to you. My men don't know the address because I want to protect them. The only person in this room who knows the address is me. I will give it to only you, general, and whatever you choose to do with it is up to you. We have done our job."

He agreed.

I took out paper from my pocket and wrote the address down, folded it, and slid it across a table to the general. He leaned back in his chair and read it, nodding, and put the paper in his pocket.

I tried to read his face. Was he involved or not? I couldn't tell. But the tension at that room was so thick you'd need a machete to cut it. Some were definitely involved.

"Mr. Robert, let me ask you. If this was happening in the United States, what advice do you have for me? What would you do?"

I told him I'd send a surveillance team to the area to keep eyes on the house and set up on all logical choke points in and out of the neighborhood. Then, at dawn, I'd send in a tactical team to hit the house and grab everyone and everything inside.

"I like that plan," he said, leaning back in his chair.

By the time we got back to our hotel, it was midnight. After many, many drinks at the courtyard bar, we all crashed in our beds. Until . . .

At 5 A.M., someone banged on my door.

"Mr. Robert!" It was the major. "We need you and your men to come with us!"

"Where are we going?"

"To the house."

"Did you find the weapons?"

"You will see," he said.

My team and I were taken in vans along the dirt roads of Guyana, passing rickety little homes and sheds, until we reached a palatial estate behind a six-foot concrete wall. Behind the wall were rows and rows of dogs in kennels. Out front, four military trucks and sixty troops lingered.

Inside, the house was destroyed. Cabinets and Sheetrock were ripped off walls, it was a mess. All the weapons and explosives were gone. Left in their wake were gun-cleaning kits associated with the specific weapons that had been stolen.

After I gave the address to the general, I

could only deduce that he gave the information to one of his men who tipped off the drug lord that they were coming, and they cleaned house.

Not everything was gone, though.

When I walked into the mansion, I was confused to see a man and a young woman there, hands handcuffed in front of them. The man wore a Muslim religious skullcap.

As it turned out, the guns were gone . . . but troops stumbled into the illicit love nest hideout of this man and woman, who were asleep when they stormed in. And it just so happened that the man was an international fugitive, wanted for an assassination attempt of the president of Trinidad in 1990.

So why did the major wake us up before sunrise and haul us across town to the mansion, when he knew the stolen stash was already gone? I think he wanted to show us that they followed up on the information I provided. And maybe, he wanted to say, with a wink — *too bad, but the weapons are all gone! Ha!*

Back at the hotel later that morning, we packed up our equipment and prepared to leave. The GDF had compromised the information I'd given them, so why would we continue working after such a charade?

As I passed through the courtyard on the

way out, the kid with the soccer ball shirt and I made eye contact. I gave him a little nod of thanks. We didn't speak. I didn't want to put him or his brother in harm's way if anyone saw us. But I could tell he knew what happened.

The next day, news of the captured fugitive was splashed all over the front pages of the local newspapers.

STOLEN AK-47S: FBI HELPS IDENTIFY SUSPECTS–TT COUP SUSPECT HELD
WANTED JAMMAT MAN NABBED IN GUYANA
WANTED TRINI PART OF
1990 COUP ATTEMPT

In the end, we didn't find the weapons or explosives, we didn't figure out who was dirty on the inside, and we didn't get the stockpile back. We might have been able to accomplish all the above had our investigation not been cut short by corruption in the Guyanese Defense Force.

But it's strange how when some things don't work out, others do.

As John keeps telling me, the universe will give us what we need, not always what we want. This is a lesson he tried to hammer home with me repeatedly.

Because a 21-year-old kid whose name I

never knew loved playing soccer, an international fugitive was caught and arrested.

I loved the fact that John Edward was right about the soccer ball. It showed me, once again, that I may not be able to trust many people out there in my travels. But I could trust John and his guides, even if their information didn't make sense to me at first.

When I got home and told John about the soccer ball shirt and the craziness of everything that happened, he didn't seem surprised at all.

"Cool!" he said.

GUYANA CHRONICLE Friday, May 5, 2006 3

Stolen AK-47s:

FBI helps identify suspects

— TT coup suspect held

THE United States Federal Bureau of Investigation (FBI) has helped local investigators identify several suspects in the case of the 30 high-powered AK-47 rifles and five pistols stolen from the Guyana Defence Force (GDF) headquarters, the Army announced last night.

And a Trinidadian terrorist suspect wanted by Trinidadian authorities has been held in a raid here by the Joint Services in the continuing search for the stolen weapons, the Army said.

The GDF said the Trinidadian being held by Police has identified himself as Mustafa Abdullah Muhammad, also known as Edmund DeFreitas, who is wanted by the Trinidadian authorities.

The man, the Army said, claimed he was a bodyguard for a known local narcotics trafficker (name given) and he was allegedly involved in the coup by the radical Jamaat Al Muslimeen group against the Trinidad and Tobago Government in 1990.

The Army said Muhammad is wanted in Trinidad for his alleged involvement in a murder attempt on a former member of the Jamaat Al Muslimeen, led by Yasin Abu Bakr.

Word of the arrest of the wanted man came as the GDF announced progress in the shocking theft of the AK-47s and pistols from a bond at its Camp Ayanganna headquarters in Georgetown.

An Army press release said the FBI is "working closely" with it in the missing weapons case.

It said the GDF investigation is progressing and several suspects have been identified.

The FBI assisted the GDF in conducting several polygraph examinations and interviews and the investigation produced additional leads that are being analysed by the FBI, the Joint Services and other organisations here and in the U.S., the release said.

The Army said the FBI is continuing to assist with the investigation.

The wanted Trinidadian

Wednesday morning, when the Joint Services swooped on a home in Nandy Park, East Bank Demerara.

A Joint Services source said several items were also seized in the raid.

The Jamaat al Muslimeen is a Muslim organisation in Trinidad with a membership of predominantly Afro-Trinidadians. The appeal of its doctrines to the poor and displaced classes of society has seen its membership and popularity increase.

Its leader Bakr led 114 members of the Jamaat in an attempted coup against the elected Trinidad and Tobago government on July 27, 1990.

Forty-two insurgents stormed the Red House – the seat of Parliament — and took the then

and most of his Cabinet hostage, while 72 of their compatriots attacked the offices of Trinidad and Tobago Television (TTT), then the only television station in the country and the Trinidad Broadcasting Company, then one of only two radio stations.

Over a six-day period members of the government, including the Prime Minister, were held hostage at gun point while chaos and looting broke out in the streets of the capital Port of Spain.

After six days of negotiation, the Muslimeen surrendered on August 1, and were taken into custody. They were tried for treason, but the Court of Appeal upheld the amnesty offered to secure their surrender, and they were released. The Privy Council in Britain later invalidated the

members were not rearrested.

About 40 people died during the coup attempt, with millions in property losses.

Present and past members of the organisation have been connected or prosecuted for serious violent crimes, including drug and gang related killings and a current spree of kidnappings for ransom of members of the Trinidad upper and middle class.

Bakr is being prosecuted with conspiracy to murder several of the group's former members who had spoken out publicly against the Jamaat al Muslimeen and its practices, and who were suspected of becoming witnesses in legal proceedings against its members.

They are under surveillance by the local National Security Agency as well as the U.S. Central Intelligence Agency for suspected terrorist relations with the Middle East, as are two other Mus-

Investigating missing weapons from the Guyanese Defense Force military base

23

Dogfights

Like the soccer ball in Guyana, sometimes it only takes one image, one word, or one fleeting thought from John to act as a key that would unlock a case or get a confession.

Until the summer of 2007, football player Michael Vick was at the height of his career — a celebrated quarterback for the Atlanta Falcons and admired by millions. A legend in his own time.

That summer, the NFL star was linked to an illegal dogfighting ring known as Bad Newz Kennels that had been operating for six years.

Vick was charged with breeding dogs on his property and training them to fight in arenas, for gambling purposes. Even worse, he was accused of brutally torturing and killing dogs with his own hands.

In an investigation that began that spring, a search of Vick's 15-acre property in Smithfield, Virginia, revealed nearly 70 dogs, mostly pit bulls, in backyard kennels. Many were injured. Police found blood, dog treadmills, scales, a breeding "rape rack," and a pry bar used to wrench a dog's jaws open.

Also behind the house, police found a mass grave filled with dead dogs.

After breeding them, Vick and his co-worker designed a "test" to see which dogs had a natural thirst for fighting, a killer instinct.

When the dogs matured to the age of one, they'd pit two pups together, rile them up, and let them go at each other. Some dogs fought ferociously; those ones were good bets for battle in the arena. Others had gentler natures. Those dogs were of no use to Vick and his operation, so they were murdered — by drowning, hanging, or beating.

Later, a forensic veterinarian for the American Society for the Prevention of Cruelty to Animals (ASPCA) would examine the dead bodies of numerous dogs from the mass graves on the site and find puncture marks, scoring on their bones, facial and skull fractures, broken necks and legs, and broken vertebrae.

The torture had become about more than just killing the dogs. To a handful at Bad Newz Kennels, it became a sport on its own, even a competition. Who could torture the dog worse? Electrocuting. Shooting. They got creative.

When details of the investigation hit the national media, the public outcry by animal rights activists, sports fans, and dog lovers around the country was immediate, vehement, and unforgiving.

Vick stood in front of a judge — "Hang 'Em High Henry" Hudson (known for his tough, hardline approach) — and swore that he, himself, had never personally tortured or killed a dog.

Was it the truth or not? He stood to lose everything if he was lying.

A trial date was set for November 2007.

Prosecutors worried the celebrity would go free unless they got an admission from Vick, so the pressure was on for the FBI to get a confession. I was asked to conduct the polygraph test personally.

Before meeting with Vick in October, I called John.

"You're going to have an issue or problem with the polygraph," he said immediately.

"What kind of issue?"

"Some confusion before the test starts."

"Okay . . ."

John paused. I could feel him watch the scene unfold.

"You need to talk to him about football," he said, matter-of-factly.

"John, I'm going to interrogate him about *dogs*."

"Yeah. I know."

"So why would I bring up football?"

Like the soccer ball in Guyana, it made no sense to me when he said it — but would later. And not for nothing, but for a guy who knew zilch about sports ("Is Whitey Bulger a baseball player?"), John gave me a hell of a lot of sports references.

"It's the way you'll get him to confess."

"But . . . how?"

"You're going to say something about football that will lead him to say something crucial about the dogs."

"I don't see the connection."

John sighed. I could be a stubborn SOB. But so could he.

"All I can tell you is what they're showing me," he insisted. "Talk to him about football. Use football terminology when you explain things. Trust me. My guides say you know how to do your job, and you do it well. Trust your instinct, you know what you're doing."

John added that there'd be a third person in the room when I got Vick to confess.

"You'll try to get this third guy on the

same page as you, in sync with you, before he talks."

I assumed John meant another FBI agent. I never imagined it would be Vick's own attorney.

"Man, you're a big guy," Vick said to me, when he walked into the polygraph room with his attorney at FBI Headquarters and shook my hand. I did tower over the guy — he was a mere 6 feet to my 6'8".

"You should have played football," he smiled.

And then we *did* talk about football a bit, but I wasn't thinking about what John said. Vick's attorney had left the room by now, and I was trying to build a rapport with the athlete.

"I played ball in high school," I told him. (And about ten years later, my son would play offensive lineman for the Miami Dolphins.)

Vick seemed nervous and afraid, and it was no wonder. On the front page of a major newspaper that morning, a journalist listed all the lucrative endorsement contracts and the millions upon millions of dollars Vick was losing because of his involvement with the dogfighting operation.

I can use his fear to lead to a confession is what I was thinking.

"Hey look, Mike," I said, very friendly. "I've been asked to talk to you today and run this polygraph. But before we even talk about a polygraph test, I'll tell you what I've been told about this case. And if anything is incorrect and you want to set the record straight, now is the time."

I was trying to give him an "out" — a way to save face — without him having to take the test, before enduring the indignity of the polygraph spitting out a ream of paper with lying lines all over it.

"Look, I don't have a dog in this fight, right?" I said.

He laughed.

"I'm a big fan of yours. Sometimes good people make bad decisions, I know that. You need to consider your situation . . ."

"Nope," he said, and dug in. "I didn't kill any of those dogs. I didn't touch them. I didn't hurt them."

I spent at least an hour trying to convince him to open up, but he wouldn't change his tune. I think he thought his celebrity might save him. That I'd be so enamored, I'd "pass" him like a schoolteacher giving a good mark to a pet student.

But the polygraph knows no favorites. It knows clear-cut truth and lies, and the body didn't lie. I was surprised Vick's attorney was even letting me polygraph his client, in fact. He must have thought Vick was telling the truth, and then he'd go back to "Hang 'Em High Henry," waving the test, saying: "He passed the polygraph!"

I reviewed the questions with Vick before starting, to make sure he understood them.

"Is your name Michael? Is today Tuesday? Are you in the FBI? Are you from Virginia? *Did you personally cause the death of any of those dogs?*"

That last one was crucial, of course. And when I went over it with Vick a few times, he answered "No."

I reviewed the questions one more time before starting the test.

"Did you personally cause the death of any of those dogs?"

"Yes."

"Yes? Mike, stop. We reviewed this question. It means did you personally, with your own hands, torture or kill any of those dogs."

"No, I didn't do any of that."

"Okay, but that's what the question means. Do you understand that?"

"Yes."

"Okay. Let's do it one more time."

I went through the list of questions again, and got to . . .

"Did you personally cause the death of any of those dogs?"

"Yes."

I put my clipboard and pen down. I remembered John's words: *Confusion before the test starts.*

"Time out, Michael. Help me understand. Why are you here today?"

"I'm here because that fucking judge doesn't believe me."

"What doesn't the judge believe?"

"He thinks I killed and tortured those dogs."

"And what's my job today, Michael? What am I supposed to do?"

I was talking to him like he was a kid because that's the impression he was giving. He was coming across like a not-too-bright, woefully educated teenager.

"You're going to give me a lie detector test to see if I'm telling the truth," he said.

"Okay, good. So, if you were me, what questions should I ask you on this test?"

He paused, shifting in his seat.

"Well . . . you might want to ask me, 'Did you hang any of those dogs?' or, 'Did you drown any of those dogs?' "

I wrote the questions down, hooked him up, and we began.

"Did you personally hang any of those dogs on that Friday in April?"

"No."

"Did you personally drown any of those dogs on that Friday in April?"

"No."

Vick failed the polygraph test — badly. And now I had to confront him about it in the post-test interview. About thirty FBI agents eagerly watched the ensuing drama from behind a two-way mirror.

"Listen, Mike," I said, as I scanned the charts on the table between us.

"There is no doubt based upon the results of this test that you've not been honest with me and we need to fix this. There's no question you were involved in the killing of these dogs. Now let's work together and figure out a way to walk this back so it doesn't look so bad on you."

He started cursing, suddenly indignant.

I immediately switched tacks.

"Hey, Mike, here's your situation. The evidence is overwhelming. This thing is going to go to trial and then, one by one, your friends are going to get up on the stand and tell the story under oath. They're going to say you were with them when these dogs were hung and tortured, and that you slammed that one dog against the concrete until he was dead. All your friends are going to tell the same story, and you're going to get up there and say, 'I don't know nothing about nothing.' "

"And here's the problem with that," I said. "There will be 12 jurors. I'm going to guess at least half of them have dogs and love dogs. So, when you get up in front of them and say, 'I don't know nothing,' you're going to have a big, big problem."

He sat with arms folded. Nope.

"I want to see my attorney."

Shit. There goes my chance for a confession out the window. I went to get his lawyer.

"Listen. Michael failed the test. I've been talking to him. It's clear he's not telling the truth."

"Let me talk to him," said the attorney.

I left them alone for half an hour. When I returned, the lawyer was in full defense mode.

"Special Agent Hilland, there's a huge problem with this polygraph. It's not a valid test, it's not admissible in court, as you are aware," he said. "And Michael tells me the questions were confusing to him. He didn't understand them."

"That's impossible."

"What do you mean it's impossible?"

"Michael gave me the questions to ask him. Isn't that right, Michael?"

The attorney looked at Michael.

"Is that right, Michael?"

Vick was silent, so I answered for him.

"Yeah, it's right. Listen . . ."

I was sitting between the two men. I turned to the attorney and began talking to him as if Michael wasn't in the room.

"We've got to help this guy. He's a hero. Children look up to him. I love your client. I don't want him walking out of here with a failed polygraph test. We've got to work together to make this right."

(Later I would remember John's words: *You'll try to get this third guy on the same page as you.*)

I was about to say more, when I glanced down at my notebook: *Talk to him about football.*

A visual hit me like a bolt of lightning. I saw Vick on the field, in slo-mo replay, running across the gridiron at the speed of light. And I knew in a flash what that link was between football and a confession that John was talking about.

This guy was insanely fast on the field. Most quarterbacks are great at throwing and he was good at that, too. But what made Vick truly special was his ability to *scramble.*

When he moved, no one could touch him. Especially when all looked lost and he was about to be sacked. That's when he'd sprint across the turf to touchdown victory.

And anyone watching could see he played with the heart of a lion — a love of the pure beauty and thrill of the game. He sped down that field like Gretzky on ice. I remembered that in the polygraph pretest, he didn't seem worried about losing money or going to jail. No wonder my other approaches didn't work. What mattered to him most was playing football. And winning. And out-running everyone else.

Talk to him about football.

"Michael, let me ask you something. You're a very famous man. Why do you think you're so famous?"

He shrugged. "Because I'm a football player."

I shook my head.

"No. There are 32 teams in the NFL and 60 or 70 guys on each team. People watching don't know who most of them are. Why are you famous?"

"Well. I'm a quarterback."

"Not it, either. There are a lot of quarterbacks in the NFL. Three or four per team. Over a hundred quarterbacks. We could march any of them down the street and no one would know who most of them are."

I leaned in.

"What is it about *you,* Michael, that makes you so famous?"

He paused, a little confused. His attorney, too, wondered where I was going with this.

"I guess I'm fast."

I smacked my hand on the table.

"That's right! You're *fast.* You have superhuman speed. There's a Nike commercial on TV right now called 'The Michael Vick Experience' about how fast you are. People love watching you because in the middle of a game when the world is collapsing around you, you scramble out of the pocket and score a touchdown. Or you find that open receiver and somehow throw the ball to him. Just when you're about to lose everything . . . you win the game."

I sat up.

"As we sit here talking, Mike, your whole world is collapsing around you. But this is not a football game. Instead of losing the game or taking a sack, you're going to lose your freedom. You're going to go to jail. You won't be able to play football anymore."

He looked in agony.

I did my leaning-in thing again.

"Michael, you can lie to me. You can lie to the judge. You can lie to investigators. It doesn't matter. But you can't lie to the man sitting next to you, your attorney. He's the only man right now that's open on the field. You've got to throw the ball to him if you want to win this."

Vick looked at his attorney and burst into tears.

"I'm sorry!" he said. "I killed all those fucking dogs. I hung them, I drowned them, I slammed them. Whatever they said, I did it!"

I sat back in my chair. The attorney looked sick. Vick sobbed.

Talk to him about football.

Eight days later, Vick's attorney announced the quarterback would plead guilty to the federal felony dogfighting conspiracy charge.

The following month, Vick was indicted by a grand jury on charges of unlawfully torturing and killing dogs.

In December 2007, Michael Vick was sentenced to 23 months in prison.

The torturing of dogs, the torturing of humans. After so many years on the job I still wasn't sure how to come to terms with the horrors humans do.

In 2008, I was promoted to run the FBI Polygraph Program in DC and moved the family to Stafford, Virginia. Soon after, I was deployed to Afghanistan.

After 9/11, the US military began conducting tactical assaults on strategic locations, going into areas they thought terrorists were conspiring or building bombs. Each time the Special Forces guys hit a location, they'd round up dozens of suspects but couldn't be sure which were terrorists and which were in the wrong place at the wrong time.

The FBI was supplying the military with polygraph examiners to help determine this, and my job was to interview, interrogate, and polygraph the suspects.

In 2002, I was at the DC FBI office when some colleagues called me over to a TV screen.

"Bob, you've got to see this," said one. They keyed up a videotape and pressed play. I couldn't believe my eyes: it was a video of the beheading of US journalist Daniel Pearl, who'd been abducted by Islamist militants in Pakistan and murdered in 2002.

I'd broken into a cold sweat and got queasy. A man was sawing another man's head off. I'd seen a lot in my life, but this was unfathomable. I turned away.

This image of Daniel Pearl was burned into my memory — as was my year searching through the smoldering rubble at Ground Zero — as I boarded the plane to Afghanistan.

I was angry. I wanted revenge. I wanted to kill anyone who *looked* like a terrorist, and in my mind, I was going to a place that was the source of evil. I was also scared and sure I'd die in this war zone.

"Should I go?" I asked John, before leaving. "A lot of bad shit could happen."

"It's going to be scary, and you'll see a lot of things, and as your brother I'm worried about you," he said. "But you will be okay. Trust your instincts and intuition. If something doesn't feel right, back out of it. If you sense something is wrong, pull yourself out. Okay?"

"Okay."

Had he told me not to go, I wouldn't have.

AFGHANISTAN DIARY, AUGUST 14, 2008

Earlier today I called my parents to say goodbye. I know they're both worried. My dad said, "Know that I will be there with you and that I am proud of you, and I love you."

I was speechless.

I was in Afghanistan for four months interrogating dirty interpreters, weeding out government corruption, and identifying bomb-making locations responsible for killing coalition forces.

I polygraphed a Taliban leader in whose eyes the hate was so hot it could burn holes through your flesh. I tested weapons smugglers and terrorists — most failed. On September 11, I took the US flags I'd packed and hung them up around the Bagram Theater Internment Facility (BTIF), the prison holding the detainees.

I got sick from drinking the water and puked day and night. An American woman went missing, kidnapped by Islamic radicals. We had suicides on the airbase. Al-Qaeda forces shot rocket-propelled grenades into our base in Kandahar, and we ran to bomb shelters. A rash of American soldiers who struggled with depression from the trauma and estrangement from loved ones committed suicide.

The birds looked different in Afghanistan, like skunks with wings. If I was lucky, I reached Alex and the kids by phone for a few minutes as they rushed to school in the morning. Caitie wore my shirts when I was away, to feel close to me.

Late one night, I was heading to a remote base near Pakistan in a small plane when, a crew member rushed over.

"We're going down!" he yelled over the engine roar, tightening a five-point harness around me.

The plane dove and shook violently,

touching the ground but not quite stopping. Explosions and gunfire surrounded the moving plane, illuminating the insight with red.

Out of the darkness, a group of soldiers ran to the plane and jumped in. Two were hoisted in, already dead. A minute later, the belly of the plane shot up like a rocket. They were US soldiers who'd been ambushed and needed extraction.

My time in Afghanistan was harrowing, but I left that country with a great gift.

On one of my final days, I visited an impoverished family who lived in an adobe mud hut. The old man, the head of the family, was so excited to have a guest he put out whatever meager food they had — a bowl of almonds, a dish of prunes. They were starving, they had nothing, and the man had tears of joy and pride in his eyes as he presented their only food to me.

Truly, my heart broke with love for this man. I was ashamed of the ignorance and anger I carried in me when I arrived in his country. I realized it didn't matter if you are from Afghanistan or the former Soviet Union or China or the United States or Pakistan.

Wherever you are, there exists only two kinds of people in this world — Good and

Bad. And not only can you find evil where you least expect it, but you can find beauty and love where you never imagine it will be.

I returned home thirty pounds lighter, a week before Christmas. The plane ride was a dream. Alex picked me up at Dulles airport, and after a shower and change into civilian clothes (blue jeans!) at home, we drove to the kids' schools to surprise Connor, now 13, and Caitie, now 11. They were expecting me to arrive a week later.

When Caitie saw me enter her classroom, she ran to me and jumped in my arms, crying. She hugged me so tight; her little body was shaking. I was choked up but tried not to show it. I carried her into the next room and hugged her for eons.

Connor was in phys ed when I got to his school. I peeked into the gym and caught a glimpse of him — my God, he'd grown so much! The teacher called him out from his dodgeball game and when he saw me, he was shocked.

"Hello, son," I said. I tried to give him a hug and kiss, but realized I was embarrassing him in front of his friends. We shook hands. There'd be time for hugging later.

That night, I took the family out for pizza.

The sense of security and peace I felt being home with my loved ones was indescribable.

TDY Assignment to Afghanistan – 2008

Contents Page

August 14th 2008 @ 10 pm – Dulles DC Thursday

– I just got through the final security checkpoint at the Airport and I'm waiting to get on the plane. Saying goodbye to Alex and the kids was terrible! Caitie couldn't stop crying and even Connor turned away a couple of times so I wouldn't see him get so upset. And most of all Alex. She's got the weight of the world on her shoulders for the next four months. I have no doubt in her abilities to handle any situation. I could not have done any better than her.

Earlier today I called my parents to say goodbye. I know they're both worried. My dad said, "Know that I will be there with you and that I am proud of you and I love you." – I was speechless. When mom got on the phone afterwards I was still upset but did my best to hide it.

I have the best family a guy could ever have.

August 15th 2008 @ 9:53pm – Doha Friday

The flight from Washington to Doha, Qatar was about 13 hours. Most slept but I couldn't. These seats are not designed for guys my size. There are 10 Agents traveling together. We all met at the Doha Airport. It was like being in a different world once we got off of the plane. The people, their dress, the smells, colors and heat (103°F at night.) The military picked us up and brought us

Afghanistan Diary, Day One: I left home with John's support and my family's love.

old to remember all of this. In the four months of separation the kids have grown up so much. I feel alot older & tired. I know this if nothing else. God has blessed me with a beautiful family and a tremendous life. They mean more to me then anything else. I would be lost without any of them.

- Alex, Connor and Carter - I love you so much and cannot tell you how proud you make me every day! Please forgive me for the separation and the times I could not be with you. Although I was on the other side of the world, I carried you in my heart every day and thought of you constantly. It's great to be home.

Love,

Dad (B)

Afghanistan Diary finale: After months of terrorists, corruption, suicides, and Al-Qaeda grenades, it was "great to be home."

Home at last, I can't believe it.

This was by far the most challenging and difficult four months I can ever remember. Being away from Alex and the kids was terrible. Time goes too quickly . . . the kids have grown up so much. I feel a lot older and tired.

I know this if nothing else: God has blessed me with a beautiful family and tremendous life. They mean more to me than anything else. I would be lost without them.

Alex, Connor, and Caitie . . . I love you so much and cannot tell you how proud you make me every day! Please forgive me for the separation and the times I could not be with you. Although I was on the other side of the world, I carried you in my heart and thought of you constantly.

It's great to be home.

Love,
Dad (B)

Flying to a remote Forward Operating Base near Pakistan: "We're going down!"

24

Lady in the Wall

Despite my wavering trust in the human race, I've always considered myself a man of faith.

I'd also become a man who believed in and asked for signs from the Other Side. This is largely due to John Edward. That night Fran willed the streetlamp to burst to life and blaze like a torch in front of me burned an indelible memory. From that day forward, I was certain we all, even I, could communicate with the world of energy.

By 2008, I'd known John for a decade, and I believed in him. Alex still thought he was a con artist, but to me he was one of the few people I could trust.

His words carried weight with me. They meant something to me.

On Mother's Day in 2008, John's words and a sign from the Other Side saved my sanity.

Alex was visiting her mother that day in

Jersey and I was home, when I heard a frantic knock at the door — one of Connor's friends. He was crying.

"Mr. Hilland, come fast. There's been an accident!"

"Is Connor okay?"

"No!"

The boys were riding their bikes, speeding down a steep hill, when Connor hurled through the air and slammed into the concrete with his head.

When I got to him about a mile away, he was curled up on the side of the road with his head split open, blood everywhere. His eyes were glazed and unfocused. I grabbed him and put him in the front seat. Caitie was in the back. I held a dishrag to Connor's head with one hand and drove with the other. Blood dripped down my arm.

By the time we got to the hospital he was unconscious. The nurses rushed him into a room as they cut the clothes off his body. I stood in the corner of the room helpless, trying to breathe. The heart monitor beeped, he flatlined — his heart stopped.

I stood there and watched my son die; I felt like I was dying with him.

Please God. Don't take my son. Take me instead. Let him live. I promise I'll be good for the rest of my life. I'm not strong enough to do this. I can't do this. You must give me a sign it's going to be okay.

The doctors pressed the paddles against Connor's chest and his body jumped on the table. His heart started beating.

The doctor took me into the room with the X-rays and CT-scans stuck up on the light board. The images look like someone's thrown a soft-boiled egg into a wall. He's saying words like "traumatic brain injury" and "brain swelling" and "skull compression" and "impaired."

Please, God, give me a sign.

"Mr. Hilland, you're in the FBI?" the doctor asked. "My father was an FBI agent for 25 years, he just retired. Don't worry, I'm going to do everything I can to take care of your son."

That was my first sign.

The second came as I was on a highway as a rainstorm began with a distraught Caitie in the backseat and Connor in a helicopter above us. We were all heading to a Level 3 Trauma Center a two-hour's drive north.

Please, God, let Connor live. Let him be okay.

The phone rang. *John.*

"Bob, what's going on?"

"My son had an accident. It's not looking good."

John was quiet. I knew he was asking his guides for information.

"Where is he now?" John asked.

"They're flying him in a helicopter to this other hospital."

I was trying to keep it together for Caitie's sake.

Another pause. Then . . .

"Your grandfather's looking out for him," John said.

I wanted to throw up. My grandfather was dead. I swerved, barely able to see the road through the water-streaked windshield. *Was he telling me my son had crossed over?*

"John, what do you mean!"

"Your grandfather is watching out for him."

Oh, God. He was dead. I couldn't hold back in front of Caitie anymore.

"John, is my son alive?!"

"Yes!"

"Is he going to be okay?"

Another pause. It lasted a few seconds but felt like an eternity. The windshield wipers squeaked. Every fraction of a second, I died a little bit more.

"Is he going to be okay?!" I repeated, more urgently.

"Yes," John said, with confidence. "He's going to be okay."

I breathed.

Connor told me later that in the helicopter, he was conscious but felt "total peace." As if someone was watching over him.

I kept praying, but I breathed easier for the rest of the drive.

After ten years, I knew that if John told me my son would be okay, he would be. And he was.

The following year, in the fall of 2009 and five days before her wedding day, 24-year-old Yale doctoral student Annie Marie Le vanished from the Ivy League university's New Haven, Connecticut, campus.

She was a petite, pretty girl of Vietnamese descent — only 4'11" and 90 pounds. In high school, Annie was class valedictorian and voted student "most likely to be the next Einstein."

She diligently worked her way through the levels of higher education with scholarships, finally reaching one of the most prestigious schools in the world. At Yale, she was studying in a graduate program to earn a doctorate in pharmacology.

Earlier that year, she'd written an article for a Yale Medical School magazine titled "Crime and Safety in New Haven" in which she interviewed the chief of the Yale

University Police about how students can prevent crime.

She wrote:

> Pay attention to where you are.
> Avoid portraying yourself as a potential victim.
> Reduce your exposure (use the Yale escort and shuttle services).
> Walk with a purpose.

Surveillance video showed Annie entering a school building on September 8 but never leaving. That building housed the school's medical lab where she worked. A search of the lab found blood and signs of a struggle . . . but no Annie.

Like Michael Vick's, this was another highly publicized case splashed on the front pages of the media, attracting frenzied public interest and empathy.

A multitude of law enforcement agencies pooled together to search for her — Yale police, Connecticut state police, New Haven police, the Connecticut State Attorney General's Office, and the FBI. A polygraph examiner in Connecticut, Cathy, was tapped to work on the case. Because her boss was off duty with a new baby, I drove up from Washington to help.

By the time I got to New Haven, Annie had been missing less than a day. The lab had been searched thoroughly, I was told, and there were no leads, suspects, or witnesses. The theory among law enforcement officials was that whoever hurt or killed Annie took her body out of the building and dumped it somewhere. Officers were searching through the nearby Hartford, Connecticut, dump where Yale's garbage goes.

Within an hour or so, the case agents identified Ray Clark as the lead suspect. Clark, also 24, was the lab's rodent wrangler. He took care of the hundreds of mice and rats in their little cages.

Not only was Clark the last known person to be in the medical lab with Annie, but he was also one of the few people who carried the type of electronic ID card required to enter thc area where Annie worked. Also, when I read his written statement of what he'd done during the hours of Annie's disappearance, something stood out to me as odd.

"And then I went to the men's room," he wrote. It sounded normal and innocuous on its own, but how he'd written it and where he placed it was not. The phrase wasn't connected to the previous sentence or the one that followed. Its interjection disrupted the flow, as if it was a Freudian slip of the pen.

Then there was the matter of his polygraph test, which Cathy was finishing up when I arrived on site.

"Are you withholding any information about Annie Le's disappearance?" Cathy asked Ray. "Do you know where Annie Le is now?"

"No," he answered both times, and failed spectacularly.

I noticed he had fresh, unusual marks on his arms and wrists. The case agents had already questioned him about it and photographed the injuries.

"Where did you get those marks?" they asked him.

"Playing softball," he replied. "I'm a very aggressive player."

This was the guy, I thought. *No doubt about it.*

On day two, I went to examine the crime scene — the medical lab. Special Agent Jim Wines and a few other Connecticut State Police investigators accompanied me. It was a nondescript, white, sterile room. The shelves on the wall were stacked with mice and the drawers filled with rats, to be used for drug experiments. It reminded me of a high school science lab. The rest of the building was a maze of hallways and similar laboratories.

The lab had been processed forensically with chemicals that exposed blood splatters and strands of Annie's hair where her struggle with the assailant occurred. After looking around, I stepped out of the building with the others as my phone rang.

It was John, calling from Ireland.

I'd left him a voicemail the night before, asking for help on the new case, but forgot he was across the ocean for an event in Dublin. While there, he intended to do some personal "spiritual" work, too. John's father, John McGee, Sr., was of Irish descent. And while John had always been drawn to his mother's Italian side growing up, he was now making it a point to explore his Irish roots and immerse himself in the culture; it was a way to continue his healing work with his father.

Fathers and sons, it was a real theme with us.

He was calling from a car on the way to his event. I moved away from the group to answer.

"John! I need your help. There's this . . ."

I didn't need to say any more, he was off and running — as fast as Michael Vick heading into the end zone.

"You're in Connecticut, right?" he asked.

"Yeah."

"You're looking for a female, in her twenties.

I'm getting an A name, like Anne Marie or Annie. Yes, Annie. She was attacked."

"Yes. She was attacked."

The other agents and officers nearby could hear bits of my conversation and looked over, wondering who I was talking to.

"Hold on a second," John said. He was putting me "on hold" to listen to his guides — like taking a call from the Other Side.

"Where are you right now?" he asked.

"I'm in the building where she worked."

"She swiped in, but never swiped out," he said.

"Yes, that's right."

His voice gained momentum.

"It's a building with a bunch of different rooms, right? And . . . mice? Yep, mice. It's a laboratory? Was she a scientist?"

"Yes. Mice, lab, scientist . . ."

"Hold on," John said. He would describe to me later what his guides were doing. They began taking him on a virtual tour through the building, left and right along the maze of hallways and classrooms. Because of his background as a phlebotomist, they were showing him all sorts of items he'd recognize — lab equipment, microscopes, test tubes.

"Where's the mini refrigerator?" he asked, with urgency.

"What are you talking about?"

"There's a mini refrigerator somewhere. Go to it. Right now. Go to the mini refrigerator!"

His tone was deliberate, clear, and excited.

I turned to the group a few feet away.

"Hey, did you come across a mini refrigerator when you guys searched this place?"

"Yeaaaah," said the crime scene captain. "How'd you know that?"

"Where is it?"

"It's down the hall, at the other side of the building."

"Show me!"

We strode back into the building and the captain led me down a hall. The others followed, like I was the Pied Piper.

"Who's Bob talking to?" someone asked, as we strode past classrooms.

"I have no idea," said another.

John's voice, from a car in Dublin across the ocean, was in my ear.

"Bob, are you at the fridge yet?!"

The captain took us on a sharp right turn into a little cul-de-sac and we hit a dead end. Tucked away in the corner of that dead end was a mini refrigerator.

"We're at the fridge," I told him.

"Okay. You should see two doors," John said. "One door on either side of the fridge — one on the right, one on the left."

"I see two doors."

"Go into the door *on the left*. She's behind that door. She's in there!"

My heart was going boom, boom, BOOM. I tried the handle and it was locked.

"Guys, did you search behind this door?" I asked the group.

They were still looking at me like I was nuts, but they could feel the energy of whatever was going on.

"I think so," said the captain, revved up.

"What's behind there?"

"Nothing!"

"Are you sure?"

I could hear John on the phone.

"SHE'S IN THERE. SHE'S RIGHT THERE!"

We opened it.

It was a noisy utility room, probably 35 feet by 14 feet, with pipes all over the place. It reminded me a bit of the pumphouse pit at Smith's factory, but that was a dark, greasy cesspool. This room was spotless and snow white.

"Guys, are you sure you checked here?"

Everyone started looking around.

I looked up.

"SHE'S RIGHT NEXT TO YOU," John said in my ear. "SHE'S TO YOUR RIGHT!"

I look up and to my right.

What tha . . .

On the pristine ceiling a few feet away — about 12 feet high — was one, perfect, sneaker footprint. It was so detailed, it looked like a fingerprint cops take when they book you.

"Whose sneaker print is that?"

"Oh, probably one of the evidence people who processed the scene," said the captain.

"Are you sure?"

"No."

I could hear John's voice in the phone.

"SHE'S TO YOUR RIGHT. SHE'S BETWEEN SOMETHING," he said. "SHE'S BETWEEN PIPES."

I put the phone to my ear: "What's on the other side of the wall?" John asked, pumped up.

"Captain, what's on the other side of this wall?"

He thought for a moment.

"A bathroom," he said. "The men's room."

I held my breath.

And then I went to the men's room, wrote the suspect, Ray, in his statement.

I ran out of the utility room toward the men's room. Everyone followed. Once inside, we searched every corner and tossed the place high and low.

"BOB, SHE IS RIGHT THERE," John kept saying.

It was like we were playing the children's game of "Hot and Cold," and John kept telling me I was hot, hot, hot, but I couldn't find the hidden object.

"She's not here, John," I said. "She's not here."

By then, John had arrived at the Helix, the venue where his Dublin event was taking place, and had to get off the phone.

After I hung up, I looked up at the group. They were waiting, confused, expectant, wondering if I was going to explain the frantic pursuit I'd taken them on.

"Bob," someone asked, "*who* were you talking to?"

"Oh, just a source," I said.

When I left the campus that day, I tried to analyze what could have gone wrong.

Well, "wrong" was the wrong word.

Annie wasn't there, that was true. Or at least, we didn't find her. But it didn't mean John was *wrong.*

I trusted and believed in him and his guides. So maybe at one point Annie was in the location John led me to, and the killer had moved her body? Much like the way he'd felt Fran's energy at the pumphouse at Smith's workplace that time.

"Keep running your cadaver dogs," I told the police officers, before I left.

If Annie was there, the dogs would pick up her scent in due time.

A few days later I drove back to headquarters. I got off the Jersey turnpike and crossed the Delaware Bridge when my phone rang.

"Bob, you're not going to fucking believe this," said Special Agent Wines, who'd been with me during the John call at the lab.

"We took the dogs into the men's room today and they went nuts."

In the bathroom, he explained, the dogs ran into a stall against the wall that separated it from the utility room on the other side. In the stall was a big metal door, a "pipe chase" where janitors and maintenance people have access to interior pipes, gauges, and valves. The dogs started pawing at this metal door.

"We looked at the lock on the door and noticed someone had jimmied it open," said the officer. "We opened it up, and there she was, Bob. Annie was *right there*."

Ray had killed Annie and wedged her tiny body up in a space within the wall between the men's room and the utility room. The day they found her, said the officer, was Annie's planned wedding day.

"But that's not all," said Wines.

It seemed Ray, the murderer, had a quirk — he loved using pens with green ink. He always carried pens with green ink. After he hid Annie's body in the wall, he realized that his favorite green pen was missing from his shirt pocket. It must have fallen into the space when he was shoving her body in, he thought. As I said before, a Freudian slip of the pen.

Not only would it be evidence against him if it was found, but he liked that pen and wanted it back. Yet he didn't want to risk opening that door and her body falling out. Which is why, we deduced, he tried to get in from the other side. He went next door to the utility room and climbed up into the ceiling with a flashlight to crawl around for his green pen.

"The sneaker print on the wall was his," said Wines.

The eerie thing about the sneaker print was this: in the article Annie wrote a few months earlier, "Crime and Safety in New Haven," she urged students that if they were accosted, they should try to remember details about what the attacker looked like to identify them later, especially the shoes.

> . . . clothing, facial hair or distinct facial details (if unmasked), and other physical features. These are the usual, but Chief Perrotti added one twist: the shoes. "The shoes are very important because they can shed the clothing along the way . . . shoes are unique."

Even after all these years, I was still amazed at John's ability. And that our long-distance detective work was as clear as if he'd been in that lab with me.

I called him right away in Ireland as soon as I hung up with the police officer. He was on his way to the Helix again for another event.

"You are not going to believe this," I said. "She was there."

"Where did they find her?"

"Between the wall, in between the pipes, right where you said to look."

"I knew it," he said. "I absolutely knew it."

Nine days after Annie Le was murdered by strangulation, rodent-wrangler and rat-keeper Ray Clark was arrested. His attack had been sexually motivated, but when she fought back, he killed her.

Annie's disappearance and murder drew so much public attention and nationwide sympathy that her funeral was broadcast live on the internet.

In March 2011, Ray Clark pleaded guilty to murder and was sentenced to 44 years in prison.

After John got back from Dublin, we went out for one of our usual steak dinners. John lived on filet mignon and French fries.

He told me about his trip and all that he'd seen, and how he'd found a new kinship with the Irish people. I gave him an update on the kids, and that Connor's brain injury had healed enough so he could start playing football in his freshman year at high school.

The perks of having a world-renowned psychic medium as your friend are that in times of emergency, like Connor's accident, he can see into the future and tell you everything is going to be okay.

But it worked the other way, too. He knew when something *wasn't* going to be okay. And whatever his guides showed him, he was supposed to relay.

"Hey, how's your marriage?" he asked, as we dug into our steaks.

"What?"

"My guides are telling me to ask you, how is your marriage?"

I wasn't alarmed by the question at all.

"It's okay," I said. As far as I knew, all was fine.

John nodded, but he looked worried.

Out on the streets of midtown Manhattan, we walked to our cars and stopped on a corner to say a quick goodbye. Like I said before, we were an odd pair — oddly alike. Standing under the streetlights, we got on the topic of our fathers and how similar our relationships with them had been growing up.

"We're like brothers," I said.

"Brothers in experience," John added. "And the universe brought us together to learn from each other and fulfill what we need to do."

But was I fulfilling it?

Months later, I rode my motorcycle — a black, gold, and chrome Yamaha V Star 1300 — from Virginia to John's new office on Long Island. He'd wrapped up two TV shows in Manhattan by now and relocated his office back to the neighborhood where he'd grown up, the area where we first met.

It was a seven-hour ride, but I liked the flying feeling of freedom — riding a motorcycle was therapeutic for me. Meditative. I sped along the highways in a black motorcycle jacket, black gloves, boots, and full helmet. I didn't dare tell Alex what was about to transpire in John's office — he was going to give me a Tarot card reading. *More hocus-pocus,* she would have said.

In the office, John shuffled the cards. The air smelled like sage.

"Ask your question," he said.

"Will I ever find Fran?" I asked.

John gave me a look, like: *I already knew you'd ask that.*

He spread the cards across the table into a messy pile, then pulled them altogether, and picked out a card. He turned it face up and laid it on the table. It was a picture of a man standing among a bunch of rods.

"The Nine of Wands," he said, tapping the card with his finger.

"What does it mean?"

"The Nine of Wands teaches patience in battle and healing. It's a about resilience, courage, persistence, and a test of faith."

"Soooo . . . does that mean I will find Fran or not?"

John paused in that thoughtful way he always does.

"They're telling me *yes* . . . but . . ."

"But what?"

"But . . . *not yet.*"

I laughed and sat back in my chair.

But they didn't say I *wouldn't* find her, right? So I kept going.

One of my final elaborate searches for Fran was in the middle of a freak snowstorm on April Fool's Day in 2012.

I went back to Smith's old house in Milford, Connecticut, with the New Haven FBI Evidence Response Team and more cadaver dogs, more ground-penetrating radar, and another excavation team. We dug next to the foundation of the house after neighbors remembered Smith digging there at the time of Fran's disappearance.

Nothing. Just a few buried, frozen animal bones, like our disappointing results from the Boone House dig in 1999.

Who was the fool, yet again? Me. I was.

I drove back to Virginia that night, and as the snow pelted my car on the New Jersey Turnpike, I yelled out loud at Fran.

"I quit! Do you hear me? I don't give a shit anymore! If you want to be found, you've got to give me a fucking sign or I'm done with you! I'm done with this case!"

I didn't see any lamplights burst to life and blaze like a torch, like I'd seen seven years earlier, the last time I asked Fran for a sign.

This time, she sent me flames on a grander scale. It was at Smith's old factory again, but it wasn't a flickering lamplight.

I got a call the next day from the owners of Carborundum, Smith's industrial factory. Somehow, in the middle of the night, the factory had caught fire and burned down to the ground in a dramatic, blinding inferno.

Whoa.

I wasn't giving up on her. *Not yet.*

25

Noah's Fighter Plane

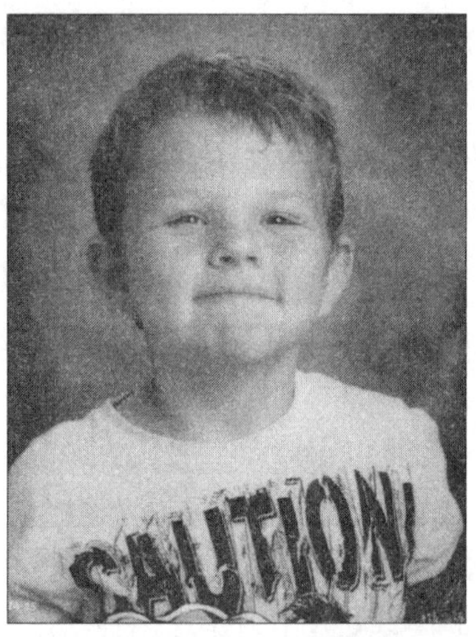

Five-year-old Noah loved Batman and Star Wars . . . *and he touched our hearts.* (COURTESY OF THE FBI)

Some cases break your heart more than others.

That's how John and I felt about a five-year-old boy with carrot-colored hair and a dimpled smile that would melt you.

Little Noah Thomas loved wearing his black-and-yellow Batman shirt and playing with his *Star Wars* X-wing fighter jet. He loved riding his Big Wheels up and down the path by his family's trailer home in Dublin, Virginia, without his coat on in the winter. His little ears stuck out like Opie on *The Andy Griffith Show,* and he gave hugs to the school lunch lady. His favorite food was birthday cake. Noah wanted to be a farmer when he grew up.

At midnight in the spring of 2015, I frantically climbed the bumpy hill behind Noah's home with John Edward in my ear, giving directions. We were looking for the little boy, who'd been missing for nearly three days.

John always excelled at keeping his emotions at bay when we worked. I was usually stoic and professional out in the field.

But this time, with this case, John and I were both gripped and driven by the same feelings of fear and love. John's son, Justin, was now 12. My son, Connor, was now 19. John and I had both grown up with absent fathers and vowed to always love and protect our own boys fiercely.

So, on the hill that day, John and I were fueled by a similar, profound, grief and urgency:

This little boy could be my son.

On the morning of Sunday, March 22, little Noah went missing from the family's single-wide trailer in Dublin, a small town in Pulaski County, four hours west of Richmond, Virginia.

Noah's mother, Ashley, had driven her husband, Paul, to his factory job earlier with Noah and his little sister, Abby, 15 months, in the car.

She returned to the trailer with the kids, she told the police, put the baby back in the crib, and fell back to sleep. Little Noah, filled with the zip of a kindergartener, stayed awake to watch cartoons.

When his mother woke up a little later, she reported, the baby was crying and Noah was gone. One of the doors of their trailer was ajar. She went outside to look for him, thinking he went outside to play, but she couldn't find him. She called 911.

By the time I got to Dublin, Noah had been missing for 24 hours.

I drove throughout the night and arrived at the Pulaski County Sheriff's Office early Monday morning for a briefing.

At the time I served as a Supervisory Special Agent in the Richmond Division. One of the programs I oversaw was Crimes Against Children.

The Pulaski County Sheriff's Office and the local FBI supervisor had set up a command post and led a team of investigators through the night. I arrived to relieve my colleague and supervise the command post.

MISSING CHILD

NOAH TERRY THOMAS

DOB: 06/26/2009

Age: 5

Missing: 3/22/2015

Sex: Male

Height: 3'11"

Weight: 60 lbs

Eyes: Brown

Hair: Red

Race: White

Clothing:

Camouflage jacket with green skulls, black pants with yellow stripes, San Diego Chargers jersey #21

Missing From:

DUBLIN

VIRGINIA

Circumstances: Last seen at his residence on Highland Road, Dublin VA

ANYONE HAVING INFORMATION SHOULD CONTACT

Pulaski County Sheriff's Office

1-540-980-7800

We posted Noah's photo everywhere,
but no tips came in from the public.

The sites out my window on the drive into town were depressing — Pulaski County suffered from a high rate of unemployment, poverty, and opioid abuse. Noah's parents, Paul and Ashley, were recovering drug addicts. The town was very isolated and rural, real *Dukes of Hazzard* country, but bleaker. A desolate wasteland. It looked like the land of the unwell.

In the 24 hours since Noah had gone missing, hundreds of law enforcement agents and volunteers searched high and low for the little boy.

The FBI's Evidence Response Team combed the area by Noah's home, the woods nearby, and the local dump. Agents interviewed parents and neighbors and scanned phone records. Search-and-rescue teams spread out on ATVs, horseback, and foot.

But when I arrived, they'd found no witnesses, leads, or suspects.

At the briefing, I ratcheted up the search. We needed to identify any sex offenders in the area and find them. I sent agents to gas stations, pharmacies, and banks in the area — any business that might have a CCTV — to get security footage.

And I called up Travis, a polygraph examiner I knew in Richmond, and told him to grab his go bag and polygraph equipment and start driving over.

It didn't take long for me to realize something was awry regarding Noah's mother, and we needed to test her. Her cell phone records and the timeline she gave police didn't match up. Agents described her as "ambiguous" when they pressed her for details about Noah's disappearance. But the biggest red flag was her 911 call, which we played out loud at the morning briefing. She had no emotion in her voice, no panic, not a spec of urgency.

Until the moment I heard that 911 call, I held on to hope that Noah was alive somewhere. After the morning briefing and Ashley's deadpan request for help, that hope was gone.

I pulled aside two investigators and asked them to set up a meeting with me and the parents, Paul and Ashley, that afternoon. I needed to see Ashley's face. I needed to see how she'd react when I questioned her.

"Tell them to get here at two o'clock," I told the investigator. "But don't tell them they're coming here to take a polygraph. Tell them they're coming because the FBI supervisor overseeing the investigation wants to meet with them personally and tell them what we're doing to find Noah. Make it a very friendly thing."

When they got to the sheriff's office, I took

Paul and Ashley into a private room to talk. Meanwhile, Travis had arrived and was setting up his machine in another room.

I began the way I usually do, showing empathy and building rapport. Ashley looked stringy-haired and pale. Paul looked sad and bewildered. After about ten minutes, I gave Ashley a test, and her first chance to tell a different story.

"I've been in the FBI a long time and I've worked many, many cases like this," I told the couple. "You need to understand there's not a lot of things that could have happened to Noah."

Ashley furrowed her forehead.

"Number one, he could have been outside and an accident happened. Number two, we could have a situation where a stranger came and abducted him. Or, number three, maybe another kind of accident happened that was unintended, something no one meant to happen . . ."

Ashley shook her head: "No, it didn't happen that way."

I was sitting knee to knee with her. I lightly touched her leg with my hand. Here was the second test.

"Ashley, I promise you I'm going to find Noah no matter what it takes. I'm not leaving until I find Noah. Period."

I've promised this before, to other parents of missing children. An innocent mother who wants her child found grabs my hand and cries and squeezes my hand tightly and thanks me.

Ashley sat there, frozen.

Nothing Paul did made me suspicious of him. But everything Ashley did — and did not do — rang alarm bells.

"I pray that my grandma and dad are taking care of Noah right now," she said, and she began crying. Rather, she *tried* to cry . . . but no tears were coming out. Crocodile tears, we call them.

Ashley's father and grandmother were dead, I knew. So, without knowing it, she was affirming that she knew Noah was dead, too.

"Hey, listen. I really need your help," I told them. "We have to rule people out from the investigation, so I need you guys to take a polygraph right now. We just want to corroborate everything you're saying and eliminate you from the investigation, you understand."

Paul nodded. Ashley froze again, like a deer in headlights.

I took her down the hall to Travis, she was the first to be polygraphed.

"Make sure to ask her these two questions," I told him:

Are you withholding information about Noah's disappearance?

Do you know where Noah is now?

Travis nodded.

I went back to the room and continued talking to Paul, trying to get more information.

"Is it your understanding that Ashley went straight back to the trailer with the children after dropping you off at work?" I asked.

"As far as I know."

"Could she have stopped somewhere else? Who else is she friends with? When was the last time you both used drugs?"As I pressed him, he grew upset. But more than anything, he was a father worried about his son and tried to be helpful.

A couple of hours later, Travis knocked on the door, and I went out in the hall.

"Mom's results were deceptive," he said, "and she's changing her story."

We never had the chance to test Paul. Ashley became outraged and fetched Paul before storming out of the sheriff's office.

"Whatever you do," I said, "make sure you follow them. Put a car on them. Don't let them out of your sight."

Wednesday morning. Noah had been missing for three days.

We'd given press conferences and posted

Noah's picture in local stores and on telephone poles. Usually, this action evokes a flurry of tips coming in from the public. Somebody sees *something.* Even with the John Smith case, we had that neighbor, Patricia Donnolly, call on the hotline with the tip that she'd seen Smith putting a bundle into a backyard grave — and that tip came in two decades after the murder!

If Noah had been taken from home, someone would have seen something.

That afternoon, I drove from the command post to Paul and Ashley's trailer in Dublin. It was time for another talk.

Paul answered the door and was hopeful when he saw me.

"Any news?" he asked.

I told him no and I glanced at Ashley, who was standing behind him. She was not happy to see me.

They invited me in, and I was shocked by what I saw. Their trailer was covered in layers of filth, cobwebs, and stains on the couch. Instead of curtains, they'd hung black garbage bags on the windows. The air was thick with smoke — both Paul and Ashley chain-smoked Marlboros. It was so foul, I wouldn't let a dog live there, never mind two children. My heart went out to those kids.

They offered me a seat on the shit-stained

couch, but I was afraid to touch anything. I crouched, instead, like a catcher in a baseball game.

"It's been three days now, and I wanted to check if you thought of anything new that would help the investigation?" I asked.

They hadn't, they said.

I asked if I could speak to each of them separately. Paul went to the back of the trailer and now I was alone with Ashley. This time, I was harder on her. Like with football player Michael Vick, I tried to give her an "out."

"Look, Ashley, I've been around a long time and I've seen a lot of things, and I know you love Noah. No doubt about it. And I know you're a good mom. Whatever happened to him, you can help me find him . . ."

Ashley sat with her left arm clutching her chest and a Marlboro in her right hand, puffing continuously, as cigarette ash tumbled onto her lap, the couch, the floor. She answered my questions with vague deflection, refusing to make eye contact.

I got nothing out of her.

At the command post that night, all the leads had dried up, so I decided to shut it down for the night. I sent the agents and officers to their hotels and homes to get rest. We were all exhausted and frustrated.

Around 10:30 P.M., I was about to leave for my hotel when I realized my wallet was missing. I started looking around, and my phone rang.

John. Thank God. I'd been trying to reach him for days.

He'd been traveling and called after landing at La Guardia. When I picked up, I didn't know he was already on the Noah case without me even telling him a word. As he drove out of the airport parking lot minutes before, his head began to throb. Information flooded his senses.

"John!" I began, "I need your help. I have a missing boy . . ."

It was like Annie Le all over again.

"Little boy, bright red hair?"

"Yeah"

"An N-name . . . not Nick, but . . . like Norman, or . . . Noah."

"Yes!"

"I feel drugs. Mom and dad and a drug guy."

"Makes sense."

"The mom's not telling you the truth. She's not being honest. Oh, man. Where are you? I'm getting a feeling like wherever you are, it's like *The Walking Dead.*"

"Yeah, that's exactly what it's like here."

"Hold on a second . . ."

I braced myself. John was putting me on hold to take a call from the Other Side, that's how I always saw it. It meant crucial information was about to come.

His next outburst was like a repeat of his finding Annie Le.

"Oh my god, Bob. He's right there. He's right there!"

My heart jumped.

"Right where?!"

"You guys literally walked over him. He's right there!"

"John, where's *there?*"

"By a trailer. They live in a trailer?"

John began describing the trailer — even the stains, cobwebs, and smoke.

"Bob. Here's what I'm seeing. When I walk out of the trailer, I want to go left. And when I go left, I feel I'm going down a hill, the property slopes down."

He paused.

"Where are the propane tanks?"

"I don't know!"

"I want to go down, behind . . . move the propane tanks, Bob, and Noah is right there. Hold on a second . . ."

I waited. I was holding my breath.

"Oh my god, Bob. Look for an X-wing fighter."

"A what?"

"It's a *Star Wars* toy. The X-wing fighter! That thing Luke Skywalker flew in *Star Wars*?"

"Oh. Okay. I have no idea what that is, but . . ."

"Bob, I literally see people walking right over Noah. They're walking right over him!"

"Holy shit."

"Where are you now?"

"At the sheriff's office."

"As soon as you get to the trailer, call me."

"What? I can't go out there now."

"Bob, you have to. You have to go *right now.*"

I'd known John for 17 years and never heard him talk with such urgency. It was close with Annie Le, but not like this.

"John, how the hell do I go out there at this time of night and justify it? It's almost 11 P.M.!"

"I don't know," he said. "Just do it. If you go out there right now, you will find him. Believe me."

Wednesday night, 11 P.M.

As I drove out to the trailer, I imagined finding Noah. I also imagined getting jammed up.

Fuck, I'm going to get fired, I thought.

The phone rang. This time, it was Jonathan.

"Jonathan! I have a missing boy . . ."

He already knew. John had called him and told him to get in touch with me ASAP. John's urgency kicked Jonathan's father instinct into gear, too.

It kicked his guides into gear, as well. He began getting all the details John got, with some new ones.

"Look for the big pile of tires," he said.

"Okay," I said.

"And down a hill, look for an open trailer with a toolbox mounted to the frame."

"Okay."

Besides the time all three of us were at the pumphouse together at Smith's factory, this was the first time the two psychics were doing a relay-team psychic race with me. Jonathan's call fired me up even more.

But after I hung up, I was still worried about how I'd explain to my superiors why I went out near midnight to the home of a victim's parents.

Then I got an idea: the missing wallet!

It could have easily fallen out of my pocket onto their filthy trailer floor when I was in baseball-catcher position earlier. Even if it didn't, it was a decent enough excuse to go.

Now all I needed was an alibi.

A mile from Paul and Ashley's trailer, we'd set up a smaller search-and-rescue command post at the volunteer fire department. They were still open. I drove over. A rotund, jolly captain was manning the post. We'd met the day of that first briefing.

"Hey, captain. Has anyone found a brown leather wallet?"

"No, did you lose one?"

"Yeah. The only thing I can think of is that earlier in the day, I was in the trailer interviewing Paul and Ashley. Maybe my wallet fell out there . . ."

I trailed off. The next moment was like divine intervention. Like all my spirit guides tapped this guy on the shoulder.

"Well, let's go out to the trailer and knock on their door," he said.

"Really?"

I couldn't had scripted it any better.

Thursday morning. Just past midnight.

Dense clouds hung low in the sky, smothering any starlight or moonlight.

The captain knocked on the door and Paul answered. I could see the glow of Ashley's Marlboro tip in the background.

"Did you find Noah?" he asked, hopefully.

"No," said the captain. "We're sorry to come out this late, but Bob from the FBI can't find his wallet. Do you mind if he comes in for a moment and looks around?"

Paul motioned for me to enter. I stepped in a few feet, shined my flashlight around, and I was done. That's all I could handle in there. I thanked them, then turned to leave.

As I stepped out the front door, I remembered John's words.

When I walk out of the trailer, I want to go left.

"Hey, I'm going to look over here for a minute," I said to the captain.

I went left, then walked along a worn dirt path at the side of the trailer that led to a steep hill.

When I go left, I feel like I'm going down a hill, the property slopes down.

I shined my flashlight across the yard and saw Noah's toys scattered across the front lawn. I passed a little green wrestling action figure and landed upon . . . a set of propane tanks.

Where are the propane tanks? John asked.

Behind the tanks, I saw a concrete slab. Beyond that, a split-rail wooden fence. Beyond the fence, the property was very steep, going down more than a hundred yards. I stood at the top of the hill by the fence and shined my flashlight to the bottom. That's where I saw Jonathan's visual:

A giant pile of tires.

An open trailer with a toolbox mounted to the frame.

Everywhere I looked, I could see what John and Jonathan had relayed, as if their descriptions were materializing in front of me.

The area beyond the fence must have been a cattle farm at one time, I thought. I could see impressions where cow's feet had sunk into the ground by six or eight inches. Now, the area looked like a dumping yard for junk.

"Has anyone searched down there?" I asked the captain, who'd followed me down the path.

"I don't know," he said. "I assume so."

I walked back to the trailer door and knocked. This time Ashley answered, cigarette dangling.

"Ashley, the property at the bottom of the hill. Who owns it?"

"My landlord," she said.

"The captain and I are going to go down there. We're going to look for Noah."

She didn't say anything.

We climbed the fence and walked down the steep hill.

The farther down we went, the darker it got.

The captain kept talking about God and

Jesus and the sins of man and salvation. I was focused on the big pile of tires Jonathan talked about, even though this junkyard was a minefield of distractions. There were about 101 ways and places a curious little boy could get into trouble here.

I passed the tires and went to the open trailer with the toolbox. As soon as I got near, I was hit by a terrible stench. Could Noah's body be in the toolbox?

"That doesn't smell so good," said the captain, close behind.

I found a rusty pocketknife on the trailer and popped the toolbox open, holding my breath. The stink of rusted tools, rotting away for years, slammed us. But no Noah.

We spread out, and each began wading through piles of shit in the dark wherever we could see stuff. It seemed endless. I still had the stench of those rotting tools in my nose and it was making me dizzy, until . . .

Opium.

Opium.

Fran's perfume.

It had been a while since she'd said hello, and here she was, telling me she was with me and offering encouragement from the Other Side.

The phone rang. *John.* Thank God.

As soon as I picked up the phone, he was on fire.

"You walked right over him!" said John, his sense of immediacy was palpable.

"What?"

"Bob. STOP WHERE YOU ARE RIGHT NOW. Turn around. Go back in the direction you came."

I turned around and started walking back to the tires.

"STOP! He's right there. You just walked over him!"

I started to backtrack. I had the phone in one hand, the flashlight in the other.

"Stop! You're going the wrong way. You need to go back up the hill. They're telling me you need to go *back up.*"

John was talking 100 miles an hour.

"Go back up the hill and look for that *Star Wars* toy — the X-wing fighter plane. Bob, the boy is there. *I'm telling you.*"

I could hear the emotion in John's voice, and that was unlike him. Noah was different for him, he later explained. The pure, guileless spirit of that red-haired little boy made the worried, loving father in both of us take over. It was personal. We felt Noah's innocence. He touched our hearts. Whatever horror befell him, his own father couldn't protect him and it was now up to John and me.

It was too late to save his life, but the least thing we could do was to find him.

He represented our sons. In a way, he was also *us.*

I climbed the steep, steep hill and my feet kept sliding and getting twisted up in the cow divots.

He had no one, I kept thinking. *He didn't stand a chance.*

At the crest, I still couldn't see the family trailer. But I could feel something. It enveloped me like a mist, but it wasn't Fran's perfume this time. It was little Noah's sweet and sad energy, leading me up the hill.

"Noah," I said out loud, my voice cracking. "I know you're here. I know you brought me here . . ."

"Who are you talking to?" John asked.

"Noah. He's with me."

Pause.

"I feel him too," said John. "We're going to find him. Stay focused. Go back up the hill! Up, up, up, they're telling me!"

"I'm almost at the top . . ."

"Okay. Do you see the propane tanks, by the toys?"

I could see that the captain spotted me from a distance and began walking up the hill toward me. And I could see a light was now on in the trailer. Ashley's silhouette was in the window. She was holding back a corner of the black garbage bag, looking out.

My flashlight beamed across her face. Our eyes met.

"Oh my god, John. I've got to go." I hung up on him.

The captain appeared as Paul and Ashley emerged from their trailer.

"Did you find anything?" Paul asked.

"It's too dark," I said, "we'll come back in the morning and search more," I said.

Ashley was not happy about this. Now she shined her flashlight on my face.

"Why are you really here?"

"What do you mean? I'm here because I lost my wallet . . ."

"Bullshit," she said. "When you came before you didn't walk down that hill. You didn't walk around my house before. You only came in the trailer. And now you're here and you're walking the property. Why are you really here right now?"

"Well, Ashley, I'm here because I'm looking for my wallet. But you know what? I'm also looking for your son. And I would think that as his parents, you'd be down there with me looking. I'm climbing through piles of shit looking for your son. That's what I'm doing."

"Do you have any specific knowledge or

information that my son is here?" she asked.

I wanted to peel her face off.

"Ashley, I have no idea where your son is. I don't know if he's at the bottom of that hill, I don't know if he's in your trailer, I don't know if he's across the street, I don't know if he's miles away. I have no idea. But I'm trying to do the right thing. I told you; I'm not leaving here until I find Noah."

She backed down a little. We were standing by the trailer and the toys on the ground caught my eye. John's last instruction before I cut him off was to look for the *Star Wars* toy.

I shined a flashlight on the toys, and then to the side of the trailer where the steep hill began.

"Hey, Paul, did Noah play back there?"

"Yeah, let me show you."

Paul walked toward the side of the trailer and I followed. Ashley and the captain were behind me. At the side of the hill there was a path worn in the grass.

Paul pointed to Noah's Big Wheels.

"Noah would ride down this path all the time," he said.

I kept walking behind the property, and the three of them followed. I saw that concrete slab from before, and a little toy basketball net that had fallen.

"Noah used to play basketball out here, and if the ball ever went down the hill, he would never leave the property. Never. He would come and get us to get the ball."

I kept walking. I pointed the flashlight across the lawn, not in front of me, where I was stepping. That's when I tripped on something. I pointed my flashlight down.

I was standing on a giant septic tank. It's large, circular lid was loose and I'd inadvertently kicked it off when my feet hit it.

I felt a chill. I had a feeling Noah was in there. I *felt* him.

I crouched down and moved the lid a few inches, shining my light inside the tank. It was filled with raw sewage that was overflowing and seeping down the hill. As I peered inside, everyone fell silent. Ashley was on my right, Paul was in front of me, and the captain was to my left. It was a moment of heavy silence.

But I couldn't see what lay underneath the murky sewage.

Something else caught my attention in the corner of my eye. I looked to my right.

Less than two feet away from the septic tank lay a *Star Wars* X-wing fighter spacecraft, angled in a way that it was pointing to the tank like an arrow.

Jesus. My blood ran cold.

"Captain, have we searched this tank?"

"I'm pretty sure the guys probed it with a stick."

"We need to search it," I said.

The captain suggested using a big branch and sticking it in. Paul agreed. Ashley was silent.

I stood up.

"No, we'll be back early in the morning to pump it out properly," I told them.

I worried we'd have trouble explaining why we were there so late, especially because Ashley was already confrontational about it. Second, I didn't want to poke Noah with a stick in the dark and potentially destroy evidence. Third, he deserved to come up from the ground in the light of day.

As we left, I told the captain: "I need you to have a car parked across the street all night. Do not let anybody leave this property."

I went to bed that night heartbroken.

The next morning, as the sun came up, the septic truck arrived to pump out the tank.

The operator was the first to see the top of Noah's head in the deep hole and went to alert someone in charge.

As soon as Noah's father, Paul, realized his son was in the tank, he grew hysterical; he tried to jump into the tank to get his boy. I would have done the same thing if it was my boy down there.

Ashley fell to the ground in a dramatic display and began pounding it with her fists.

"Fuck you, god!" she yelled.

I stood back and watched as workers in Hazmat suits set up a large, metal frame — like a tripod — over the tank's hole.

One of the workers was lowered into the tank and, using a winch, the others lifted the boy out. Noah's cherubic face was covered with waste, he looked like he'd been playing in the mud after a rain. He was wearing Spider-Man boots.

I felt a sense of relief that he wasn't missing anymore, that he wasn't lost.

Searching the septic tank by the family's trailer home: "He's right there!" John insisted. (COURTESY OF THE FBI)

What would have happened had I not talked to John and Jonathan when I did? There had to be a reason why John was so insistent I come out here late at night. Maybe someone was planning to move Noah's body?

Instead, John saw the arrow — *Star Wars* X-wing fighter jet — pointing in Noah's direction, inches away.

I knew one thing for sure. Noah wasn't alone.

The moment I smelled Fran's perfume on the hill, I felt a sense of comfort.

If what I've learned watching John Edward all these years is true, then Noah's loved ones on the Other Side were there to greet him when he crossed over.

Maybe even Fran was there to take his hand.

That thought made me smile.

I still hadn't given up trying to find her.

And Caitie, now 18, wanted to help.

She and Connor had seen me on TV shows like *Forensic Files* and *20/20* talking about Smith and other cases. Caitie was especially intrigued.

She was a lot like me: focused, OCD organized, passionate about causes, citing injustices and wanting to save the world. She loved psychology and trying to figure out why people acted the way they did (she would later get an undergraduate degree in neurobiology and a master's degree in psychological counseling).

And she was also the only other person in the house, my only ally, who understood and embraced John Edward's ability. In fact, when I took her to one of his events and she met John, he told me later that she had psychic potential. That her astrological stars were aligned for her to do that kind of work, if she desired it.

"Dad, it's all about *energy,*" Caitie would explain. Oh, boy, I thought. Wait until her mother hears *this.*

She told me about how her beloved, deceased dog "visited" her at night as she slept and curled up next to her in bed. Then, a one-on-one phone reading with Jonathan Louis sealed the psychic deal. He told her she was the most "emotionally aware" member of the family.

That I can believe.

So, I shouldn't have been surprised when I walked into her sanctuary in the basement one day and found her sitting cross-legged on the floor, surrounded by my boxes of newspaper articles, old police reports, notes, and photos. She had everything spread out on the carpet, much the way John spreads his Tarot cards on the table, and was sorting everything into neat, chronological piles.

"I'm going to solve the Smith case for you," she said, scanning a document in her hand. "I mean, Dad. Seriously. You've been consumed by this case for as long as I can remember and you're not going to let it go until you die. I better help you figure it out."

Yep. She was my daughter all right.

Caitie stayed holed up in the basement for days, scrutinizing reports and taking notes. I peeked in around day three.

"Solve it yet?"

She looked up, serious.

"Dad, you and John Smith have a lot in common."

"What?"

"He's really smart like you, that's obvious. But you have a savior complex and he's like your dark alter-ego."

"My *what?*"

She went back to her investigation and I slowly closed the door. Maybe there was some truth to what the kid was saying.

A few months later, I got back to my own search for Fran.

In what would end up being my final, formal dig on the case, I returned to the Carborundum factory in New Jersey with Newark's Evidence Response Team, the NJ State

Police, and West Windsor Police officers.

With an excavation team and ground-penetrating radar, we cracked the area outside the pumphouse. We crawled through water pipes and up ladders inside the water tower. We found nothing.

I climbed as high as I could go up a big tube and looked around. Who the hell is going to drag a dead body all the way up here?

There's no way. And for the first time in 17 years, I thought:

It's not going to happen.

When I left the burned-down factory that night, all I had of Fran was the lingering scent of her perfume, following me like a shadow.

EPILOGUE

Letting Go

BOB HILLAND
August 2023

By the time I watched Noah being pulled from the septic tank, I'd spent most of my life fighting for justice for the powerless, voiceless victims of this world.

Whether I was beating up bullies or chasing bad guys in cop cruisers or interrogating terrorists in foreign lands or trying to keep Smith in prison or looking for Fran, I wanted to help the preyed upon and hunt down the evildoers.

Sometimes I found justice; other times I did not, like in Noah's sad story.

Ashley was later convicted of multiple counts of felony child abuse and neglect, though the court would find there was insufficient evidence that she left her son unsupervised with "the knowledge and consciousness that injury would result."

I poured my soul into my cases and cared about the people involved despite the outcome.

Today, images flash through my mind from the last thirty years like pages in a photo album: Janice's face in the lime green nightgown, Fran's face in the pumphouse, newlywed Jennifer on the honeymoon cruise, the soccer player in Guyana, Annie Le in the wall at Yale, and Noah in his Spider-Man boots.

"Certain people are called upon, chosen, to do very difficult and special things," John told me at our first meeting.

"Chosen by who?" I asked.

"God. The universe. A higher power."

After decades of fighting for the side of Good, I have learned many lessons, and this is one of them: Chasing Evil is not about how many bad guys I put behind bars or how many cases I crack when no one else can. It's about the human journey in doing so. It's about the energies around us, both good and bad, and being a soldier for the side of honor. It's about understanding we are all connected.

When I smelled Fran's perfume on Noah's hill, I felt she'd come to comfort me and Noah. John had other ideas.

"She came to say hello, but also good-bye,"

he said. "It was Fran's way of showing you that she was with you and you didn't need to search for her anymore."

Not search for her?

This was the endless debate. Would I find her or not? Should I keep looking for her or not? For years, Fran was the elephant in the room as John continued to help me on other cases.

In 2018, I got another lead. By then I was an instructor at FBI headquarters in Quantico, and out of the blue, I got a call from Smith's third wife. She had new information to give me.

The three days Smith went missing in 1999 — the disappearance that got me thrown off the case — he'd gone missing from home, too, and "he reappeared covered in dirt and thirsty," she said, "like he'd been living out in the woods for days."

Back then, we all assumed Smith spent those days trying to get to his brother to kill him for cooperating with the FBI. But now I had a new theory: After the murder, he hid Fran's remains in the gray cylinders by the industrial factory — which is why we felt her presence there, and why John saw the cylinders at our first meeting.

But what if . . . what if . . . he took Fran's remains with him to California in something also cylinder-shaped and stored them. And what if, during those three missing days, he fetched the remains and buried them somewhere? It would explain him reappearing covered in dirt.

But buried them where?

I got Jonathan on the phone: "I'm being pulled to the Southeast," said Jonathan, "about an hour from Escondido. I'm looking for a store where I can buy a tool, like a hardware store, a place Smith has been before . . . I see him with Fran's dismembered remains in buckets, he buries them off-trail in a secluded area, on a Woodline . . ."

Buckets. Buckets were cylinder shaped!

I looked up Google Maps and found a location that sounded like Jonathan's description. I was ready to get my shovel and go. But there was no convincing my boss, or my wife, to let me go cross-country for yet another potentially fruitless dig.

Stop searching for her? Who would I be if I was not searching for Fran? What would be my purpose?

I wasn't sure.

When John's guides would no longer offer insights into Fran's whereabouts, I would try to slip her into our conversations.

I would, in effect, try to trick John's spirits

guides into giving me information. I was supposed to be an expert at that, after all.

"What's up with Fran?" I'd ask.

He'd shake his head.

"Bob, she's fine. Just because you haven't found her, doesn't mean she hasn't transitioned. She's not the one who is earthbound and stuck. It's you."

After seventeen years, it was time to let my obsession go.

In the years to follow, I would let go of other things as well.

In 2019, Alex and I ended our marriage. The strain of the Smith case — "the other woman," as John once called Fran — was too much. Alex always called the FBI "the other woman," too.

I remembered John's words at our first meeting:

"You are a man of extremes," he said. "There's no middle ground in your world. You will make it your mission to get this guy at all costs. That could mean your personal life, your family, your status at work . . ."

The price fighting for Good, and against Evil, was high, indeed. But I had signed up for it.

One day in 2016, a year after Noah, I was driving home from work and I suddenly felt a heaviness smother me. A despairing energy wrapped itself around me so oppressively, I couldn't breathe.

I called John.

"I feel like I'm under attack!"

He was about to go onstage at an event and instructed me to call Jonathan immediately.

"Something's not right," I told Jonathan, and described what I was experiencing.

"Listen, there's nothing the Dark Side would like better than to take you down," he explained. "But you need to know that your spirit guides are always surrounding you. So, ride the wave. Let it hit you and knock you down, then get up."

We talked for an hour as I drove. During that time, Jonathan taught me how to recognize signs from my guides, be they warnings or nudges of encouragement.

I reminded myself: I was not alone in this fight.

Soon after the ending of my marriage came another finale — after 23 years with the FBI, I retired.

But the monumental letting go was to happen this year, in 2023.

Back in 2019, I brought the Mercer County, New Jersey, prosecutor, three of his assistants, and several investigators to the FBI Academy in Quantico, Virginia, and presented them with more than enough information to indict and convict John Smith for Fran's murder.

He'd been up for parole once already and I wanted to make sure there wasn't a second time. If released, he was still young and healthy enough to hurt new victims.

The head prosecutor agreed and a grand jury was impaneled. I spent a day testifying, and it was the first time I'd seen Smith's pale, shark-eyed face in a decade. He didn't look like a monster anymore; he looked like a frail old man whose energy had dissipated. The dragon had been slayed.

While I was on the stand, he looked up at me only once. I winked.

In November of that year, Smith was indicted for Fran's 1991 murder.

I was anxious for the trial to come, so we could put this monster away forever. But like many trials during the COVID era, it kept getting pushed.

And then, a shocker. On June 28, 2023, I got a phone call from the Mercer County Prosecutor's Office with news: at noon that day, they entered into a non-prosecution agreement with John Smith in which he admitted he'd wrapped Fran's body in a blanket and put it in a dumpster at Carborundum.

"It's over," said one of the prosecutors.

Because a judge ruled that Smith's murder conviction of Janice could not be used as evidence in the upcoming trial, prosecutors didn't think they stood a chance at conviction.

"Without it," said the prosecutor, "he doesn't look like a killer. He just looks like a bad husband."

I couldn't believe my ears.

Their deal meant that unless I found Fran's body, he could never be prosecuted for her murder. It meant there was now a possibility that he'd get out of prison the next time he was up for parole. All that, and he didn't even have to admit that he'd killed her — or how.

I felt like someone pulled my insides out. I was gutted.

"You gotta talk me down," I said to John when he answered the phone. "I'm spinning."

I told him the news.

"All the time and energy I put into this case for 25 years!" I lamented. "The time I spent away from my wife and kids. For nothing! All flushed down the toilet."

"It wasn't for nothing," said John. "Think about all the women whose lives you saved by putting Smith in jail."

"He's lying about Fran's body."

"I know."

"He played the system. How is this right, John?"

"I know you're upset, Bob, but you have to understand. This is about the balance of Good and Evil. And the earthly justice system pales in comparison to the universal justice system. I wouldn't want to have Smith's karma."

"So, it was supposed to end this way?"

John paused, checking with his guides.

"Energetically, this was supposed to be the outcome."

It was hard for me to accept. I'd promised Fran and Janice that I'd put him away forever.

"Bob, it's the universe's way — and Fran's way — of saying 'thank you.' Now you have to let go. You need to pave a new path."

I still fought it.

"I've seen you evolve so much since our first meeting," said John. "If you can let go of this, you will be one of the greatest students of the universe that I have worked with."

I was quiet.

"I know you were trying to save Fran, Bob. But in the end, I think Fran is saving you."

Saving me?

After we hung up, I thought about John's

words. As I tried to sleep that night, I remembered something.

A decade earlier, he'd given me as a birthday present a Skype session with a famous astrologer he knew, Maggie Kerr. I'd given her my place, date, and time of birth, and from that, she drew up a natal chart for me, a snapshot of the stars and planets the moment I was born.

"You've been on quite a journey," she'd said, as she examined a page of circles, lines, numbers, and symbols.

"Your soul has been involved in spiritual work for many, many lives. You've been involved in compassionate service. A spiritual warrior."

"It says that?"

"Yes. Look here," she'd said, holding the chart up to the screen.

"You've gone to bat on behalf of others less fortunate or compromised during your history. That's why you have this instinctive urge to use your energy to protect and care for others in victim positions in this life."

"Interesting."

"But you need to learn boundaries. You are getting ready to move forward. You must trust your soul to guide you where you need to go."

"Can I ask a question?"

"Yes."

"I've been looking for this one woman who is dead. Her name is Fran. She haunts me. I have to find her."

Maggie searched the chart until her eyes locked onto an answer.

"No," she said, shaking her head. She held up the page to her laptop screen again.

"Do you see this?"

I looked at the converging lines and squiggles.

"Here is your search. But it's not really a search for this woman, Fran, as you say," said Maggie. "Because we live in a symbolic universe. Your search for Fran," she said, "is really a search *for yourself.*"

The plan for me was already charted, shown to me years ago. And today, John was reminding me of the plan.

You have to let go, my friend. You need to pave a new path.

It was that same lesson, over and over, that he keeps trying to teach me: The universe will give us what we need, not always what we want.

So maybe I don't find Fran, I thought. But at age 55, I finally find myself.

I could live with that.

Tomorrow I'll have new battles to fight, new wrongs to right — with John, and on my own. As Jonathan said, I have to ride the wave, get knocked down, then get back up.

I turned out the lights.

"Thank you, Fran," I said out loud, in case she was listening.

I shut my eyes and fell into a long, peaceful slumber.

JOHN EDWARD
January 2024

It's been seven months since Bob and I got the news about John Smith and his agreement with the Mercer County Prosecutor's Office.

When I reflect on that moment, I feel the same way Bob did when he got the call; gutted. The deal feels unjust and karmically wrong, and it was a devastating blow to Fran's memory, to her family, and to Bob's undying dedication to find her and bring her home. It encapsulates everything that's wrong with the legal system — even humanity — in our world today.

But as someone who works with energy, when I put on my metaphysical glasses and look at the big picture, I see it differently.

As I told Bob on the phone that day, the universe has a justice system more profound and enlightened than we'll ever have on earth. Energetically, this was the correct outcome for everyone involved so they could learn the lessons they needed to learn.

What do I mean by that? I truly believe that every struggle serves a purpose and gives us an opportunity to adapt, transform, and evolve. Moments of struggle or loss give us the chance to choose to either stagnate or leap forward and learn.

Bob is choosing to learn.

After his initial, gut-wrenching reaction to the Smith news, he understood that letting go of Smith and Fran signified a spiritual growth for him. And that it was time to free himself from his self-imposed passion project, from the prison he'd been living in.

The way Bob watched me go from a guy doing readings in his Long Island office to international recognition with syndicated shows, events around the world, and my own TV platform (www.evolveplusTV.com), I have witnessed him advance and transform in every respect: His language, his perspectives, his philosophies have all widened beyond the obvious and logical. He isn't *Dragnet*'s "Just the facts, ma'am" Joe Friday anymore.

Where Bob was once fuzzy about boundaries and acceptance, he has a sharper focus now. Along the way, his myopic view of getting John Smith and finding Fran became more about *finding Bob* and seeing life from an aerial perspective.

Having said that . . .

I still don't rule out finding Fran.

This is because of the one subtle piece of information my guides gave me during that first reading with Bob in 1998 — that Fran had breast implants with serial numbers on them. It was one of the first details my guides showed me about Fran, and I can't think of any reason why they'd show me such a specific detail unless she was going to be found and identified that way.

(Plus, I need to prove my dear friend, psychic Shelley Peck, wrong. She always insisted Fran would never be found. I don't want to get to the Other Side and watch her perform the *I-told-you-so* dance for eternity.)

Fran's presence was so strong at the pumphouse, I wonder if someday there will be new construction going on there and she will be unearthed.

When I put on my metaphysical glasses, my view is that we *did* find Fran. Not her body, but for sure her spirit. Bob, Jonathan, and I all connected with her.

Even though I still think there's a chance Bob will find Fran, I don't go out of my way to mention it. He's paving a new path, and that's good — I don't want to interrupt it.

When we've chatted over the last seven months, it's been about our families and the state of the world — normal conversation between brothers. Sometimes, he'll slip in a question about Fran. *Have you heard anything from your guides about her? Do you think we should go to California and dig?* He can't help himself.

I shake my head.

"You've graduated," I tell him. "In the same way you can't go back to high school and redo your senior year. You've moved on."

And he knows it's true, for the most part.

I've been a teacher of energy for most of my life, and now, with this book, Bob becomes a teacher, too.

This is the beginning of his new work; shifting how law enforcement look at energy and approach problem-solving. Perhaps he will teach his colleagues about balance in their personal lives.

Life lessons are challenging, difficult, and overwhelming. It takes fortitude and focus to navigate them. Bob is a great example of fortitude in human form, which is why I wanted to tell our story.

It's possible he'll always see the letting go of Fran, Smith, his marriage, and the FBI as "deaths" to be grieved — energetic spiritual divorces, of sorts. But he's an example for you, the reader, that letting go does not mean you failed. Quite the opposite.

As for me, working with Bob for more than two decades helped me examine my issues with my own police officer father. I was able to revisit deep traumas of my own and work through them. Like Bob, I sought acceptance and approval from patriarchal figures because of my father. He and I have both found healing in this area.

My hope is that readers who picked up this book for the true-crime journey will also reflect on their own lives and think about what they need to embrace, learn, shift, transform, or release to allow something greater to happen, to reach the next level.

When I first met Bob, I told him that certain people are called upon to do very difficult things, and he was about to join the battle between Good and Evil.

I don't think the universe is done with Bob Hilland yet. There is plenty more work to be done, and the world needs this good soldier on the side of honor to keep fighting.

I also don't believe he and I have finished our work together as a team.

I'm sure — I *know* — that when the time is right and the spirt world is ready, we'll hear from them.

The Other Side knows how to reach us.

ACKNOWLEDGMENTS

A special thank you to Katrina (Kat Jenus) for not only choosing to share genetics in this lifetime, but helping me to facilitate helping so many others.

Justin Edward — I'm so proud of the man you've become and in choosing to make the world a better place through medicine.

Olivia Edward — you're a super nova in the world and I can only imagine how you will continue to brighten up the paths of all those who are lucky to be in your orbit.

And to Sandra, where I've said it before, and I will say it again . . . there could be no JOHN EDWARD if it wasn't for the support and family foundation you've created. Thank you for sharing me with the world for 30 years

Natasha Stoynoff — thank you for capturing my words and voice like no other could. From pop culure and books, to travel

— you've always been cheering from the sidelines.

Bob Hilland — wow, we did it!

Captain Jack (my father) — I hope after 22 years of watching me do this in spirit and honoring your profession I've made you proud.

— John

I would like to acknowledge all of the victims and their families — never lose hope. And to those pursuing justice — never give up.

— Bob

ABOUT THE AUTHORS

John Edward is an internationally acclaimed psychic medium, bestselling author, and worldwide lecturer who pioneered the psychic phenomena genre with his highly successful television program, *Crossing Over with John Edward,* in 2000. His books, tours, personal readings, and online forums (www.evolveplusTV.com) have helped people connect to and understand the spirit world for more than three decades. For more info about John Edward go to www.JohnEdward.net or join www.evolveplusTV.com.

Robert Hilland has served the law enforcement and intelligence communities for 34 years — first as a police officer, then for 25 years as a special agent and instructor at the FBI. His expertise as an investigator has drawn him into prominent criminal cases around the world. He currently provides training to agents and investigators serving the United States intelligence community.

Natasha Stoynoff is an award-winning journalist, *New York Times* bestselling author, and screenwriter. On staff at *PEOPLE* magazine for a dozen years and a freelancer for *TIME, The Washington Post, USA Today,* and *AARP,* she has collaborated on 16 books.

The employees of Thorndike Press hope you have enjoyed this Large Print book. All our Thorndike Large Print titles are designed for easy reading, and all our books are made to last. Other Thorndike Press Large Print books are available at your library, through selected bookstores, or directly from us.

For information about titles, please visit our website at:

http://gale.cengage.com/thorndike